Palgrave Studies in Audio-Visual

Series Editor
K. J. Donnelly
School of Humanities
University of Southampton
Southampton, UK

The aesthetic union of sound and image has become a cultural dominant. A junction for aesthetics, technology and theorisation, film's relationship with music remains the crucial nexus point of two of the most popular arts and richest cultural industries. Arguably, the most interesting area of culture is the interface of audio and video aspects, and that film is the flagship cultural industry remains the fount and crucible of both industrial developments and critical ideas.

Palgrave Studies in Audio-Visual Culture has an agenda-setting aspiration. By acknowledging that radical technological changes allow for rethinking existing relationships, as well as existing histories and the efficacy of conventional theories, it provides a platform for innovative scholarship pertaining to the audio-visual. While film is the keystone of the audio visual continuum, the series aims to address blind spots such as video game sound, soundscapes and sound ecology, sound psychology, art installations, sound art, mobile telephony and stealth remote viewing cultures.

More information about this series at
http://www.palgrave.com/gp/series/14647

Paul Mazey

British Film Music

Musical Traditions in British Cinema, 1930s–1950s

palgrave
macmillan

Paul Mazey
Department of Film and Television
University of Bristol
Bristol, UK

Palgrave Studies in Audio-Visual Culture
ISBN 978-3-030-33552-6 ISBN 978-3-030-33550-2 (eBook)
https://doi.org/10.1007/978-3-030-33550-2

Cover image: Belle Chrystall and Niall MacGinnis in *The Edge of the World* (Michael Powell, 1937), Everett Collection Inc / Alamy Stock Photo

This Palgrave Macmillan imprint is published by the registered company Springer Nature Switzerland AG.
The registered company address is: Gewerbestrasse 11, 6330 Cham, Switzerland

For Christopher

Acknowledgements

Many people offered me advice while I was working on this book and I am grateful to all of them, particularly to those who read and commented on drafts at various stages. Their generosity with their time, and their recommendations have undoubtedly improved the quality of this study, and any faults that remain are mine alone.

Jan Brookhouse read early drafts of this research and provided useful feedback. At the University of Bristol, Liz Bird encouraged me to undertake this research, and I am grateful to her and to other faculty members who have been consistently supportive. I am particularly indebted to Kristian Moen and Alex Clayton for their comments and for a suggestion that significantly improved the structure of this study. I am grateful to Guido Heldt for offering me the benefit of his experience on musical and film music matters, and to Pete Falconer for his advice on revisions. I owe a particular debt of gratitude to Sarah Street for her unfailing support, guidance, and encouragement throughout this process, which has made it a rewarding and pleasurable experience. I would also like to thank the Arts and Humanities Research Council for funding this research and the helpful staff at the British Film Institute's Reuben Library and Special Collections.

I am grateful to Kevin Donnelly for his inspiring work on British film music and for his enthusiasm for this volume. At Palgrave Macmillan I would like to thank Lina Aboujieb for her efficiency in dealing with my many questions. Last, but very far from least, I would like to thank Chris Drew for his support, and his willingness to explore with me the byways of British film history.

Contents

List of Figures

CHAPTER 1

Introduction

The music heard in many British films has an intriguing quality, a sound that colours the music, and in its turn the films themselves, with a particularly national hue. This quality causes the music to register as a marker of Britishness as strongly as more obvious indicators such as British accents and British settings. The central concern of this book is to explore the nature of this quality and to understand how it creates this effect. The answer, I will argue, lies in the connections between British film music of this era and historical traditions of music in Britain. While all film music exploits existing musical forms, British film music is notable for the extent to which it embraces styles of music that are culturally significant in the history of British music. This book traces the ways that British film music draws upon the heritage of British music, and reveals how British film culture mines a rich and emotionally resonant seam of connotations evoked by the musical styles it adopts. By investigating the intricate intersections between the film industry and the musical establishment, it proposes that the evolution of British film music can be best understood when considered in relation to the traditions and history of musical activity in Britain.

This work explores film music in British cinema from the 1930s to the 1950s, a period that represents something of a golden age for British film music, and for British film itself. Not only did film music practices develop and become established in the British industry during this era, but it was also the time when cinema played its most central role in the cultural life

P. Mazey, *British Film Music*, Palgrave Studies in Audio-Visual Culture, https://doi.org/10.1007/978-3-030-33550-2_1

of the nation as the foremost medium of mass entertainment. In these decades, cinema was more popular and more attended than at any time before or since. This era witnessed the impact of the Second World War, when films provided first information and propaganda in support of the war effort and later entertainment and escapism from its privations. The postwar years saw cinema attendances climb to their highest ever levels, and also a peak in the popularity of British films with British audiences. This changed during the 1950s, when the spread of television began to usurp cinema's position as the primary entertainment medium. With older audiences increasingly dwindling, film production declined and the industry sought to entice younger viewers. The resulting shift in the cinema-going demographic brought an equivalent alteration in the types of films being produced, and a notable rise in social realism and horror. This in turn saw a change in the nature of film music with a movement away from the traditional orchestral sound and towards a more contemporary idiom of modernism, jazz and popular music. The film industry sought to offer what television could not, and while traditional scoring continued in the epics that promised colour and big-screen spectacle, it developed in alternative directions in the genres aimed at the adolescent and young adult audiences.

The more modern scores of the following decades strike a contrast with those of the era that preceded them. These had been characterised by the diversity of music the films contained, and by the range of composers involved, including the eminent concert composers of the time. The concert composers brought to their scores their own musical voices and with them the sound of contemporary British art music. In addition, they brought to the film world a connection with the musical establishment, and a link to the Victorian campaign to raise the quality and appreciation of British music, a campaign that initiated a revival of creative activity that has been dubbed the English Musical Renaissance. The aim of the architects of the English Musical Renaissance was to establish a school of composition in order to foster a national style of music and to raise the standard of music and musical appreciation. The first step was accomplished with the opening of the Royal College of Music in May 1883, which, together with the existing Royal Academy of Music, was a place where the next generation of composers and musicians could not only learn their craft, but also take up the challenge of developing an accessible musical language that would draw its inspiration from the heritage of British music.

The direct involvement of concert composers illustrates the diversity of the film music soundscape in Britain and demonstrates the flexibility of the process wherein the British industry evolves its own aesthetic practices in the arena of film music. At a time when Hollywood films had captured international cinema markets, and America protected its own domestic market, the British industry resisted the Hollywood template in respect of film music. This represents an achievement of some significance, and demonstrates a clear artistic vision on the part of the filmmakers responsible. The film music practices that developed within the British industry impart a feel to British films that subtly differentiates them from the Hollywood films that dominated British screens during this period. K. J. Donnelly notes that 'in terms of overall sound and function', British film music 'often appeared superficially similar to that in Hollywood films' (2007, 8). All national film industries use music to create similar effects. Music may be employed, for example, to aid a film's continuity; to create atmosphere and set the scene; to intensify emotion and dramatise subjectivity; to animate and enliven onscreen action; to unify the film and to guide audience response. However, the music itself can vary widely in both its style and how it is used within a film. These variations highlight different practices and conventions in national industries, and the filmmakers' choices reveal cultural concerns that allow us to read the music as an element which inflects a film with a national character. The disparities between British and Hollywood film music make theories pertaining to Hollywood methods inappropriate to the British industry, other than to confirm different approaches and to make a case for research into the way music is produced within specific national film industries.[1]

The first book-length study into the production and use of music in the British industry, John Huntley's 1947 *British Film Music*, appeared at a historical high point for British cinema and reflects both the level of confidence and the scale of ambition for film music that existed at the time. This is illustrated by Music Director Muir Mathieson's belief that, while Hollywood may have been technically 'more advanced, or at least infinitely "slicker"', the 'average score written here has more intrinsic musical value' (1944, 9). With his classical musical education, Mathieson strove to raise the standard of film music within the British industry, notably by pioneering the practice of commissioning concert composers to score British films. The European composers who established the Hollywood score looked to the late-Romantic idiom of an earlier period rather than to the modernism of much contemporary Continental art music. In Britain, the composers associated with the English Musical Renaissance had similarly drawn upon earlier periods of British music in seeking an accessible musical language and consequently their music was appropriate for the popular medium of cinema. Sixty years after Huntley's contemporary assessment, Donnelly (2007, 14) notes that British film music is to some extent differentiated from its Hollywood equivalent by the 'considerable influence' it received 'from the languages of concert music'. It is upon this foundation that this work builds and expands through a wider exploration of these influences and the ways they enrich the soundscape of British cinema. The involvement of concert composers in the British industry gave rise to a level of tension between the different musical worlds and their working methods and this tension sparked debates over the place of music in the British film. The debates centred on two related issues. First, whether music that retains too great a degree of autonomy may, by serving its own musical ends, undermine the film it accompanies and, second, whether the music should be judged separately from the film.

On the first point, the debate over whether it may be harmful for film music to pursue its own musical logic stems from the concern that in so doing, it may draw attention to itself to the detriment of the film. While dismissing the idea that music should be 'criticised on the ground that it is "too good"', the English composer Gerald Cockshott concedes that it 'may be unsuitable because it is too *developed*' (1946, 2, emphasis in original). The conflict between the worlds of film and music arises partly as a consequence of the power of music in film, and its status as an area not completely within the control of the director. Cockshott reports an unnamed director who finds 'composers as a class difficult to deal with', being 'chiefly anxious that their music *will* stand out from the film so that other producers will notice it and it may be issued separately, on gramophone records' (1946, 8, emphasis in original). A similar complaint is made by producer John Croydon, who accepts the desirability of commissioning eminent composers but criticises those who 'write their music with one eye on concert hall receipts' and in consequence 'the unity of the film suffers' (quoted in Huntley 1947, 161).

On the second point, whether the music should be judged separately from the film, commentators tend to agree that, as the music is written to be heard in the film, it is not possible for it be assessed outside of that context (Huntley 1947, 21; William Alwyn in Manvell and Huntley 1975, 222). Arthur Bliss takes the opposing view that the music should be judged 'solely as music' (Huntley 1947, 160). In 1942, William Walton expressed the opinion that film music 'should never be heard without the film' (Hayes 2002, 140), although he was to alter this view, a shift perhaps not unconnected to the commercial benefits of recordings and concert suites. In 1960 he writes to his publisher that he had 'either forgotten or not realised that they were such money-makers after the initial payment' (Hayes 2002, 316). It is also true that as Walton gained in experience, his film music increased in confidence and autonomy and therefore it became more suitable to be adapted for the concert hall.

The Hungarian-born composer Miklós Rózsa began scoring films in the British industry prior to his successful career in Hollywood, and his case highlights differences in film music practices that were already apparent in the mid-1930s. Rózsa, a trenchant commentator, notes that he accepted his first commissions for scores

> without any idea of how to set about it … I managed to find one or two books on film music and film-making in a bookshop on the Charing Cross Road, one by Kurt London and another translated from the Russian (1982, 66)

The young composer turned for guidance to the earliest published volumes on film scoring, Kurt London's *Film Music* (1936) and *Music for the Films* by Leonid Sabaneev (1935). Both books adopt an instructional tone, and both are critical of practices that were to become established elements of classical Hollywood music: the scoring of dialogue and the close synchronisation of music and onscreen action (1935, 20, 49; 1936, 125). The range of choices in the use of music, the differences in style and aesthetic approaches between national cinemas were thus apparent to the earliest commentators. Even in the relatively early development of the synchronised sound film, we witness a divergence between practices in Hollywood and those in Britain (and more widely in the industries of other European countries), practices that profoundly affect the films of this era and the music they contain.

Although much writing on film music reflects the dominance of the Hollywood product and its characteristics, aspects of the wider debates may be applicable to the context of the British film. One such area is the relative neglect in scholarly writing on film music, and three main factors account for this. The first is the marginal status that film music occupies between the separate disciplines of music and film. Muir Mathieson asserted that criticism of film music falls between the film and music critics, and ends up being 'nobody's baby' (Huntley 1947, 7), a point also made by Hans Keller, who stated in the 1947 pamphlet 'The Need for Competent Film Music Criticism' that 'the film critic should know as much about music as the film music critic must know about the film' (2006, 13).

The second factor that accounts for there being little writing on film music is the visual bias of cinema, in which the primacy of the image can lead us to undervalue the sound and music that give it meaning. This process is eloquently described by the French theorist Michel Chion. Chion uses the term 'added value' to describe the self-effacing nature of film sound, whereby

> a sound enriches a given image so as to create the definite impression … that this information or expression 'naturally' comes from what is seen, and is already contained in the image itself. Added value is what gives the (eminently incorrect) impression that sound is unnecessary, that sound merely duplicates a meaning which in reality it brings about (1994, 5)

Image and sound enjoy a reciprocal relationship, although the combined effect of the two is attributed to the image alone, for sound 'ultimately reprojects onto the image the product of their mutual influences' (1994, 21). This creates 'the impression that we *see* in the image what we are in fact *audio-viewing*' (Chion 2009, 213, emphasis in original). Chion reassesses the role of sound and music in film and reframes the relationship between sound and image with a welcome clarity.

Chion's description of the way the image absorbs the credit for the combined effects of sound and image is connected to the third factor that leads to music being undervalued in cinema—confusion over the way music is apprehended by the cinema audience. Writers are broadly in agreement over the seemingly paradoxical nature of how the audience experiences film music. It must be heard, although not actively listened to; it must be audible, but not occupy the forefront of the audience's awareness. Music must not 'attract attention to itself at the expense of the screen' (Sabaneev 1935, 22), or unsettle a filmgoer's 'concentration on the picture', which it might do if it 'diverged from the picture' (London 1936, 37). The music should be 'heard unconsciously by spectators engrossed in the action' (Levy 1948, 98), but it must not distract the audience by drawing attention to itself. The aesthetic decisions made within individual industries in response to these challenges reflect the differing opinions of practitioners working in Britain and in Hollywood.

Although Hollywood set a remarkably homogenous template for film music as a result of its standardised mode of production, practitioners in the British industry did not seek to emulate it. Not, I would suggest, that the filmmakers in Britain set out with any oppositional intention, but rather that they held different views on how music might be used most effectively. Two clear areas emerge where opinions differ: the quantity of music and the weight and style of its orchestration. The contemporary practice, according to Cockshott (1946, 6–7), was 'to use too much and score it too heavily' in a hangover from the silent period, a point echoed by Manvell and Huntley (1975, 45). With regard to the style of orchestration, Cockshott deplores the overly romantic elements of the Hollywood score: 'the fanfares, the harp arpeggios, the sentimental solo violin, the luscious string tune' (1946, 7). His comments seem to be aimed more at the formulaic elements of the Hollywood score, and to reveal less of a concern with the size of the orchestral forces than with what he considers the excessive sweetness of their orchestrations. Sabaneev (1935, 32) and French composer Maurice Jaubert (1938, 110) similarly criticise the Hollywood system of using orchestrators to arrange the compositions of others, a view shared in Miklós Rózsa's assessment that the music being produced in Hollywood 'all sounded much the same' (1982, 95).[2]

The different approaches to film music in Britain and Hollywood are the subject of Jan Swynnoe's 2002 publication *The Best Years of British Film Music, 1936–1958*. Swynnoe explores the same historical period as this work, although her book takes the form of a comparative analysis of the two industries. Apart from Swynnoe, Donnelly has been something of a lone voice in writing about music in the British industry of this era. However, in spite of there being little recent work on this period, much contemporary writing took place. At the time, film music was attracting a measure of attention in Britain which resulted not only in Huntley's *British Film Music*, but also in his regular column in the BFI's *Sight and Sound*, and articles by Huntley and others in the *Penguin Film Review*. In addition, regular articles appeared in music journals such as *The Musical Times* and *Tempo* by knowledgeable practitioners and commentators including Hubert Clifford, Muir Mathieson, Ernest Irving and Hans Keller.

The focus of this book is firmly on the British industry, although the different practices in British and Hollywood film music are briefly considered in the first part of the second chapter. Here I begin to explore the aesthetic conventions that evolved in British film culture, introduce the main practitioners in the British industry and examine their links to the musical establishment. The chapter concludes with a variety of examples that illustrate the expressive power achieved in the films of this era, and how the British system was able to accommodate an assortment of musical styles. Each of the four subsequent chapters analyses a recurring musical type. Chapter 3 considers music in a pastoral mode, music that blends with landscape imagery to offer visual pleasure, and to evoke its many connotations. Folk song is the subject of the fourth chapter, which explores how its quality as pre-existing music lends authenticity to depictions of communities across the British Isles. Chapter 5 investigates the use of choral voices, their connections to religious and mystical feelings and their relation to the British tradition of choral music. Chapter 6 examines the march, with its military connotations, its historical links to the British military bands and its ceremonial functions. Each musical style is tied to the heritage of British music, and they are included in scores in ways that variously reflect both notions of restraint and the documentary impulse in much of the filmmaking of this time. In order to bring clarity to the field of investigation I have imposed rather artificial boundaries between the musical styles, although there is some drift across the musical areas, and this interaction is in itself expressive. The pastoral aesthetic, for example, permeates folk song and much choral music, while folk song is often heard in choral arrangements that encompass the connotations of both folk song and choral music. Although this complicates the clear categorisation of these styles, it enriches their expressive potential by its cumulative power. When considering examples that freely traverse these borders, I have been guided by the associations most strongly conveyed when deciding where to place them.

The case studies included here tend to favour the work of the better-known British concert composers for the more noted 'prestige' projects. This is a consequence of the composers' concert work being in many instances clearly aligned with their work for films, and therefore a connection may be most clearly drawn between these two areas. The makers of prestige films, those with larger budgets and greater ambitions towards quality, tended to commission scores from celebrated composers as a means of imbuing a film with a sense of artistic value. The prestige films were often the most marketed and promoted at home and internationally, the most discussed, sometimes the most popular and therefore among the most influential films of the era. In addition, the prestige films, perhaps in deference to the eminence of their composers, welcomed music that retained the character of the composer's style and its own musical logic. Although the emphasis on these quality films may reinforce the accepted canon of British films, I hope to reveal a wider picture in respect of British film music. To this end I aim to shine a light upon some of the more (I might say unjustly) neglected scores and films in order to reflect the breadth of filmmaking in the British industry.

Before moving on to a consideration of each musical area, I would like, in the next chapter, to lay the groundwork for the subsequent argument by enlarging upon the nature of musical practice in the British industry of this era, introducing some of its key practitioners and demonstrating how their contribution to British film culture could be both expressive and poetic.

Notes

1. For example, psychoanalytic theories that call on the hypnotic, trance-like quality of the wall-to-wall Hollywood scores of the 1930s and 1940s (Gorbman 1987, 55), or those that explore the uses of Romanticism in Hollywood scoring (Flinn 1992, 24) serve to highlight the differences between British and American film music.
2. Miklós Rózsa was initially wary of the American system of orchestrators. He recalls that, on his arrival in Hollywood to complete work on *The Thief of Bagdad* (1940), union rules compelled him to use an orchestrator for his subsequent films. The orchestrator had to be a union member, and Rózsa himself could not join the union until he had spent a year in Hollywood (interviewed in Brown 1994, 278).

References

Brown, Royal S. 1994. *Overtones and Undertones: Reading Film Music*. Berkeley: University of California Press.

Chion, Michel. 1994. *Audio-Vision: Sound on Screen*. Trans. Claudia Gorbman. New York: Columbia University Press.

———. 2009. *Film, A Sound Art*. Trans. Claudia Gorbman. New York: Columbia University Press.

Cockshott, Gerald. 1946. *'Incidental Music in the Sound Film' Pamphlet*. London: British Film Institute.

Donnelly, K.J. 2007. *British Film Music and Film Musicals*. Basingstoke: Palgrave Macmillan.

Flinn, Caryl. 1992. *Strains of Utopia: Gender, Nostalgia and Hollywood Film Music*. Princeton: Princeton University Press.

Gorbman, Claudia. 1987. *Unheard Melodies: Narrative Film Music*. London: British Film Institute.

Hayes, Malcolm, ed. 2002. *The Selected Letters of William Walton*. London: Faber.

Huntley, John. 1947. *British Film Music*. London: Skelton Robinson.

Jaubert, Maurice. 1938. Music on the Screen. In *Footnotes on the Film*, ed. Charles Davy, 101–115. London: Lovat Dickson Ltd.

Keller, Hans. 2006. In *Film Music and Beyond: Writings on Music and the Screen, 1946–59*, ed. Christopher Wintle. London: Plumbago Books.

Levy, Louis. 1948. *Music for the Movies*. London: Sampson Low.

London, Kurt. 1936. *Film Music: A Summary of the Characteristic Features of Its History, Aesthetics, Technique, and Possible Developments*. London: Faber & Faber.

Manvell, Roger, and John Huntley. 1975. *The Technique of Film Music*. London: Focal Press.

Mathieson, Muir. 1944. Aspects of Film Music. *Tempo* 9: 7–9.

Rózsa, Miklós. 1982. *Double Life: The Autobiography of Miklós Rózsa*. Tunbridge Wells: The Baton Press.

Sabaneev, Leonid. 1935. *Music for the Films: A Handbook for Composers and Conductors*. Trans. S.W. Pring. London: Sir Isaac Pitman & Sons Ltd.

Swynnoe, Jan G. 2002. *The Best Years of British Film Music, 1936–1958*. Woodbridge: Boydell Press.

CHAPTER 2

Aesthetic Conventions: Distinctiveness and Diversity

Music in British films often displays a level of aesthetic diversity that makes it difficult to single out its defining characteristics and conventions. As a result, although we experience music and film as an integrated audiovisual unit, it can be useful to consider the nature of the music separately to the way it is used within a film. These two interrelated factors, the music itself and how it is employed, combine to create meaning and multiple effects within a film. Both are pertinent to the central concern of this chapter, which is to investigate the distinctiveness of much British film music, to understand the industry conditions that enabled it to develop in the way that it did, and to demonstrate the expressive potential that was possible within this system. Before going on to introduce the key practitioners in the British industry and to look more closely at examples of their work, the chapter begins to explore the characteristics of British film music by pinpointing some areas of divergence between British and Hollywood film music.

The British Score and the Hollywood Score

Music in British cinema of this era is in some respects similar to that associated with Hollywood cinema and in other respects quite different to it. Points of convergence and divergence are found in both the intrinsic qualities of the music and in the way it is used within the film. When film music practice in Britain deviates from the norms adhered to by the dominant

P. Mazey, *British Film Music*, Palgrave Studies in Audio-Visual Culture, https://doi.org/10.1007/978-3-030-33550-2_2

Hollywood product, the departures offer insights into how the British industry responds to the particular challenges it faces and how it comes to accommodate a more diverse musical palette. Moreover, divergences in practice reveal areas where the British industry in certain respects establishes separate conventions in film music, whether as a result of aesthetic differences or economic necessity.

The aim of the Hollywood score was to provide narrative clarity, and the conventions that governed its use were based on this guiding principle. It was designed to be as unnoticed as the continuity editing of which it forms a constituent part. The music featured 'a high degree of direct synchronisation between music and narrative action', its sound 'was largely symphonic; its idiom romantic; and its formal unity typically derived from the principle of the leitmotif' (Kalinak 1992, 79). Exemplified by the major work of Max Steiner, Hollywood scores employed leitmotivs and close synchronisation with onscreen action, scored (usually by orchestrators) in a lush, late-romantic style. In the Hollywood score, 'every mood and action [was] rendered hyperexplicit' (Gorbman 1987, 1), and the remarkable consistency of the means by which this was achieved makes it relatively straightforward to summarise its defining characteristics. When Gorbman (1998, 45) writes of the reliance of the Hollywood score on 'such devices as *ostinati*, 'stingers', and mickey-mousing' in order to maintain close synchronisation between music and action, she reminds us of the debt that all film music owes to the classical repertoire, particularly to opera, and to the conventions of silent film scoring.

While the music written in the British industry equally reflects its musico-dramatic forbears, it displays a greater diversity of form and musical character, and it is less reliant upon close synchronisation and leitmotivs. The British film typically uses less music, and the music is generally less tied in a moment-to-moment relationship with onscreen action. Ralph Vaughan Williams has written of two styles of film scoring. In the first, 'every action, word, gesture or incident is punctuated in sound', and the composer notes that this closely synchronised scoring calls for 'great skill and orchestral knowledge and a vivid specialised imagination'. The second method, which Vaughan Williams favours, is to 'ignore the details and to intensify the spirit of the whole situation by a continuous stream of music [which] can be modified … by points of colour superimposed on the flow' (1945, 161). Vaughan Williams's two styles broadly align with the models adopted in Hollywood and British scoring respectively. In contrast to the standard Hollywood score, the British score generally embodies a more restrained, even understated approach, although the wider array of variation it displays presents a challenge to its categorisation based upon standardised elements, for overall it is marked by a diversity that is the result of a greater freedom *from* standardisation.

In common with Hollywood and other European film-producing countries, the British score usually employs a Western orchestral sound, although with a variety in terms of instrumentation that extends from the single instrument nondiegetic score of *The Third Man* (Carol Reed, 1949) to the full symphonic force of Vaughan Williams's music for *Scott of the Antarctic* (Charles Frend, 1948). British scores differ from their Hollywood counterparts both in the intrinsic qualities of the music they employ, and in their greater freedom from the conventions that govern its use. For example, a convention generally adhered to by the Hollywood score is the use of music as a continuity device during transitions between scenes (Gorbman 1987, 73), whereas spatial and temporal ellipses in British films are frequently achieved without musical smoothing. Similarly, the potential 'jarring effects' that result from the disruption of chronological linearity occasioned by the flashback find music 'compulsively used' in the Hollywood film (Flinn 1992, 109). British films, in contrast, display a greater flexibility and may bridge their flashback transitions without music. They might instead employ a dissolve and voiceover (*The Woman in Question* (Anthony Asquith, 1950)), dialogue that ends on a dissolve (*While I Live* (John Harlow, 1947)), or a simple cut and continued voiceover (*Kind Hearts and Coronets* (Robert Hamer, 1949)).

The differences between the scores produced in Hollywood and those produced in Britain can be attributed to the different production methods that evolved in each industry. The Hollywood industry was organised along the lines of a large factory. Its rigorously controlled production line yielded efficiency and consistency, and in standardising its production methods Hollywood also standardised to some extent what was produced. The economies of scale enjoyed by the major studios both enabled and required them to employ teams of full-time composers, orchestrators and musicians to create scores that complied with the expected and successful formulae. The more humble resources of the much smaller British studios precluded salaried composers and instead scores were commissioned on a film-by-film basis. This practice had two significant benefits for the standard of music in the British industry. First, it enabled composers to be employed for projects that were considered suitable to their style. Second, the freedom from the constraints imposed on Hollywood composers to provide scores built upon leitmotivs and close synchronisation, combined with the 'longer scenes and slower cutting' typically found in British films of the 1930s and 1940s, enabled the use of more 'autonomous music' (Donnelly 2007, 38). This allowed composers from different walks of musical life to work in the film industry. More significantly, the music itself, free from the homogenising influence of the Hollywood orchestrators and the necessity to shadow every detail of onscreen action, was able to retain more recognisable elements of its composer's individual style, and to maintain its own musical logic; to be 'genuine music' (Rawsthorne 1975, 36). While it would be an oversimplification to suggest a complete lack of variation in Hollywood scoring techniques, British scores embrace a greater variety of musical voices, and their music is generally used more sparingly and is less wedded to each contour of screen movement.

Composers in the British Film Industry

The majority of composers in the British industry combined their film work with other activities, either writing popular music, light music, incidental music for theatre and radio, or art music for concert performance. While this was undoubtedly an economic necessity for the composers, it nevertheless enlivened the range of film music by the influences of these other fields, and is a further element of divergence in industry practice between Britain and Hollywood. Composer Malcolm Arnold notes that in America, composers were generally obliged to choose between writing for film and writing for the concert hall, owing to the geographical distance between their respective centres, Hollywood and New York, and the contractual arrangements with the film studios, whereas

> composers in London are not tied by contract to any company, and they can accept work on the basis of writing for one film. We have much more freedom (quoted in Schafer 1963, 149–50)

Just as actors in the British industry were able to combine their film work with theatrical engagements in the West End,[1] composers were able to work in a number of musical arenas.

The eminent concert composers who wrote film scores during this period tend to draw a disproportionate amount of critical attention, for a number of reasons. Audiences and commentators may pay more attention to the music in a film if the composer has a certain cultural standing. The filmmakers may promote the music of a noted composer as a 'featured aspect' in the film's opening titles and in its wider publicity, and accordingly the music may be permitted to take more of a foreground role within the film itself (Donnelly 2007, 2). In addition, the cultural cachet that a composer can confer upon a film is called upon by filmmakers who wish to lend their project a mark of quality, and the more celebrated composers therefore tend to be associated with the higher-budget 'prestige' productions, releases that are in any case more heavily marketed and that shoulder a greater burden of box-office expectation both nationally and internationally.

The origin of using more autonomous music both to promote a film in wider cultural spheres and to confer upon it an aura of highbrow respectability can be traced back to *Things To Come* (William Cameron Menzies, 1936). H.G. Wells adapted his own book and was closely involved in the production for Alexander Korda's London Films. His approach was innovative. 'The music', wrote Wells, 'is a part of the constructive scheme of the film ... [It] is not intended to be tacked on; it is part of the design' (quoted in Huntley 1947, 39). Wells himself met the composer Arthur Bliss in the spring of 1934 and invited him to provide the film's score. With hindsight, it adds prescience to Bliss's article, written more than a decade earlier in 1922, in which he bemoans the state of film music at that point, and looks forward to the 'proud day' when composers might be 'featured as the sound producing experts on a real life multi-million dollar movie' (1991, 220).

Bliss's musical score was composed prior to the shooting of the film in accordance with Wells's treatment and detailed ideas, for the author felt strongly that the film should be built around the music. In October of 1934, Wells wrote to Bliss:

> I am at issue with Korda ... on the question of where you come in. They say – It is the Hollywood tradition – 'We make the film right up to the cutting then, *when* we have cut, the musician comes in and *puts in his music*'.
>
> I say Balls! ... I say 'A film is a composition and the musical composer is an integral part of the design. I want Bliss to be in touch throughout' (reprinted in Bliss 1970, 104, emphases in original)

Ultimately, only the extended montage that depicts the rebuilding of Everytown was edited to Bliss's pre-composed score (Frayling 1995, 37–40). Wells's vision was otherwise forced to give way to practical considerations and the music was rearranged and edited to fit the needs of the screen (Riley 2010, 254). In spite of this, the film is notable not only for introducing Bliss to the cinema, but also for pioneering the practice in the British industry of commissioning film scores from eminent composers. It was also an early example of a score being arranged for concert performance. Bliss's *Things To Come* suite received its premiere at the Queen's Hall Proms in 1935 prior to the film's release, and it was issued on a Decca gramophone recording with the London Symphony Orchestra under the composer's baton. Perhaps most significantly, though, by opening the film world to the concert composer, *Things To Come* initiated the evolution of a more fluid and flexible approach to film music, occasioned by the adjustments necessary to customary methods of working. These exploratory negotiations between the concert world and the film industry sought to accommodate and at times to foreground the composer's contribution in a way that acknowledged the value of music to the film. The working relationships between film industry and art music depended to a large degree upon the ministrations of the music directors, who formed the point of liaison between the two.

The music on the soundtrack of *Things To Come* was conducted by Korda's young Scottish music director, Muir Mathieson. The British industry practice of commissioning scores individually for each film magnified the importance of the music director's role, and Mathieson made it his mission to raise the standard of music in the British film. In 1934, at the age of twenty-three, Mathieson took over as the music director of Alexander Korda's London Films. Korda had recruited him from the Royal College of Music (RCM) where Mathieson had studied piano and composition under Arthur Benjamin and conducting under Malcolm Sargent. Mathieson had insisted that Korda allow him to commission 'first-rate composers' for every score, rather than require Mathieson himself to provide his own 'indifferent music' (1947, 59). Miklós Rózsa remembers Mathieson as a 'competent and serious musician' who was 'very experienced at synchronising music and action' (1982, 69). Mathieson worked with the forces' production units and the Crown Film Unit during the war and later on a freelance basis with a number of companies under the Rank umbrella. The young music director had clear ideas about his aspirations for music in the British industry, and these did not include an emulation of Hollywood music. Although he acknowledged its excellence in 'technique and the very lighter type of music', he found among it 'very little that is worthwhile' (1947, 62). His musical training facilitated his acting as a liaison between the world of music, and particularly the concert hall, and the world of film, for it was Mathieson who largely pioneered the practice of commissioning art composers for film work.

Concert composers were also commissioned by Ealing Studios, where Ernest Irving had been the music director since 1933, the time of its earlier incarnation as Basil Dean's Associated Talking Pictures. Michael Balcon recalled Irving as 'a musicologist and classical scholar' who lived in 'Dickensian chaos' (1969, 147). Irving had been an experienced conductor and music director for theatre and operetta before he discovered a gift for fitting existing music to silent films and moved into film work. A third prominent music director was Louis Levy at Gainsborough Studios. Levy had risen through the ranks of the cinema orchestra to become a music arranger and director for silent films, before joining Gaumont-British Studios at the end of the silent era.

The responsibility for all of the musical aspects of a film rests with the music director—nondiegetic and diegetic music, researching specialised instruments, training actors to portray musicians convincingly, arranging, supervising, and frequently conducting recording sessions (Manvell and Huntley 1975, 200–201). Muir Mathieson has detailed the process with reference to Laurence Olivier's *Hamlet* (1948). It begins when the music department receives the final shooting script:

> This is immediately read through, and a note made of the more obvious points at which music will occur – trumpet calls, for example, and scenes showing musicians or, possibly, unusual instruments. Close contact is maintained with the composer from now on, and any specialised items discussed with the director and producer (1948a, 63)

The music department offers any necessary advice 'on musical or choral scenes' once the shooting begins, and arranges any music required on set. When the 'rough cut' of the film is ready, it is screened for the music director, composer, director and editor to determine 'where music is required and what form it should take'. The editor then compiles for the composer a sheet of exact timings of the sections for which music is needed. Finally the music is recorded, in this case with the Philharmonia Orchestra under Mathieson's baton, 'in short sections … though the music sections usually covered several shots for greater effect'. The importance accorded to the music for *Hamlet* is evident in the music sessions being attended not only by composer William Walton, but also by Olivier, and the film's editor, Helga Cranston. The music director's role as the point of connection between the worlds of music and film requires a broad technical knowledge of both, and a close working relationship with the composer and the director.

While the attention attracted by eminent concert composers undoubtedly raised the profile of film music within the British industry, their overall contribution is not large when taken as a proportion of the total output. British film music is characterised by the range of composers employed and the diversity of their musical endeavours outside of the film industry. Although it requires a measure of generalisation, the composers for the films included in this study may be grouped into three broad categories: those who specialise in popular lighter music; those who combine film work with serious music but enjoy greater success in the film world; and those concert composers who take on film score assignments.

Among the composers of light music are Richard Addinsell and Charles Williams. Addinsell composed the popular 'Warsaw Concerto' for the film *Dangerous Moonlight* (Brian Desmond Hurst, 1941), worked regularly in the theatre with Clemence Dane and put his melodic gifts to good use in a lasting collaboration with Joyce Grenfell. Charles Williams provided music for many films before it was the accepted practice for individual composers to receive a credit (notably Hitchcock's *Blackmail* (1929)) and he went on to score *While I Live*, which includes the popular piano piece 'The Dream of Olwen'. Williams specialised in melodic light music, and his work has been taken up for theme tunes, for example, by the long-running radio programmes *Dick Barton, Special Agent*, and *Friday Night is Music Night*, and also to accompany the early television interlude 'The Potter's Wheel'. Alongside Addinsell and Williams, Hubert Bath (composer of the 'Cornish Rhapsody' from *Love Story* (Leslie Arliss, 1944)) and Hans May (the composer for several of the Gainsborough melodrama films) were most associated with light music.

Among composers in the second category, those who undertook film work as well as writing for the concert hall, are William Alwyn, who wrote prolifically for film, and Brian Easdale, who is known for his work with Powell and Pressburger. Into the third category fall Arnold Bax, Arthur Bliss, John Ireland, Constant Lambert, Ralph Vaughan Williams, and William Walton, together with Alan Rawsthorne and Bernard Stevens, who were primarily concert composers who accepted film commissions. Benjamin Frankel proves an exception to this categorisation. Frankel studied composition, piano and violin, began his career as a musician and arranger for jazz and dance bands, wrote prolifically for films and also maintained an output of serious music that included eight completed symphonies and embraced twelve-note composition.

The assortment of musical activities the composers engage in outside of the film world belies a remarkable consistency in their musical education. Of more than fifty composers who provided film scores in this period, thirteen received their musical education on the continent and reflect the transnational influence of European émigrés, who either settled in Britain (Francis Chagrin, Allan Gray, Hans May, Mátyás Seiber), moved on to Hollywood (Miklós Rózsa), or worked internationally (Georges Auric). A further ten attended varied schools—Alan Rawsthorne, for instance, studied at the Royal Manchester College of Music, while Leighton Lucas was largely self-taught. William Walton left Oxford without a degree, although he regards his years as a chorister at Christ Church Cathedral 'a musical education in itself' (quoted in Schafer 1963, 73). The remaining composers display a greater uniformity in their musical education. Nine, including William Alwyn and Charles Williams, attended the Royal Academy of Music, while four RAM attendees, Hubert Bath, Arnold Bax, Jack Beaver, and Eric Coates, all studied under Frederick Corder. Seventeen composers attended the Royal College of Music, across several generations of musical luminaries. Ralph Vaughan Williams and Gustav Holst both studied under the founding members Hubert Parry and Charles Villiers Stanford. Holst went on to teach Arthur Bliss and Anthony Collins. Stanford also taught Arthur Benjamin, Arthur Bliss, John Greenwood, John Ireland, and Gordon Jacob. Gordon Jacob in turn taught John Addison, Malcolm Arnold, Brian Easdale, Antony Hopkins, Bernard Stevens, and Cedric Thorpe Davie. Further exploration reveals inter-relationships (see Fig. 2.1)—the English composer Armstrong Gibbs (1889–1960), although not involved with film, had studied under Vaughan Williams at the RCM, and then taught at the institution between 1921 and 1939, when one of his students was Brian Easdale.

A web of connections emerges in which each generation of composers learns from the previous generation and teaches the next. While not in itself unusual, this passing-on of a musical heritage suggests a more consistent and uniform musical education across the board of this group of composers than the specialisms in my rough categorisations above might indicate. Moreover, it exposes a connecting thread between those who originated the mission of the English Musical Renaissance and the

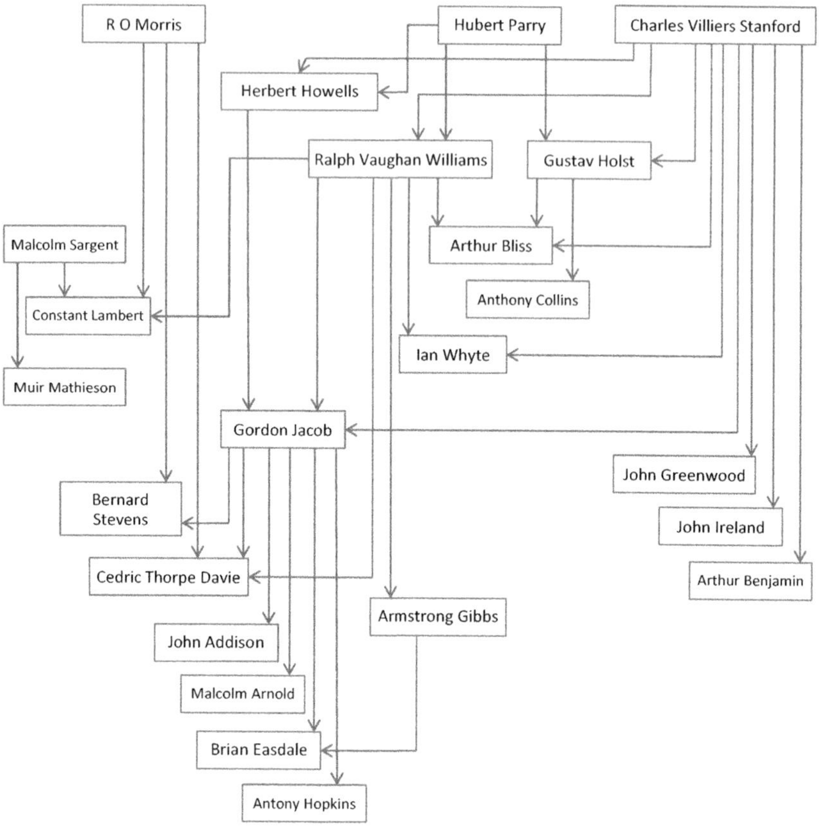

Fig. 2.1 Composers and their tutors at the RCM (Arrows connect tutors [above] with students [below])

composers of succeeding generations to whom they passed the baton. The close links between the architects of the Renaissance, the composers in the second tranche of that movement, and the younger composers explains the engagement of the latter with the historical traditions of British art music, traditions that they are able to call upon in their subsequent film music.

In spite of this apparent parity and uniformity in the musical training of the film composers, there nonetheless exists in musical discourse a hierarchy of cultural value that places film music, together with lighter music, some distance below concert music (Palmer 1971, 20). A composer who is strongly associated with film music may struggle for recognition in the world of serious music. Mervyn Cooke notes that the reputations of William Alwyn, Malcolm Arnold, and Benjamin Frankel have suffered as a result of their involvement with film music (2008, 226). In the case of Arnold, Jackson concurs with this view, although he also notes the opportunity it provided the composer to 'try out techniques and devices', and to gain 'experience of conducting and … financial security' (2003, 55). Asked whether a young composer might 'jeopardize his talents by writing for the films', Arnold himself responded that it might be

> a bad thing to be completely submerged in the film world – bad even for your film-music – but a certain amount of it can be very good for a young composer (quoted in Schafer 1963, 151)

Vaughan Williams similarly felt that film work was a 'splendid discipline', particularly for those who were 'apt to be dawdling in their ideas, or whose every bar is sacred and must not be cut or altered' (1945, 160). This sentiment is echoed by Arthur Bliss who believed it 'good for a composer's technique' (1970, 106). Mathieson observes the benefit to a composer of their work being heard quite quickly after it has been written, something that cannot be taken for granted with music written for the concert hall (1944, 9). For an aspiring serious composer, then, undertaking film work may have had a positive impact on technique and a negative impact on reputation.

William Walton addresses the issue of reputation in a 1938 letter to his publisher Hubert Foss, at the Oxford University Press. Gabriel Pascal had approached him to write music for the film *Pygmalion* (Leslie Howard, Anthony Asquith, 1938), and two further projects for the then princely sum of £1650. '[It] all boils down to this', the composer writes, 'whether I'm to become a film composer or a real composer'. Making clear that he regards film work as a means to a financial end, he continues: 'I think I can safely wipe out films, which have served their purpose in enabling me to get my house etc.' (Hayes 2002, 115). Walton declined Pascal's offer and *Pygmalion* was scored by the Swiss composer Arthur Honegger. It was only with the outbreak of war, and the consequent reduction in musical life in London that Walton returned to film work. Films then served a dual purpose of providing Walton with an income[2] and a means for him to avoid being called up for active military service (Hayes 2002, 119–120).

A notoriously slow worker, Walton found the deadlines of film music a challenge. In December of 1943, he wrote to composer and orchestrator Roy Douglas that *Henry V* (Laurence Olivier, 1944) was 'more of a bloody nuisance than it is possible to believe … there's going to be the usual hell of a rush' (Hayes 2002, 147). The short deadlines of the film studio are repeatedly cited as a concern by concert composers. Vaughan Williams, explaining how busy he has been in a letter to composer Gerald Finzi, writes 'the gestation period of a film composer seems more like a cat than a human' (Cobbe 2002, 354). John Ireland, composing for his only film, *The Overlanders* (Harry Watt, 1946), reports that although it is 'terribly hard, *cruel* work', he finds it

> very interesting and exciting … – but the amount of work is fantastic. I get up at 6 every morning – and work till 1 or 2 a.m. – *every* day! (quoted in Richards 2000, 201, emphases in original)

Ireland's enthusiasm for film work is not shared by Arnold Bax. Mathieson (1948b, 324) reports that it took 'quite a bit of persuasion' to convince him to write music for the documentary *Malta G.C.* in 1942. For his next commission, David Lean's *Oliver Twist* (1948), Bax complains of being 'inveigled (not to say bullied)' into writing the score. Not only did the composer find 'no music in the subject at all' but there was 'the usual inconsiderate rush' (quoted in Foreman 1983, 346). Four months later Bax was no happier, and writes that he is 'still plagued' by the film, 'for which [he] struggled in agony to provide music' (ibid.). Overall, Bax found film an unsatisfactory medium for the composer, complaining that his music ended up being 'largely inaudible, toned down to make way for—in many cases—quite unnecessary talk' (quoted in Huntley 1947, 160), and, perhaps unsurprisingly, *Oliver Twist* remained his only feature-length score.

Bax may have taken some solace in the fact that, in addition to the publicity he garnered from his *Oliver Twist* score, it was also one of his most financially profitable undertakings (Foreman 1983, 346). Arthur Bliss concedes that the 'chief incentive' to undertake film work is financial, 'as a composer is likely to make far more money in a little time by this sort of work' than is possible from concert composition (quoted in Huntley 1947, 160). Ernest Irving recognises this position, and suggests that a composer might earn a sufficient sum 'on film music' in a quarter of a year to enable him to spend the remaining three quarters on his own work, 'however uncommercial' (1959, 162). This was certainly the case for Walton, whose widow reports that the fees from his first film (*Escape Me Never* (Paul Czinner, 1935)) 'helped to pay the mortgage' while the composer worked on his First Symphony (1988, 87). Thus, the film studios provided composers with a commercial outlet for their work, one that could prove extremely lucrative, and in this respect, it is possible to view film commissions as a positive aspect of a composer's portfolio, in that they enabled their less commercial activities.

The majority of film composers working in the British industry at this time also contributed scores for documentary films, and, for some, this was their introduction to the film studio.[3] The short documentary films not only provided a training ground for future feature film directors, notably Alberto Cavalcanti and Harry Watt, but they also gave a number of British composers, particularly those more associated with the concert world, the opportunity to try their hand at film music composition. Malcolm Arnold, Arnold Bax, Brian Easdale, Gordon Jacob, Constant Lambert, and Alan Rawsthorne all scored documentary subjects prior to taking on feature commissions. Benjamin Britten had worked on nearly two dozen short documentary films for the General Post Office (GPO) Film Unit before scoring his only feature film, *Love from a Stranger* (Rowland V. Lee, 1937),[4] and he continued to work on documentaries until 1946 (Oliver 1996, 222–4). Documentary productions enabled composers to discover whether film work suited their particular talents and abilities, and allowed the music directors to gauge their potential for feature subjects. In contrast, Benjamin Frankel, Richard Addinsell, John Greenwood, and Clifton Parker had all scored for feature films before working on documentaries.

Under the leadership of John Grierson at the Empire Marketing Board Film Unit and its successors the GPO Film Unit and the Crown Film Unit, the British documentary movement exerted a significant influence on British film culture and particularly on its use of music. Although Grierson saw film primarily as a means to an educational end, he nevertheless 'encouraged and supported aesthetic experimentation' in filmmaking (Aitken 1990, 144). Muir Mathieson welcomed the documentary makers' innovative approach in mixing elements on the soundtrack to create 'a coherent whole, not a mere aural accompaniment to the visuals on the screen' (1944, 9). In the documentary, he explains, 'sight and sound are entirely dependent on each other', with the result that 'music plays a doubly important part, providing, as it must, a larger than usual share of the entertainment' (1948b, 323). Mathieson's role as the Music Director of the Crown Film Unit is emblematic of the shared personnel and creative cross-pollination that occurred between the documentary arm of the British industry and British feature production. In its previous incarnation as the GPO Film Unit, it had, in the 1930s, commissioned music from art composers, including Maurice Jaubert, Darius Milhaud, and Marius-François Gaillard. Benjamin Britten provided his influential scores for *Coal Face* in 1935 and *Night Mail* in 1936, each containing the composer's rhythmic interpretation of W.H. Auden's verse to accompany onscreen movement. Alberto Cavalcanti, the director of *Coal Face* and sound director of *Night Mail*, finds a 'poetic effect' in such audiovisual melding, where

> Out of the conflict between the objectiveness of the picture and the subjectiveness of the commentary comes a third thing, a dramatic feeling which is different in essentials from, and I think deeper in effect than, either of the two elements which are combined to create it (1985, 102)

The inventive environment of the documentary unit offered composers 'an outlet for experiment and initiative not possible under the restrictions of commercial cinema', and engendered a more creative approach to film music within the wider industry (Huntley 1947, 106, 103). With the onset of the Second World War, the realist aesthetic of documentary was to have a profound effect on British feature production, on the nature of music in the films and on how it was employed. The characteristic approach was a restrained one that favoured an understated use of music rather than one that might be deemed excessive.

The Aesthetics of British Film Music

British films, in comparison with their Hollywood counterparts, typically employ less music and thus adopt an aesthetic of restraint. Gerald Cockshott praises this approach, and believes music to be 'more effective the more sparingly it is used' (1946, 7). While this may be regarded as an economic imperative, and at times it no doubt was, there are instances where a decision was made to use less music than was available, and these indicate that restraint can be a purely aesthetic choice. David Lean, for example, decided against using all of the music that Arnold Bax composed for *Oliver Twist*. Bax had written music to accompany the opening storm that Oliver's mother struggles through, and this was completely removed, 'apart from a few string harmonics when briars are silhouetted against the darkening sky' (Parlett 2003, 8). Instead, the soundtrack contains only natural sounds and sound effects, and this sequence thus parallels the opening of Lean's *Great Expectations* (1946), in which the howling wind and creaking of the trees are heard without musical accompaniment.[5] Elsewhere in *Oliver Twist*, parts of the score were used in a heavily truncated form, for example, only the concluding fanfares of a cue written for the aftermath of Nancy's murder are used to accompany the montage of 'wanted' posters being put up (Parlett 2003, 12). Bax was not experienced in composing for the cinema, having previously only provided music for the documentary short *Malta GC* (1942). To assist the composer, Lean wrote extensive notes on where he wanted music and what he wanted it to do, a sample of which is reprinted in Manvell and Huntley (1975, 90). Lean is extremely detailed in this extract, indicating not only exactly when he wishes the music to begin and end, but also in explaining what he hopes it will achieve. The director's selectiveness in reducing the amount of music used in the final cut of the film is therefore all the more notable.

When music is not heard as a constant background accompaniment, a contrast may be drawn between its presence and its absence that accentuates both its use and the musical silence when it is not used, and increases the audience's awareness of the music. Chion confirms that the significance of music to a film is 'in no way proportional to the number or length of the cues', and that music used intermittently 'is likely to make a difference when it does occur' (2009, 417). In British cinema, where musical accompaniment is infrequently heard in a constant stream, a greater emphasis may be placed upon the strategies that are employed to introduce and to end music cues. Muir Mathieson notes that 'the transition from music to speech is of the greatest importance to the flow of the sound track' (1944, 9). British films tend rarely to use the practice of the music 'sneaking in', where the music starts at a low level and gradually increases in volume. Instead, the dramatic impact of music as it starts or ends is often heightened through its introduction or cessation in tandem with a narrative sound, action, or both. Music may be introduced in synchronisation with the sharp sound of a diegetic event, which provides a similar experience to a sting, and this occurs notably when the music continues through a montage of different shots.

For example, the music that accompanies the montage sequence that depicts Narcy's (Griffith Jones) brutal physical assault on Sally (Sally Gray) in *They Made Me A Fugitive* (Cavalcanti, 1947) begins with sudden urgency when he first strikes her, and quickly builds to an orchestral tumult as she falls to the ground. After a series of quickly cut shots that alternate between Narcy, Sally and Cora (Rene Ray), who listens at the door of the dressing room where the attack takes place, the image darkens and becomes degraded with light speckles that reflect Sally's perspective. As the violent onslaught continues, Narcy is shown from Sally's point of view and his image spins, first anti-clockwise then clockwise, in a visual representation of her experience. Marius-François Gaillard's frenzied music indicates the continuation of the assault when the image rests on Cora outside of the room, and when the music slows and becomes calm, we understand that the physical violence has subsided. The close synchronisation between music and action at the beginning of the sequence ties the soundtrack to the image track. This enables the music to represent the action when it is not directly shown on screen, to hold together the montage of shots, and to express the ferocity of the attack. The initial alignment between action and music both justifies and naturalises the presence of nondiegetic music on the soundtrack.

Music that holds together a montage sequence may also begin in synchronisation with diegetic action, and in a similar way the coincidence between music and action will create a bond between the two that allows the image a greater freedom to be expressive rather than explicit. In *Odd Man Out* (Carol Reed, 1947), William Alwyn's urgent music begins on the action of Dennis (Robert Beatty) as he runs towards the police in order to draw their attention away from the injured Johnny (James Mason). The driving intensity of the music is joined on the soundtrack by the sound of the police whistles as the chase begins. The ensuing montage comprises shots from high and low angles, canted compositions and inserts of the reactions of the residents in the streets Dennis runs along. The chiaroscuro lighting, glistening wet streets and distorted shadows thrown against brick façades prefigure the similar imagery that Reed would employ in *The Third Man* (1949) for chase scenes through the streets of war-torn Vienna, and the retrospective comparison highlights the engagement of Alwyn's music in these scenes in contrast to the cool aloofness of Anton Karas's zither score in the later film. The close relationship initially established between Alwyn's music and the onscreen action maintains the narrative thread of the sequence and liberates the image from the requirement to explain each turn of the pursuit.

Just as music may begin in synchronisation with a diegetic sound or action, it may also end with a diegetic sound or action. The flexible music that Benjamin Frankel provides for a dialogue scene between Adam (Kieron More) and Felix (Burgess Meredith) in *Mine Own Executioner* (Anthony Kimmins, 1947) ends abruptly as Felix snaps his cigarette lighter closed. More strikingly perhaps, music may not simply end suddenly, but its interruption by diegetic events may subvert our expectation of its musical resolution. In *The Broken Horseshoe* (Martyn C. Webster, 1953), a fast version of Wilfred Burns's main theme is heard as Fenton (Robert Beatty) enters a hotel reception only to break off mid-phrase when he rings the desk bell. In contrast, John Wooldridge's soft background music in *Appointment in London* (Philip Leacock, 1953) is gradually drowned out by the engine noise of an aeroplane that fills the soundtrack before it takes off. This provides a more discreet ending to the cue, more akin to music sneaking out, and in consequence is less dramatically expressive.

In a variation on the visual motivation for the presence of music, its absence may be prompted by sudden darkness on screen. In *Odd Man Out*, the theme associated with Johnny is heard as he hides in the shadowy corners of a bunker when a young courting couple enter and talk. The music grows louder as the man lights a match and approaches Johnny, then synchronises with the action of the match going out after Johnny tells them to clear out, and pauses to leave a moment of silent darkness before it resumes softly as they go. In *Oliver Twist*, Parlett (2003, 9) notes the unnerving atmosphere of the music Bax provides to accompany Oliver's first night among the coffins at the funeral parlour, conjured by 'strings playing *sul ponticello* [on the bridge], baleful muted brass and skeletal xylophone'. The scene ends with a short flourish on woodwinds after Oliver blows out the candle. The music in both scenes accentuates the visual contrast between light and dark and also equates silence with the eerie emptiness of darkness on screen. The absence of light on screen leaves us nothing visual to experience as we await its reintroduction, and places us (in the cinema at least) in the same position as the characters in the narrative.

The sting or stinger—a sudden, shocking musical blast that shatters a hitherto calm and quiet atmosphere, and the reverse sting, in which music ends abruptly to leave a sonic void, use music in a way that specifically draws attention to its sudden presence or absence. Although its use as a dramatic device is found across generic boundaries, Donnelly identifies the stinger as a staple of the horror film genre, and describes also the primal, physical effect it may exert upon the audience (2005, 93). The stinger not only represents the sudden shock felt by characters in the narrative, it recreates the experience for the audience.

The stinger may dramatise the subjective experience of a character, as happens explicitly in *The Long Memory* (Robert Hamer, 1953) when Davidson (John Mills) closes in on Pewsey (John Slater), the man who had caused him to be wrongfully imprisoned. The front door is filmed at a low angle from inside and Pewsey mumbles to himself as he puts the cat out. William Alwyn's main theme is heard in a dark, foreboding guise as the door opens to reveal the figure of Davidson approaching, although initially Pewsey, bent over with the cat, does not notice him. Only when he grasps the situation, pulls back and struggles with the door do the stinging chords begin, spinning in confusion and panic as he closes the door and manages to secure the bolt and barricade it with the hallway coat stand. Through its close synchronisation with his realisation, the stinger expresses Pewsey's subjective experience and his terror. This contrasts with the film's earlier musical restraint, for, as Johnson notes, up to this point the tension has been ratcheted up using only sound effects (2005, 252).

Both the subjective terror of the young Duke of York (Andy Shine) and the fury of Richard (Laurence Olivier) are expressed through an extended stinger in *Richard III* (Olivier, 1955) when the boy arouses Richard's sudden volcanic anger. The music starts with a percussive crack as, filmed from a low angle that represents the boy's point of view, Richard turns and fixes him with a malevolent stare. Walton's cue continues through a cut to the reverse shot of the boy as he stumbles backwards, and the music subsides to leave a cold silence that expresses the discomfort of the gathered witnesses. In these examples, the stinger is shockingly full-blooded, at the loudest and most startling end of the spectrum. As a result of the transparent bluntness of the effect, it tends to be used sparingly and reserved only for highly dramatic moments, as it is the most extreme method of using a musical accent to mark a narrative event or subjective experience.

Similarly, the dramatic effect of the reverse sting, in which the music breaks off abruptly to leave a sudden silence, may be modulated by the volume and intensity of the music employed. The reverse sting has the effect of throwing into sharp focus the image that accompanies the ensuing silence, and the sound or particularly the dialogue that breaks it. In *Brighton Rock* (John Boulting, 1947), the device builds a sense of expectation in the audience prior to the introduction of Pinkie (Richard Attenborough). Hans May's winding melody on a solo violin is heard as Dallow (William Hartnell) climbs the staircase to show Pinkie the newspaper headline that indicates the reporter who brought about the demise of the former leader of his race gang would be in Brighton that day. As Dallow enters the room, the camera privileges Pinkie's point of view, and in the foreground we see only Pinkie's hands, playing 'cat's cradle' with a piece of string. The music builds in volume with shimmering cymbals and low brass as Dallow presents the newspaper to Pinkie, and then breaks off abruptly to leave silence as the image cuts to a close-up of Pinkie's dead-eyed, silent reaction. The cold cruelty of Pinkie's character is conveyed through the sudden musical emptiness that is prompted by this, his first appearance in the film.

A reverse sting may be used to emphasise the dialogue that fills the silence it creates. In *The Woman in Question*, John Wooldridge provides music with a loud stinging start as Pollard (Charles Victor) throws a scarf around the neck of Agnes (Jean Kent) in his flashback memory of her murder. As the music continues, the screen is filled with an extreme close-up of Pollard's perspiring face as he speaks of the bitterness he felt when she rejected him. The music ends abruptly with a short drumroll to leave silence before he looks up and says 'You laughed at me'. The music is understood as a dramatic representation of the violent struggle between them; therefore, its end marks the end of the struggle and of her life. Pollard speaks the last line aloud to himself, and no longer looks at Agnes. The reverse sting throws into relief the image, sound or dialogue that fills the emptiness of the void it creates, and marks it as significant. In this scene, and the one described earlier from *They Made Me A Fugitive*, the violence that cannot be shown on screen is depicted in the music in a cinematic parallel of the operatic convention of representing musically violent events that occur offstage, for example, the beheading of John the Baptist in Richard Strauss's *Salome*.

On a lighter note, a reverse sting may create a humorous reversal of mood, and an example occurs in *Hobson's Choice* (David Lean, 1954). Willie (John Mills) overhears Maggie (Brenda De Banzie) extolling his virtues as she extracts him from his engagement with Mrs Figgins's daughter. The camera rests on a close-up of Willie while an orchestral surge of romantic music builds as Maggie tells Mrs Figgins (Madge Brindley) that she loves Willie. Willie seems dazed with emotion and as the music swells as though to a rousing finale, it breaks off abruptly when Mrs Figgins's hand enters the frame to slap his face and jolt him from his reverie. The sequence exploits our familiarity with the film music convention of using a rising arc of uplifting sound to mirror a character's subjective experience and thus confounds our expectation of how the scene will end. The joke sends up a cinematic convention, and achieves its effect by exploiting the ability of cinema to limit our perspective and then to reveal what we had not seen coming.

The scoring of dialogue scenes is an area where differing conventions developed between the practice in the British industry and that in Hollywood. Although dialogue was privileged above music and other sound effects in the Hollywood film, the underscoring of dialogue was deemed necessary to express the 'emotional depth' of characters, while melodrama films depended on music to convey an emotionally heightened atmosphere in which their equally heightened dialogue would be acceptable (Gorbman 1987, 66–67). In British films, the scoring of dialogue is again characterised by both diversity and restraint. British films vary more in their use of music in dialogue scenes, and tend either to limit its use or to dispense with it altogether, complying with Cockshott's recommendation that if music is to accompany dialogue, the 'merest musical suggestions' will suffice (1946, 6). Sabaneev (1935, 20) adopts a similar stance, feeling that music 'should cease or retire into the background' during dialogue, although he was writing at a time when the technology for recording and mixing sound was less sophisticated and his opinion may be based as much on technical as on aesthetic concerns.

As British films do not adhere strictly to a convention of using music with dialogue, it tends to be more noticed when it does occur. William Alwyn felt that the practice of composing music to underscore dialogue in films had prepared him well for his later operatic word-setting (Johnson 2005, 263), and the comparison with opera is apposite. The correlation between film music and opera is most apparent where the underscoring of dialogue imbues a sequence with the heightened emotional atmosphere associated with operatic expression, although it may also be invoked to describe music that adds meaning or inflection to the spoken word, or that which weaves dialogue into a musical fabric that both regulates the pace and rhythm of a narrative and also unifies the audiovisual experience of the film. I would like to look more closely at examples of how words and music have been brought together to expressive, poetic, and sometimes comic, effect. The cinematographer Desmond Dickinson has noted that the soliloquies in Olivier's 1948 film of *Hamlet*

> were planned to a great deal of movement, so that audiences listening to an uninterrupted speech would not become restive, since the screen would be

taken up with all kinds of action to hold their attention. If the actors were not moving around, then the camera was (1948, 31)

This attention to movement is paralleled in the music that accompanies these scenes. Walton explains that in Hamlet's soliloquies, the 'incidental musical effects ... varied their orchestral colour according to the shifts of his thought' (quoted in Manvell and Huntley 1975, 93). Walton associates a musical theme with Hamlet's introspection, and he introduces it on low strings for the Prince's first soliloquy. The theme emerges after a diegetic brass fanfare as the King, Queen and gathered courtiers disperse, and Christopher Palmer (1990, 6) remarks on the violence of the contrast 'between the bright, brash blare of the brass and the dark dourness of the double-basses'. In a high-angle framing, Hamlet appears a small central figure in the bottom of the image. As the camera moves down to a closer shot of him, the lugubrious low strings mirror its slow movement, and continue through a cut to an extreme close-up of Hamlet's profile.

Hamlet turns his face slowly towards the camera, pausing at a three-quarter view as the first lines of his soliloquy are heard in voiceover: 'O, that this too, too solid flesh would melt, thaw and resolve itself into a dew', and then expressing the emotions contained in his words, he looks slowly upwards at the mention of 'the everlasting', rises and remains still for 'How weary, stale, flat and unprofitable/Seem to me all the uses of this world!', before he walks to the end of the table and interjects diegetically the line 'Nay, not so much, not two' (see Fig. 2.2). The mobile camera tracks his progress to the chairs that the King and Queen had previously occupied as he recalls the haste with which his mother has remarried. He speaks diegetically again, then his voiceover resumes as the camera returns with him to his chair, moves fluidly into a briefly held close-up before it glides away towards the corridor that will take us to the next scene.

Walton's widow recalled that an assistant editor, Helga Keller, praised Walton's ability to underscore dialogue by incorporating Olivier's vocal tone 'as if it were just another musical instrument only needing the accompaniment of his particular orchestration' (Walton 1988, 96). In the same way, Hans Keller (2006, 179) applauds the effectiveness of the music in this soliloquy, particularly in the transition from music to speech where it presents the speech as 'a logical element in the unfolding of the texture', and also the fugal form of the music that offers the listener 'known quantities' in the repeating patterns on the strings as the soliloquy progresses.

Fig. 2.2 Hamlet's soliloquy heard in voiceover in *Hamlet*

Olivier's solution to the cinematic presentation of the theatrical soliloquy, partly delivered as internal monologue and partly spoken out loud, invests each spoken line with a sense of spontaneity, 'as if the thought had suddenly pushed itself to the forefront of his consciousness' (Sinyard 1986, 3), while the rendering of his thoughts in voiceover portrays Hamlet's essentially introspective and isolated character. Chion (2009, 342) notes the different vocal delivery that Olivier establishes for internal and external expressions in his later 'To be, or not to be' soliloquy. It is also relevant that at the point in the latter scene when Hamlet reverts to internal monologue, the low strings of Hamlet's introspection theme return to the soundtrack in recollection of their initial association with his first soliloquy. The recurring theme marks the contemplative nature of the character's inner musings. The innovative technique of rendering the soliloquy partly as internal monologue and partly as spoken dialogue had been originated by Olivier in *Henry V* (1944), although the device has been taken up by many subsequent film directors (Geduld 1973, 67).

Walton's scoring of the soliloquys has the effect of weaving the spoken sections into a broader musical pattern, in which the words seem to arise naturally from the musical foundation. While this may be facilitated by the poetic metre of the source text, Chion has observed that the same may be true of sound effects, which are often 'incorporated into the music'. The music then 'locks them into their proper place in the score, as in opera' (2009, 77). The connection to opera is again appropriate, for film music has the ability to arrange other sound elements according to musical principles, to punctuate sound effects and dialogue, or to use sound effects and dialogue for its own musical punctuation. An example of this is Walton's scoring of the celebrated 'Battle of Agincourt' scenes in Olivier's *Henry V*. Hubert Clifford (1944, 174) notes the 'long "crossfade"' that brings the music to prominence after it opens with the diegetic French drums, brass calls and the sound effects of the horses' hooves and the clinking of armour, and also the wisdom of suppressing the sound effects to allow the music its head as the charge progresses with a pounding momentum.

The climax to the Agincourt sequence, Palmer notes, is not in the music, but in 'the sound of the arrows as they … curve across the sky and strike among the French lines', and the music drops out to allow this to dominate the soundtrack (1972, 250). Walton scores the diegetic sounds into the musical shape of the sequence and exploits the expectation of the musical arc to dramatise the action. The sequence is justly praised, and its debt to the 'Battle on the Ice' sequence in Eisenstein's *Alexander Nevsky* (1938) widely acknowledged, although Eisenstein apparently 'hated Olivier's film' (Sinyard 1986, 3).[6] However, whereas Eisenstein had edited his footage to synchronise with Prokofiev's pre-composed music, Walton was required to write the music to match the rough cut of the film. In May of 1943 he wrote to Roy Douglas about the process:

> I've been working on the battle of Agincourt, & luckily didn't get very far as all the footages were rearranged two days ago & they forgot to tell me! So I must now start again … 10 mins of charging horses bows & arrows [sic] (Hayes 2002, 145)

Walton himself knew Eisenstein's film, and wrote to the producer of *Henry V*, Dallas Bower, in January 1942 that he had 'very much enjoyed' it, which suggests that he may have seen it on Bower's recommendation (Hayes 2002, 136). Bower had been an assistant director on *As You Like It* (Paul Czinner, 1936), which had starred Olivier and for which Walton had provided the score. It was Dallas Bower, acting as Czinner's personal assistant, who had put forward the suggestion to the director that Walton be commissioned to write his first film score for *Escape Me Never* in 1935 (Lloyd 1999, 109).[7]

The accomplishment of Walton's scores for Olivier's Shakespeare films demonstrates a development of the composer's technical abilities, of his growing assuredness in the medium, and they are recognised as high points in British film music. Nevertheless, scores conceived on a less grand scale, in characters equally appropriate to their subjects, also contain music that works with dialogue to point up particularly dramatic, theatrical or comic moments. A playful use of music with dialogue lightens the mood at the beginning of *Pimpernel Smith* (Leslie Howard, 1941), when the seemingly eccentric academic Smith (Howard) calls over the museum attendant Jordan (Arthur Hambling) to berate him for neglecting to dust the statue of Aphrodite. John Greenwood's music matches the mood of the action, lightly bustling as Smith spots the dust and puts on his spectacles, then as he turns and calls 'Jordan', the strings immediately mimic the tone and shape of his utterance. He calls again and the musical echo repeats in a lower key, whereupon, having added a comic lilt, the music retires to allow the dialogue to continue unscored.

In *Great Expectations*, music substitutes rather than echoes shouted names. Mrs Joe (Freda Jackson) returns excitedly to the forge with news of Pip's invitation to Satis House. The music marks the jaunty progress of her pony trap, in a scene from which all diegetic sound is removed. As she stands and calls to Joe and Pip, her diegetic voice is replaced by the blasts of brass instruments, which in themselves resemble the sounds of a cow or donkey and tend to sound amusing (Dyer 2010, 131) (Fig. 2.3). This comic rendering of the shrewish blast and bray of her shouting also punctures her self-importance and undercuts the unpleasantness of her character. The substitution of Mrs Joe's voice with musically mimicked animal sounds is especially notable because it reverses the formulation of an earlier sound montage in which Pip imagines the cattle chiding him as he runs to deliver the file, food, and drink he has stolen for the convict Magwitch. The disapproving utterances on the soundtrack are arranged so that they seem to emanate from the cows he passes in the field.

In addition to gently marking spoken words, music may engage more closely with speech patterns to reflect and emphasise their contours. In a montage sequence in *Pygmalion* (Anthony Asquith, Leslie Howard, 1938) that compresses the education of Wendy Hiller's Eliza, Higgins (Howard) beats out on the glockenspiel the rhythm of the phrase 'How kind of you to let me come' for her to repeat. He speaks the phrase and instructs her

Fig. 2.3 Dialogue replaced by musically mimicked animal sounds in *Great Expectations*

to listen carefully, then plays the eight notes of the syllables. As Eliza attempts the phrase, we hear the musical rhythm again in Arthur Honegger's nondiegetic score, first in time with her words and then as Higgins shakes his head. He plays the notes again, and the nondiegetic accompaniment returns as Eliza now successfully matches the rhythm. The earlier part of the montage sequence has been intercut with two scenes of Freddy (David Tree) calling to see Eliza, and on each occasion Higgins instructs Mrs Pearce (Jean Cadell) to 'Throw him out!'. When Mrs Pearce enquires a third time, Higgins simply plays the rhythm of the three syllables of 'Throw him out!' on the glockenspiel, and as Mrs Pearce passes the message on, they recur three further times in the nondiegetic score, in progressively descending pitch. The montage sequence exploits the musical rhythms of spoken language that are employed in Higgins's educational system.

A similar rhythmic mimicry of patterns of speech creates a disturbing effect in *The Rocking Horse Winner* (Anthony Pélissier, 1949). Our view of the discussion of the family's money troubles ends when Hester (Valerie Hobson) firmly restates the words she has already used: 'There must be more money!'. As she shuts the door William Alwyn's music starts with a sudden flurry, then continues more gently to restate a six-note figure echoing the rhythm of the spoken phrase over tremolo strings, and as a series of dissolves carries us higher up the shadowy staircases, the musical phrase alternates with whispered voices that reiterate 'There must be more money!'. The musical phrase and the whispers climb to the nursery, where Paul (John Howard Davies) pauses and looks intently at his rocking horse, as though searching for the source of the sounds. He turns to his young sisters, who hear nothing, and the image cuts to an extreme close-up of Paul, in profile, before he turns to face the camera as the sound montage of music and whispers increases in volume and intensity. The camera's slow movement towards him emphasises his startled look (Fig. 2.4). On a sombre drum beat the image cuts to the horse's head with the same camera move closing in slowly, then Paul looks into the horse's mouth, as though seeking to understand, and the scene ends with a fade to black as the whispers of 'more money, more money' also fade. Alwyn's musical handling of the sequence introduces the 'money' motif that will recur

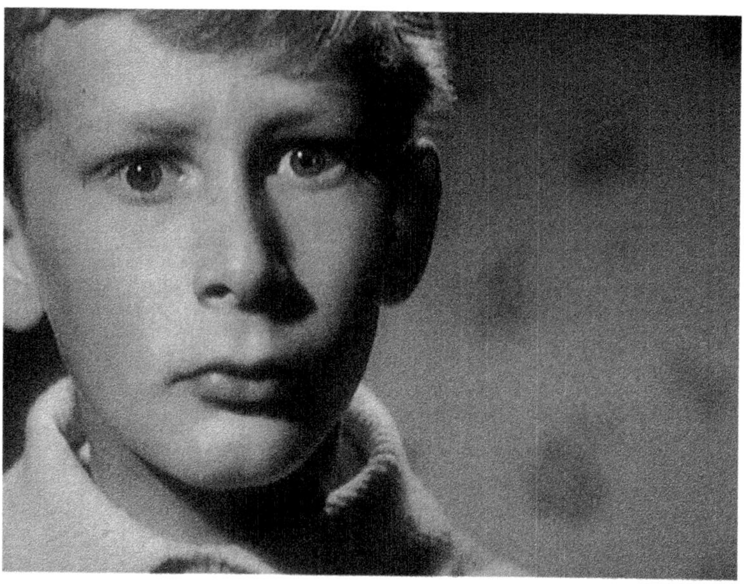

Fig. 2.4 'There must be more money' sound montage in *The Rocking Horse Winner*

throughout the film, made all the more memorable by its association with the spoken words, and its connection to the supernatural aspects of the narrative. Johnson finds an 'almost perfect congruity' between sound and image in this sequence, in which Alwyn expresses 'inner meanings that cannot be implied by the imagery alone' (2005, 210, 208).

The montage sequence from *The Rocking Horse Winner* illustrates a balance between moments of closer and looser synchronisation. Here, the closer synchronisation provides the audience with a sense of reassurance and offsets the 'potentially disturbing' moments without synchronisation (Donnelly 2014, 8). The sequence begins with a strong point of synchronisation: the orchestral chord coincides exactly with the diegetic sound of the closing door. The whispered voices as the camera ascends the stairs suggest the subjectivity 'of the ghostly voices themselves' (Johnson 2005, 210) and the lack of direct synchronisation maintains an ethereal atmosphere. As the camera draws closer to the nursery, the voices subside and allow the motif in the music to dominate, and as the image cuts to Paul the voices return with greater force and clarity and state the phrase once. It is then repeated musically twice, the second restatement coinciding with Paul's point-of-view shot of his sisters. The voices return when the image cuts back to the close-up of Paul and continue to echo until the scene ends. Broken down in this way, it is possible to see that Alwyn has brought to the montage sequence a musical logic and caused the editing of the shots to appear motivated by a musical impulse that locks the images into a broader musical framework without sacrificing the supernatural aspect of the sequence. Moments of close synchronisation reinforce the unity between score and screen and naturalise the presence of music. In a montage sequence, the close synchronisation of some parts of the sequence binds together the music and the image and reinforces their connection through parts of the sequence that are less closely aligned. Thus, during montage sequences, there may be an ebb and flow of closer and looser synchronisation that wraps image and sound in unity without requiring a sonic duplication of every action depicted within the frame of the image.

The unvarying alignment of music and image, where every onscreen element or action is slavishly repeated by the musical score, known as 'mickey-mousing', is one of the devices associated with the Hollywood score (Gorbman 1998, 45). As its name suggests, it is derived from animation, and its excessive employment may render a dramatic score 'too obvious' and cartoonish (Manvell and Huntley 1975, 91). However, the technique can also have the effect of lightening onscreen events, and music that accompanies comic situations is often closely aligned with onscreen action. This is exemplified by Richard Addinsell's score for David Lean's film of Noel Coward's *Blithe Spirit* (1945). The film's main title music is bouncy and upbeat, busy with a ping-pong effect where one section of the orchestra responds to the other as it builds to a climax that suggests lightness and comedy. The first scene opens on the hallway of the house and the music sets off at fast pace before the maid Edith (Jacqueline Clark) bursts through the door at a run, jogs briskly up the stairs and along the landing and into her mistress's room. The music stops abruptly as she comes to a halt. Ruth (Constance Cummings) reminds her to slow down and be calm. The music matches her pace as she sets off at a run, and duly slows in tandem with her movement as she leaves the room. The close synchronisation between music and movement in these opening scenes establishes the connection between the music and the image at the outset. It is reserved, though, for the moments of broader physical comedy—Manvell and Huntley (1975, 150) note that the tempo of the music for Madame Arcati's (Margaret Rutherford) bicycle ride is 'nicely attuned to her somewhat irregular journey'. Elsewhere in the film, Addinsell's music is more evocative and less closely aligned with the image, particularly in the shimmering waltz tune associated with the ghostly Elvira (Kay Hammond). Addinsell's closely synchronised music heightens the physical comedy of the film by marking and augmenting the comic action in the manner of music associated with silent slapstick film, and circus or music hall performance.

While brightly orchestrated music that matches the tempo of onscreen movement frequently has the effect of rendering comic the antics of the characters it accompanies, particular actions may also be emphasised musically for comic effect. In a sequence from *Woman Hater* (Terence Young, 1948), Lambert Williamson's scoring gently underlines the comic elements. Before Terence (Stewart Granger) enters and introduces himself to Colette (Edwige Feuillère), the music follows her actions as she gets something in her eye, and dabs it with a handkerchief in front of the mirror. When Colette speaks to Terence, she winks at him and the action is marked in the music and immediately repeated in the underscore. As she sits and reiterates her desire to be by herself, she winks a second time, and again the action is emphasised in the music and softly repeated as a musical echo. Each time the brief two-note phrase, in imitation of Colette quickly closing and opening one eye, is first heard in synchronisation with the action of the wink and then restated as the image cuts to show Terence's surprised

Fig. 2.5 Musical emphasis of comic action in *Woman Hater*

reaction (Fig. 2.5). The music magnifies the wink and accentuates the comedy. It enables Colette's winking to be a subtle movement by clarifying the action and Terence's reaction, and it regulates the comedic timing of the scene.

Isolated moments of close synchronisation may also dramatise and intensify onscreen action. In the montage sequence that opens *The Overlanders*, orchestral blasts synchronise with the impact of the axe blows on the corrugated metal water tank as the family, fearing Japanese invasion, set fire to their home and move on. The synchronised blows confirm the correlation between sound and image, and enable urgent music that is not directly synchronised with action to hold together the following scenes of the house being set on fire. The faster dramatic music accompanies static shots of the family waiting on the cart, and energises the shot of the father walking to the cart at a fairly leisurely pace. As the music becomes calmer the image dissolves from a close-up of the wasted water to the horse-drawn cart making its way. Here the music slows to a funereal pace and acts to dampen down the pace of movement in the frame. Sabaneev notes that music 'often dictates its rhythms and tempi to the screen' and that the rhythm of the images are 'regulated by the music' (1935, 21). This example illustrates clearly that the music acts first to accelerate the momentum and make the action appear faster and more dramatically exciting, and then to slow it down and to score the melancholy feeling of the scene rather than the pace of travel. John Ireland resists the temptation to match the beat of the horses' hooves in an onomatopoeic manner.[8]

The onomatopoeic musical reflection of the rhythm and sound of horses' hooves in motion is perhaps one of the most recognisable instances of nondiegetic music that augments or even replaces diegetic sound. The ease with which music is able to mimic other sounds was exploited by silent film, although Donnelly notes that the form it takes may be highly 'stylised ... [and give] little more than a hint or an echo' of the imitated sounds (2005, 93). Chion finds that representative sounds are accepted by the audience not necessarily if they 'reproduce' the original sound, but if they 'render (convey, express) the feelings associated with the situation'. Furthermore, if the sound is synchronised with the onscreen event, a 'spontaneous and irresistible weld' is produced that bypasses 'any rational logic' (1994, 109, 63).

The Captive Heart (Basil Dearden, 1946) contains an example of this 'weld' in the scenes of the rail transport that carries the prisoners-of-war to the camp. In the first shot, the train slows as it pulls into the station, in silhouette against the late afternoon sky, accompanied by the diegetic sounds of the train's steam engine and the squeal of its brakes. At the cut to the next shot, the guard slides open the door of the cargo carriage, and Alan Rawsthorne seamlessly substitutes the diegetic sound of the sliding door with wavering string figures that form a brief musical prelude to the trudging march that accompanies the scenes of the men's onward journey on foot to the camp. The strings synchronise with the action of the door opening and their momentary quivering sound creates no mismatch with the image of the door opening. If anything, there seems a logical connection between the movement of the sliding door and that of the bows on stringed instruments.

However, such a connection is unnecessary for audience acceptance. In *Above Us The Waves* (Ralph Thomas, 1955), Arthur Benjamin scores the frogmen's ascent in a tall cylindrical water tank with rising figures on harp, strings and percussion. The music expresses the movement of the water and the air bubbles that surround them as they rise, and it ends with the return of the diegetic sound as they break the surface. Here, the music renders the 'feel' of the image, the shimmering look of the water and the effervescence of the air bubbles, rather than reproducing realistic underwater sound. The ascending musical figures make sense with the images of the men floating upwards to the surface in the same way that descending scales conventionally accompany parachute jumps and falls.

The first parachute jump in *Against the Wind* (Charles Crichton, 1948) illustrates a further step that music may take in replacing diegetic sound. Softly trembling strings join the fading sound of the aircraft engine as Philip (Robert Beatty) parachutes to the ground. Leslie Bridgewater marks his landing with a pizzicato note, although on screen we see only a dissolve between a shot of him descending and a shot of him running to retrieve the parachute from where it has fallen. The music here may convince us that we have seen Philip land, although in reality we have only heard a musical representation of the event. The music, substituting for sound, may make us believe that we have seen something that we have only heard, although at a further remove because we have not even heard the sound of the landing, only a note of music that, it is suggested, synchronises with the action.

A poetic variation of this formulation occurs towards the end of *The First of the Few* (Leslie Howard, 1942). As the terminally ill Mitchell (Howard) rests in the garden in the background and his wife Diana (Rosamund John) walks slowly along the path towards the house (and the camera), William Walton introduces a gentle lyrical strain on violin. Behind Diana we see Mitchell's arm fall lifelessly from the armrest of his chair. A moment later a pizzicato string marks the moment of her realisation as she stops with a sharp intake of breath. Diana has walked through the sunlight into the shadow cast by the house and the image now cuts to a close-up of Mitchell's resting face bathed in sunlight that fades to shadow. In a highly poetic rendering, both characters have moved from the light into the darkness. The pizzicato note marks not a diegetic sound, but emphasises a silent moment of awareness and emotion. Its simplicity creates a moment of elegiac beauty that enables a greater narrative economy and provides a clarity that the images alone would lack.

The brief musical marking of emotion in *The First of the Few* is extended in other films into an expression of operatically heightened feeling. An example is found in Alfred Hitchcock's *Waltzes From Vienna* (1934), a film that fictionalises Johann Strauss's composition of 'The Blue Danube'. Strauss's sweetheart Resi (Jessie Matthews) visits his father's orchestral rehearsal to persuade him to play his son's music. The older composer (Edmund Gwenn) is dismissive and in frustration Resi climbs onto the podium, picks up the music pages from the stand, and throws them into the air. Hardened, Strauss turns back to his orchestra, taps the music stand with his baton and then raises it to resume the rehearsal. The music begins with a building drumroll as Resi runs from the room, directly towards the camera. As she runs, she moves in and out of light and darkness in a highly expressionistic rendering of her emotional turmoil. There is a seamless cut to a matched composition as she moves closer to the camera, momentarily blurred before coming into sharp focus as she stops dead when the grand double doors close behind her, the action synchronised with a clash of symbols. The close-up reveals her tear-stained face as she stands still in the corridor. After a moment's silence, the sound of another woman singing 'The Blue Danube' is heard emanating from another room. The close framing registers her emotion as softly she says to herself 'My song'.

During the editing of *Waltzes From Vienna*, the director was interviewed for *Cinema Quarterly* and he used the forum to explain his experiments with music in the film. Hitchcock considered the introduction of sound a great opportunity, as it brought the 'accompanying music ... entirely under the control of the people who made the picture'. Not only was the editing of the images prepared in advance of the shooting, but 'the musical cuts were worked out too'. Hitchcock notes the effectiveness of silence, and the way it may be 'heightened by the proper handling of the music before and after' (reprinted in Gottlieb 1995, 242, 244), and this is evident in the sequence described. Although achieved over two set-ups, the scene is conceived as a single movement, in which Resi's frustration and humiliation as she rushes from the rehearsal room are, after a brief silent bridge, compounded by her feelings of betrayal as she hears the song, dedicated to her, and which she has been trying to promote to Strauss's father, sung by another woman.

This stylised and expressive sequence foreshadows a similar scene in *The Tales of Hoffmann* (Powell and Pressburger, 1951), in which Antonia (Ann Ayars) tries to escape from the malign offices of Dr Miracle (Robert Helpmann). When the doors lead her back to the same room, she runs towards the camera and falls from a precipice in a painted landscape and descends in slow motion into a dark abyss, only to awaken on the floor of the chamber from which she had sought to run. In common with Resi in *Waltzes From Vienna*, the distraught Antonia flees a dark-coated male authority figure whose image remains in the background of the shot (Fig. 2.6). Both

Fig. 2.6 Resi's flight in *Waltzes From Vienna* (above) echoed in Antonia's flight in *The Tales of Hoffmann* (below)

sequences are edited to fit the requirements of a musical climax. In the earlier film, this has the dramatic simplicity of a drumroll topped with a cymbal clash (reminiscent of a circus performance); in *The Tales of Hoffmann* the scenes accompany the climax of the trio 'Pour conjurer le danger' ('To ward off danger') for Miracle, Antonia's father, and her lover, Hoffmann. Both scenes harness a stylised theatricality to create an effect that is only possible with cinematic means.

The element of theatricality is pertinent to a consideration of this era of British cinema for, even in the limited number of films discussed above, we can see the role music plays in negotiating and reconciling the conflict between an established British literary and theatrical tradition with the pull towards the more realist modes espoused by the British documentary movement. The tension between these seemingly contradictory models, of a heightened form of expression on the one hand and a more restrained one on the other, breathes life and energy into British film music. The involvement of composers whose musical specialisms lie in other areas, whether in lighter or more serious music, fosters an atmosphere of creative flexibility that enriches not only the palette of music, but also the ways it is used in British films. Perhaps of greater significance, though, is the consistency in the musical education and training of the composers who work in the British industry, a consistency that belies the variety of musical paths they then follow. The links between the architects of the English Musical Renaissance and the composers of the succeeding generations establishes a direct connection between the revitalisation of British concert music and the subsequent flowering of this golden age of British film music. The result of these connections will be the subject of the chapters that follow, as I explore how British films employ styles of music that invest their scores with a national resonance by evoking the historical cultural associations of the music. The first area for closer study is music in a pastoral idiom, a mode at the forefront of the English Musical Renaissance and one whose influence on British concert music is hard to overstate, as it engaged with such a wide range of national cultural preoccupations in this era.

Notes

1. Margaret Lockwood, for instance, recalls working in the film studio during the day while appearing each evening on the West End stage (1955, 42–3, 47)

2. In December 1939 Walton writes to the composer John Ireland that he has a film commission 'which seems to be the only money I shall earn next year!' (Hayes 2002, 127).
3. Of the fifty-one composers in this study, thirty-three also scored documentary films, ten of whom worked on documentaries before scoring their first feature film.
4. *Love from a Stranger* was based on a play by Frank Vosper which in turn was based on a short story by Agatha Christie. Britten's score includes music from Grieg's 'Peer Gynt Suite', and Michael Oliver hears in the film's opening storm scenes a 'clear anticipation of the storm music [in *Peter Grimes*]' (1996, 59).
5. The scraping metallic sound of the lamp blowing in the wind outside the workhouse finds an echo in the augmented sound effects that accompany the swinging shop signs in the opening scene of Lean's 1954 adaptation of *Hobson's Choice*, a sequence that intentionally mirrors the beginning of *Great Expectations*.
6. The connection between the battle sequences in *Alexander Nevsky* and *Henry V* is noted by, among others, Roger Manvell (1971, 39), Neil Sinyard (1986, 3), Kenneth S. Rothwell (1999, 55), and Mervyn Cooke (2008, 170). In his autobiography, *Confessions of an Actor*, Olivier himself notes that *Henry V* was 'littered with petty larcenies' from Eisenstein (1982, 162).
7. Dallas Bower had also been instrumental in promoting the idea of a film of *Henry V*, having prepared a script for a possible BBC Television production in 1938, upon which the film script was based (McFarlane 1997, 81).
8. Onscreen horse-drawn journeys tend to be accompanied by music that matches the rhythm set by the hooves. This musical mirroring of the pace of onscreen movement is found in horse-drawn journeys in many films including *The Flemish Farm* (1943), *A Canterbury Tale* (1944), *Tawny Pipit* (1944), *The Years Between* (1946), *The Brothers* (1947), *The Loves of Joanna Godden* (1947), *The Mark of Cain* (1947), *They Made Me a Fugitive* (1947), *Jassy* (1947). In *So Long at the Fair* (1950), the tempo of Benjamin Frankel's 'Carriage and Pair' explicitly mimics the gentle trot of the horses pulling the onscreen carriage.

References

Aitken, Ian. 1990. *Film and Reform: John Grierson and the Documentary Film Movement*. London: Routledge.

Balcon, Michael. 1969. *Michael Balcon Presents … A Lifetime in Films*. London: Hutchinson.

Bliss, Arthur. 1970. *As I Remember*. London: Faber & Faber.

———. 1991. "Those Damned Films!" *Musical News and Herald*, 18 February 1922. In *Bliss on Music, Selected Writings of Arthur Bliss 1920–1975*, ed. Gregory Roscow. Oxford: Oxford University Press.

Cavalcanti, Alberto. 1985. Sound in Films. In *Film Sound: Theory and Practice*, ed. Elisabeth Weis and John Belton, 98–111. New York/Chichester: Columbia University Press.

Chion, Michel. 1994. *Audio-Vision: Sound on Screen*. Trans. Claudia Gorbman. New York: Columbia University Press.

———. 2009. *Film, A Sound Art*. Trans. Claudia Gorbman. New York: Columbia University Press.

Clifford, Hubert. 1944. Walton's Henry V Music. *Tempo* 9: 173–174.

Cobbe, Hugh, ed. 2002. *Letters of Ralph Vaughan Williams, 1895–1958*. Oxford: Oxford University Press.

Cockshott, Gerald. 1946. *'Incidental Music in the Sound Film' Pamphlet*. London: British Film Institute.

Cooke, Mervyn. 2008. *A History of Film Music*. Cambridge: Cambridge University Press.

Dickinson, Desmond. 1948. Camera and Lighting. In *The Film Hamlet*, ed. Brenda Cross, 29–35. London: Saturn Press.

Donnelly, K.J. 2005. *The Spectre of Sound: Music in Film and Television*. London: British Film Institute.

———. 2007. *British Film Music and Film Musicals*. Basingstoke: Palgrave Macmillan.

———. 2014. *Occult Aesthetics: Synchronization in Sound Film*. Oxford: Oxford University Press.

Dyer, Richard. 2010. *Nino Rota: Music, Film and Feeling*. London: British Film Institute.

Flinn, Caryl. 1992. *Strains of Utopia: Gender, Nostalgia and Hollywood Film Music*. Princeton: Princeton University Press.

Foreman, Lewis. 1983. *Bax: A Composer and His Times*. Aldershot: Scolar Press.

Frayling, Christopher. 1995. *Things to Come*. London: British Film Institute.

Geduld, Harry M. 1973. *Filmguide to Henry V*. Bloomington: Indiana University Press.

Gorbman, Claudia. 1987. *Unheard Melodies: Narrative Film Music*. London: British Film Institute.

———. 1998. Film Music. In *The Oxford Guide to Film Studies*, ed. John Hill and Pamela C. Gibson, 43–50. Oxford: Oxford University Press.

Gottlieb, Sidney, ed. 1995. *Hitchcock on Hitchcock, Selected Writings and Interviews*. Vol. 1. Berkeley: University of California Press.

Hayes, Malcolm, ed. 2002. *The Selected Letters of William Walton*. London: Faber.

Huntley, John. 1947. *British Film Music*. London: Skelton Robinson.

Irving, Ernest. 1959. *Cue for Music*. London: Dobson Books.

Jackson, Paul R.W. 2003. *The Life and Music of Sir Malcolm Arnold: The Brilliant and the Dark*. Aldershot: Ashgate.

Johnson, Ian. 2005. *William Alwyn, The Art of Film Music*. Woodbridge: The Boydell Press.

Kalinak, Kathryn. 1992. *Settling the Score: Music and the Classical Hollywood Film*. Madison: University of Wisconsin Press.

Keller, Hans. 2006. In *Film Music and Beyond: Writings on Music and the Screen, 1946–59*, ed. Christopher Wintle. London: Plumbago Books.

Lloyd, Stephen. 1999. Film Music. In *William Walton: Music and Literature*, ed. Stewart R. Craggs, 109–131. Aldershot: Ashgate.

Lockwood, Margaret. 1955. *Lucky Star*. London: Odhams Press.

Manvell, Roger. 1971. *Shakespeare and the Film*. London: J. M. Dent & Sons.

Manvell, Roger, and John Huntley. 1975. *The Technique of Film Music*. London: Focal Press.

Mathieson, Muir. 1944. Aspects of Film Music. *Tempo* 9: 7–9.

———. 1947. Music: Introducing Muir Mathieson. In *The March of the Movies*, ed. Leslie Mitchell and Harry Alan Towers, 54–62. London: Sampson Low.

———. 1948a. Recording the Music. In *The Film Hamlet*, ed. Brenda Cross, 63–64. London: Saturn Press.

———. 1948b. Music for Crown. *Hollywood Quarterly* 3 (3): 323–326.

McFarlane, Brian. 1997. *An Autobiography of British Cinema*. London: Methuen.

Oliver, Michael. 1996. *Benjamin Britten*. London: Phaidon.

Olivier, Laurence. 1982. *Confessions of an Actor*. London: Weidenfeld and Nicolson.

Palmer, Christopher. 1971. British Composers for the Film. *Performing Right* 6: 20–28.

———. 1972. Walton's Film Music. *The Musical Times* 113 (1549): 249–252.

———. 1990. Booklet Notes to 'William Walton: Hamlet & As You Like It', Chandos CD CHAN 10436 X.

Parlett, Graham. 2003. Booklet Notes for 'The Film Music of Sir Arnold Bax', Chandos CD CHAN 10126.

Rawsthorne, Alan. 1975. The Celluloid Plays a Tune. In *Twenty British Composers*, ed. Peter Dickinson, 30–36. London: J & W Chester.

Richards, Fiona. 2000. *The Music of John Ireland*. Aldershot: Ashgate.

Riley, Matthew. 2010. Music for the Machines of the Future: H.G. Wells, Arthur Bliss and *Things To Come* (1936). In *British Music and Modernism, 1895–1960*, ed. Matthew Riley, 249–268. Farnham: Ashgate.

Rothwell, Kenneth S. 1999. *A History of Shakespeare on Screen*. Cambridge: Cambridge University Press.

Rózsa, Miklós. 1982. *Double Life: The Autobiography of Miklós Rózsa*. Tunbridge Wells: The Baton Press.

Sabaneev, Leonid. 1935. *Music for the Films: A Handbook for Composers and Conductors*. Trans. S.W. Pring. London: Sir Isaac Pitman & Sons Ltd.

Schafer, Murray. 1963. *British Composers in Interview*. London: Faber and Faber.
Sinyard, Neil. 1986. *Filming Literature*. Beckenham: Croon Helm.
Vaughan Williams, Ralph. 1945. Composing for the Films. In Vaughan Williams, Ralph. 1963. *National Music and Other Essays*, 160–165. London: Oxford University Press.
Walton, Susana. 1988. *William Walton: Behind the Façade*. Oxford/New York: Oxford University Press.

CHAPTER 3

Pastoral Music: Representations of Landscape

The gentle nature of pastoral music belies the intense emotions it can arouse, and the breadth of connotations its expressive devices can encompass. This chapter explores the use of pastoral music in British films in the light of its multiple associations and the predominant position it came to occupy in British music. A range of films combine music in a pastoral idiom with landscape imagery in a way that foregrounds the natural environment. These films celebrate the idea of landscape, and in celebrating the British countryside they value the things that it stands for; tradition, history, and communities living close to the land with a shared national identity. Entwined with these ideas is a symbolic connotation that takes on a greater significance in times of conflict, that of the landscape's stability, tranquillity and resilience, its mythical resistance to change. These cultural associations are magnified in the audiovisual coupling of pastoral music and landscape imagery on screen, an area in which the intersections between British concert music and British cinema are readily discernible.

The involvement of concert composers in British cinema is particularly relevant to films that foreground their landscape settings. This engagement occurred in the wake of an era when the musical establishment in Britain had set out to construct a recognisably national style of composition (a thorough critical account is offered by Hughes and Stradling 2001). At the forefront of the movement was Ralph Vaughan Williams, who developed a musical style that drew upon the earlier English traditions of Tudor music and folk song and embraced pastoral modes of

P. Mazey, *British Film Music*, Palgrave Studies in Audio-Visual Culture, https://doi.org/10.1007/978-3-030-33550-2_3

expression. Central to the second phase of the English Musical Renaissance from the turn of the twentieth century was the desire to establish a verifiably English musical idiom that would differentiate English music and demonstrate its freedom from the Continental, and particularly German, influences that had come to dominate European art music in the previous centuries (Hughes and Stradling 2001, 117; Howes 1966, 22). In meeting these criteria, the pastoral emerged as 'the dominant discourse of music in Britain' after the outbreak of the Great War, aided by the wide appeal afforded by its 'nonmodernist aesthetic' (Stradling 1998, 183). From the first stirrings of the undertaking in the last quarter of the nineteenth century, the revival sought a musical language that was accessible to the general musical public, one that would be able to maintain the place of music in the cultural life of the nation. Thus the mode of expression of this group of composers, the generation of George Butterworth, Ralph Vaughan Williams and Gustav Holst, while deemed backward-looking and increasingly out of step with modernist developments in concert music, was nevertheless appropriate to the commercial imperative of a cinema that depended upon the patronage of a broad popular audience. Moreover, in its musical expression of sensitivity to the landscape, the pastoral style was fitting for films that foregrounded and valorised their natural settings.

Eric Saylor (2008, 39) questions how we might define English pastoral music, given that it is generally discussed on the basis of what it is assumed to represent rather than how it represents it, and even then in quite broad terms. Frank Howes, for example, writes of music that is 'gentle, undramatic … [the] strong and persistent musical equivalent of the English landscape' (1966, 261), and Michael Trend describes a 'musical language that was associated with [the composers'] feeling for the English landscape' (1985, 8). Such vague descriptions do little justice to the pastoral style and overlook its intricate synthesis of musical ideas and contemporary concerns. This can contribute to the critical dismissal of the pastoral as a mere sentimental retreat from modernism (Saylor 2008, 40–41). Musically, the pastoral idiom came to be characterised by uncomplicated and lyrically flowing melodies with moderately slow tempi and a seemingly improvised quality. It is connected stylistically to the Swiss tradition of the *ranz des vaches* or *Kuhreigen*, melodies originally used by herdsmen in the Alps to call in their cows. These were either sung or played on the alphorn, and were built upon repetitions of gently lyrical themes with a freely improvised feel (a genuine example is heard, appropriately, in the slow section of the overture to Rossini's *Guillaume Tell*). Saylor compiles a list of features found in English pastoral music that includes 'quiet dynamic levels' and a 'proclivity for string-dominated timbres, with secondary emphasis on the upper woodwinds' (2017, 20). Geoffrey Chew notes that wind instruments came to symbolise the 'fluting or playing of reed pipes by classical shepherds' and those found most in pastoral modes are flutes and oboes, 'often in pairs' (2001, 223). In general, Saylor summarises the 'pastoral effect' as

> one of gentle understatement, restraint, and calm, characteristics frequently associated with the peacefulness of the English countryside but applicable to other settings as well: ceremonies of mourning or remembrance, for example, or spiritual introspection (2017, 20)

Saylor's reference to remembrance and spirituality is pertinent to the haunting and often elegiac nature of the pastoral style, and I will explore these ideas more fully in my consideration of choral settings in a pastoral mode in the fifth chapter. The British films that combine music with landscape imagery to produce a pastoral effect employ cinematic techniques to emphasise the presence of landscape on screen. British film production in this era was largely a studio-based undertaking, and extensive location shooting was rare. Filming on location incurred additional expense and offered filmmakers a level of freedom from studio control, and consequently, as Sue Harper has noted, landscape representations were 'a minority subject and practice' (2010, 151). Although films that prioritise their settings and employ music as a significant element to foreground the natural environment are more of an occasional feature in British film culture, the effects that are prominent in the small group of films I explore here are found to a lesser degree in a much wider array of films. The techniques are sufficiently potent for their effect to be registered when employed in a less sustained and developed manner. Before moving on to a detailed analysis of these films, I would first like to consider briefly some more general themes regarding landscape, the construction of the 'rural myth', and how cinematic representations of the natural environment engage with broader cultural traditions of the pastoral.

Landscape is a mediated representation. Our understanding of what constitutes a landscape is connected to notions of aesthetic pleasure and therefore to decisions about what is included and what is not. Landscape representations across art forms are the result of 'selection, interpretation and omission', and are 'never neutral in intention or reception' (Harper and Rayner 2010, 16). Cinematic landscape representations, then, are always 'invested with value, meaning and significance' (Higson 2006, 240). The connotations of landscape are complex and multiple, and landscape is imbued with a range of symbolic values that may merge and overlap to create composite meanings. Images of the English countryside tend to signify a connection to the past, and from this stems its association with a sense of timeless continuity, tradition, and values seen as rural, such as community and non-materialism. Stephan Kohl (2006, 187) records that, prior to the Great War, it was widely (and erroneously) believed the countryside was becoming depopulated at a troubling rate, and this lends to rural images an additional sense of loss, as well as a concomitant sense of urgency. The historical increase in urbanisation and the adjustment to urban living fuels a corresponding idealisation of rural life as less complicated, and, in its apparent resistance to the tide of modern industrial advances, one that is somehow more 'natural' (Andrews 1999, 151). In this way the image of the countryside not only becomes the focus of nostalgic yearnings for a simpler past, but also offers itself as a blank page onto which we may project any of the qualities or values we imagine ourselves to have lost in the transition to modern urban life.

In addition, the landscape becomes a focus for displaced feelings of attachment, a 'surrogate for more politicised notions of nationhood' (Pugh 1990, 1). The concept of nationhood is raised by Ralph Vaughan Williams in his description of music as 'the expression of the soul of the nation'. The composer defines a nation as a community 'spiritually bound together by language, environment, history, and common ideals and, above all, a continuity with the past' (1963, 68). The similar terminology used for landscape imagery and music is indicative of the similar cultural positions that both occupy as bearers of a specifically national feeling. Both landscape and music evoke a familiar sense of place and the reassurance of historical continuity that confirms a sense of belonging within a shared national identity. Fowler and Helfield suggest that cinematic representations of rural life act as a barometer of national feeling, with positive depictions revealing a nation 'heavily invested in the past and nostalgic for its values, ideals and comforts' (2006, 10). Looked at this way, rural settings in cinema may be viewed as a form of escapism, a nostalgic and backward-looking retreat into an idealised vision of a simpler past.

However, to see only indulgent nostalgia in pastoral representations is to ignore the tensions that animate them and to disregard what they have to say about the present and the future. Insofar as the pastoral represents an idealisation, a celebration of the past as a romanticised Golden Age, it must also imply the possibility of a better future (Gifford 1999, 36). Therefore, in addition to a view of the past, the pastoral also offers a utopian vision upon which to model the future. The continuity with the past that spiritually binds together Vaughan Williams's imagined community does not represent simply a nostalgic yearning for times gone by, it also acknowledges a shared history that remains relevant to contemporary life. Hughes and Stradling note that the composer was influential in espousing the view that 'the future for English Music was to be found in its past' (2001, 75), in folk song, Tudor polyphony, and pastoral modes. However, this was not merely an attempt 'to put the clock back and re-enter a vanished world', but a way of 'making the past present' (Mellers 1989, 28). In a similar way, Nanette Aldred observes that the past is privileged in *A Canterbury Tale* (Powell and Pressburger, 1944) through 'the motifs of the English landscape, the craftsmen and the village', and the effect of this is to render the present unknowable 'except by reference to the past' (1987, 118). This promotes a sense that the past inheres in the landscape, that the history of the land is inscribed in it (and at the same time contradicts the myth of a timeless and unchanging landscape). The English landscape, 'to those who know how to read it aright', the historian W. G. Hoskins argues, 'is the richest historical record we possess' (1985, 14). Powell and Pressburger conceive *A Canterbury Tale* as an exploration of materialism and idealism, a way to explain 'the spiritual values and the traditions we were fighting for' (Powell 1986, 437). The filmmakers send their characters on a pastoral retreat not to indulge in landscape nostalgia but in order to raise contemporary issues.

Natural cinematic landscapes draw upon the visual traditions of landscape painting and they carry with them the connotative aspects of these antecedents. Filmed landscape scenes reveal the influence of the visual arts in their composition and lighting, as well as in their attention to detail. Michael Powell, for instance, recalls how cinematographer Erwin Hillier would beg him to wait for clouds to come into the frame when filming *A Canterbury Tale* (1986, 443). On a deeper level, the impact of landscape in British cinema is intensified by its centrality in other spheres of artistic endeavour in Britain, most notably the landscape tradition in painting,[1] which tends to promote rural scenery in an idealised pastoral mode. The alignment of landscape scenes in cinema with fine art, and in particular with a dominant genre of British painting, enables British cinema to draw upon the iconography of the earlier art form in order to access established and deeply ingrained associations relating to the rural landscape. Andrew Higson summarises this as the view that England 'had ancient roots in the countryside and the countryside therefore represented tradition, stability, and tranquillity, a refuge from modernity' (2006, 242). So pervasive is this rural myth that filmmakers employing visions of rural England are able to lay claim to a sense of continuity with the past, and also to 'proclaim a deep sense of national identity' (ibid.).

The purely visual nature of landscape, coupled with the visual bias of cinema, can lead us to undervalue the part that music plays in the audio-visual presentation of cinematic landscapes. Chion stresses the ability of music to create and expand space through its own suggestion of expansiveness. The 'fragmentation of editing', he finds, may cause landscape scenes to seem 'oddly shrunken' on screen, a condition that natural diegetic sound is powerless to rectify, and music is often introduced to 'restore the missing sensation of immense natural grandeur' (2009, 409). The interaction between music and landscape in cinema remains a largely unexplored area. For Harper and Rayner, sound and music are integral to cinematic landscapes. Music stresses the 'performative nature' of cinema, but is often 'purely evocative' (2010, 19), and the subject is not investigated further in connection with British cinema. Among writers on American film music, Eisler and Adorno (1994, 13) mention landscape shots only to berate Hollywood composers for the 'stale programmatic patterns' followed by the music that accompanies them. In their key texts on classical Hollywood film music, neither Claudia Gorbman nor Kathryn Kalinak specifically mentions landscape, although both refer to music that is used to mark cinematic spectacle, which must include, but not be limited to, landscape scenes. Gorbman identifies music that lends an epic dimension to the images it accompanies, which, 'rather than involving us *in* the narrative, places us in contemplation *of* it' (1987, 68, emphases in original). Kalinak additionally notes that in moments of pure spectacle the music is accorded priority over naturalistic sound, with the result that the spectator's awareness of the music increases (1992, 97).

In Western visual art, landscape gradually moves from the background to become the main subject in the development of the genre of landscape painting that we understand today. In cinema, Martin Lefebvre theorises a parallel movement whereby a shift occurs on screen between space understood as 'setting', that is, as 'the location for some unfolding action', and space that is offered as 'landscape', for 'aesthetic contemplation and spectacle' (2006, xviii). Space that is liberated from narrative imperatives may therefore emerge as 'autonomous landscape' (2006, 23). Accordingly, Lefebvre posits two viewing modes that operate in cinema: a narrative mode and a spectacular mode, which film viewers alternate between, thus 'allowing them both to follow the story *and*, whenever necessary, to contemplate the filmic spectacle' (2006, 29). Lefebvre overlooks the key role that music plays in marking these different modes. His proposed viewing modes broadly align with the two separate types of spectator bonding that Gorbman finds are fostered by film music: first, that which invites the audience to identify with characters in the narrative, and second, that which places them in contemplation of cinematic spectacle. Music used in the latter way permits the audience to relax during moments of spectacle, in the knowledge that the image may be enjoyed without further narrative information being offered until the music alters to cue this in. The spectator is more likely to be aware of music during moments of spectacle, when its use 'punctuates a pause in narrative movement in order to externalize, make a commentary on it' (Gorbman 1987, 68). This alternation between narrative and spectacular elements is theorised in the influential work of Laura Mulvey. For Mulvey, the male gaze of the cinema finds visual pleasure in the spectacle of Woman, whose presence on screen threatens to suspend the progress of the narrative: 'to freeze the flow of action in moments of erotic contemplation' (1975, 11). Spectacular landscape scenes risk the same suspension of the narrative drive, and the visual pleasure to be found in landscape also complies with Mulvey's formulation of '*to-be-looked-at-ness*' (1975, 11).[2]

Many of the films considered in this chapter contain pastoral scenes, in the sense that they combine music and imagery in a way that romanticises the natural environment. The term 'pastoral' may be understood in a number of ways, and its usage has widened over time. From its original description of a poetic form wherein shepherds rhapsodise about love and the beauty of the countryside, it has expanded to encompass all art forms that portray country life in an idealised fashion (Gifford 1999, 1–2). It may be broadly defined as a genre that presents 'rural life or is expressive of its atmosphere' (Chew 2001, 217). The pastoral form is based upon oppositions between town and country, retreat and return, and its frequently allegorical nature is aimed at a 'knowing' urban audience. Although the films discussed here may be more generally categorised as those in which the natural environment plays a significant role, some also manifest key elements of the pastoral form. As well as containing imagery and music that is pastoral in nature, they may adopt the form of retreat and return that the pastoral text epitomises. In this respect, *Love Story* (Leslie Arliss, 1944) is exemplary. The film juxtaposes the city and the country through the contrast it makes between the unhurried calm of the camera's journey through the Cornish countryside in its title sequence and the opening shots that establish Trafalgar Square, and again when the journey is reversed in the fast dissolve between a London bus and the view from Lissa's (Margaret Lockwood) hotel room in Cornwall. In *Love Story*, nondiegetic music is associated with the country—the title music briefly carries over the dissolve to a pan shot of barrage balloons in the sky, and its final notes fade into the Westminster chimes as the image dissolves again, to the top of Nelson's Column silhouetted against the sky. The next dissolves, to an establishing shot of the façade of the National Gallery and then to a poster advertising a concert, introduce the piano playing that is quickly revealed as Lissa's diegetic performance. *Love Story* proceeds without music until Lissa's mention of the sunshine, wind and the Cornish rocks that transports the narrative to Cornwall. The film represents Lissa's 'retreat' to Cornwall both as an escape from the pressures of her modern urban life, and as an experience that yields insights into that life. Furthermore, it promotes the notion of the country not only as a location where the slower pace of life may allow romance to blossom, but also as a site of healing and restorative powers, a place where both Lissa and Kit (Stewart Granger) can come to terms with their diagnoses. The pastoral text can act 'as a form of pastoral escape' for its largely urban audience, and, more than this, it can deliver to that audience the insights that are characteristic of the retreat and return structure of its literary and dramatic incarnations (Gifford 1999, 74). In this way, the pastoral cinematic text not only draws upon landscape imagery and music in a pastoral mode, but it can also in itself embody the allegorical form associated with the pastoral.

Music and Landscape Emphasis

The opening section of *Love Story* illustrates a recurring feature of films that foreground their landscape settings. These films signal the importance of their landscapes in their title sequences or introductory scenes by employing camera techniques that emphasise its expanse. P. Adams Sitney (1993, 107–8) identifies three modes employed in cinema to emphasise landscape: the long shot, the panoramic sweep ('pan') and the moving camera. The first of these, the long shot, emphasises scale and adopts the pictorial conventions of landscape painting and still photography. As in these still forms, *repoussoir* elements may be included at the sides or in the foreground of the shot to indicate depth and to guide the viewer's eye into the image. The long shot may function to establish the setting if it is followed by closer views (1993, 108). The other two techniques that emphasise landscape move beyond the limitations of the still picture to exploit the potential of cinema's moving image. The panoramic sweep imitates the movement of the spectator's eyes across a landscape. It promotes scale by raising awareness of 'the landscape extending in all directions beyond the edges of the screen' (Sitney 1993, 107). Pan shots often serve as establishing shots either during or immediately following a film's title sequence, where they mark the significance of the location to the narrative.

Composer Alan Rawsthorne notes that title music is perhaps the only music the audience will hear consciously, and it is of 'the highest importance' to 'establish the mood of the ensuing drama' (1975, 33–4). Consequently, the music accompanying a film's opening pan shots will interpret the landscape and indicate whether it is a place of safety or danger. For example, *Tawny Pipit* (Charles Saunders and Bernard Miles, 1944) begins with a pan from clouds in a summer sky across idyllic English scenery to reveal a group of birdwatchers, wrapped in a pastoral ambience created by Noel Mewton-Wood's gentle woodwind tune. By contrast, *Sea of Sand* (Guy Green, 1958) depicts a perilous desert journey. Clifton Parker's score opens on a drumroll, and continues in a solemn tone while the camera pans across a barren desert landscape as the titles appear on screen. Such dangerous terrains can also provide visual spectacle. *The Drum* (Zoltan Korda, 1938) opens with a series of leisurely pans across a dramatic mountainous landscape accompanied by John Greenwood's expansive music, inflected with an Eastern lilt, which establishes the location before the action of the film begins. A pan can also contribute to the narrative logic of the film. The cattle drive in *The Overlanders* is introduced by a montage that comprises a wide establishing shot, a slightly closer shot and then an extended slow pan from left to right. The pan shot emphasises both the grandeur of the open landscape and the challenge faced by the drovers as it slowly takes in the cattle, horses and riders. The pan establishes the left-to-right direction of travel that is maintained throughout the film, while the tempo of John Ireland's jaunty tune energises the shots and endows the montage with a sense of forward momentum that the images of the steadily paced herd would otherwise lack.

Whereas the long shot and the panning shot emphasise the scale and expanse of the landscape, the moving camera provides a more immersive experience for the spectator. When the camera moves through the landscape in a film's title sequence, the audience is transported into the environment of the film and the location is marked as particularly significant. The pace of the music usually mirrors the speed of the camera's journey. Thus, the leisurely pace of travel along the country lane into the village during the title sequence of *Went the Day Well?* (Alberto Cavalcanti, 1942) is reflected in the tempo of William Walton's music. Similarly, William Alwyn's title music for *Great Day* (Lance Comfort, 1945) advances steadily in unison with the camera's progress along the village street. The slow movement suggests the apparently unhurried pace of country life and taps into the characteristic pastoral opposition between the city and the country. Music that accompanies the moving camera in the body of a film tends to synchronise directly with the pace and rhythm of travel. In *A Canterbury Tale*, for example, when Alison (Sheila Sim) pauses in the horse-drawn cart to admire Colpeper's house, Allan Gray's gentle music stops and restarts in alignment with her progress, and in this way the music naturalises its presence on the soundtrack.

Similarly, in *The Flemish Farm* (Jeffrey Dell, 1943), Duclos (Clifford Evans) walks along a country lane that is accentuated both by the camera moving backwards to keep him in the frame, and by the straight lane being filmed from both aspects to reveal it extending away into the distance in both directions. The tramp of Duclos's walk is matched by the robust march rhythm employed by Vaughan Williams, which echoes his setting of Robert Louis Stevenson's 'The Vagabond', part of the composer's *Songs of Travel* cycle. The march rhythm is interrupted by darker tones when Duclos is stopped at the Nazi checkpoint and resumes only when he is on his way again. At a later point in the film, a montage sequence brings together both musical matching of movement, and its use in a panning shot. The segment depicts Duclos walking, cycling and obtaining lifts in a cart and a truck, merged on screen with ticker-tape messages and a poster offering a reward for the return of the regimental flag he is secretly carrying. The extended montage begins with a gunshot, immediately followed by a clash of cymbals that ushers in urgent and fast-paced music with stabbing strings. The striking urgency of the strings, together with the way the energy momentarily drains from the music to leave extended low chords before resuming, prefigures Bernard Herrmann's string score for Alfred Hitchcock's *Psycho* (1960) and particularly the lower figures heard after the attacker leaves during the shower scene. The music that accompanies these scenes gives way to a more lyrical pastoral effect when Duclos arrives in picturesque sunlit countryside and the camera pans across a hill to reveal in the distance a cottage where he will find help. The change in tone, and the release of tension it brings, is also conveyed through a shift in the orchestral arrangement as the darker strings are replaced by a gentle tune on oboe and flute, instruments particularly associated with the pastoral. The music guides our response to the open landscape while the filming techniques accentuate both the scale of the setting and Duclos's vulnerable position within it. This use of music in a pastoral mode that romanticises the landscape is an isolated effect in the varied score that Vaughan Williams supplies for this war film. In the next section, I will turn my attention to a small group of films from the 1940s in which pastoral modes are employed in a way that both highlights the natural environment and offers insights into the sensitivities of the characters by exploring their relationship with the landscape.

Landscape Representations Through Music in the 1940s

The 1940s was a significant decade for British cinema and for British film music. During the years of the Second World War, cinema admissions in Britain rose steadily to a peak of 1.6 billion in 1946, while British films enjoyed an unprecedented popularity with home audiences (Dyja 1999, 30; Thumim 1991, 247). The Ministry of Information sought to capitalise on the propaganda potential of cinema and encouraged film subjects that would help to mobilise the population in support of the ideals that were being fought for. At the same time, the practice in the British industry of commissioning scores on a film-by-film basis allowed concert composers to take on film work as a means both to maintain an income during a time of reduced general musical activity and to make a contribution to the war effort. One of the fortunate results of this combination of factors was that a sense of purpose and creative energy infused much of the film-making of the period.

I would like to explore one particular area of this activity by analysing four films that illustrate how music of a pastoral nature is used with landscape imagery to express a range of meanings with contemporary significance. Two of the films—*The Life and Death of Colonel Blimp* (Powell and

Pressburger, 1943) and *A Canterbury Tale*—have scores composed by Allan Gray. The remaining two—*49th Parallel* (Powell and Pressburger, 1941) and *The Loves of Joanna Godden* (Charles Frend, 1947)—are scored by Ralph Vaughan Williams. While these films are not unique among British films of this time in combining landscape scenes and music, when explored together they demonstrate a consistent pattern in the way their music creates meaning in the context of the film. The films use their scores not only to signal visual spectacle, but also to express the subjectivity of their characters and to exploit a range of qualities associated with the landscape.

Film music can perform several functions simultaneously, and consequently it can foreground landscape in subtle but significant ways. For instance, music that provides continuity between different shots can also emphasise landscape. Music used prominently to accompany landscape scenes becomes associated with the landscape depicted, and its continued use on the soundtrack when the landscape no longer dominates the image maintains the 'idea' of the landscape in the minds of the audience. An example of this occurs in *49th Parallel*, a film whose narrative charts the progress of a group of Nazis as they seek to escape detection in Canada, and depicts their encounters with different groups of people. The episode I will look at details their conflict with the communal ideals and pacifism of a Hutterite community. A montage of scenes depicting the wheat harvest of the Hutterites is loudly accompanied by bright music that Michael Kennedy likens to folk dance (2004, 6). At the end of the montage sequence, the music slows in tempo and the same tune is repeated on the flute, which gives it a more lyrical, pastoral feel, as on screen Peter (Anton Walbrook) stands surveying the wheat field in a location shot. The image cuts to a closer shot of Peter, filmed in a studio in front of an indistinct background (Fig. 3.1). Swynnoe (2002, 148) notes that the establishing shot lends 'an impression of space' to the ensuing dialogue, assisted by Vaughan Williams's music. I would enlarge on this to propose that the music, which carries on softly during the scene, not only masks the rupture between location and studio shots but also maintains the aural 'image' of the landscape and therefore the illusion of its continued presence. The music here acts as an element of what Michel Chion has described as 'extension', whereby the boundaries of the scenic space may be constructed for the spectator, and varied, not only by what is seen but also by what is heard (2009, 477). Just as the sound of thunder in a later scene reminds us of the scale of the landscape beyond the Hutterite community

Fig. 3.1 Location shot (above) and studio insert (below) in *49th Parallel*

as a storm approaches, so the music in this sequence holds in the mind of the audience the expansive landscape with which it is associated. Therefore, the music acts as a continuity element that holds together the montage sequence and it also maintains the aural impression of the wider landscape when it is no longer depicted.

In addition, the character of the music expresses the values of the Hutterite group. The uplifting bounce of the music that accompanies the scenes of the harvest reflects and reinforces the cheerful willingness of the workers in the field. Its slowing tempo suggests the work coming to an end and the passage of time to the late afternoon, in tandem with the rhythm of a working day, while the pastoral reiteration of the theme on the flute promotes the sense of a celebration of the natural environment and its bounty, and of satisfaction at being close to the land. In this way, *49th Parallel* vividly contrasts the values of those seen as living in harmony with nature (particularly the Hutterite community, but also in other episodes the Hudson Bay trappers and traders, and Leslie Howard's gentle aesthete) with those of the Nazi group. The group's disintegration, the film suggests, occurs as the result of its imposition of a deeply flawed ideology. While the Hudson Bay and Hutterite communities are co-operative groups with shared collective ideals embraced freely by their members, the Nazi group are forced to comply with the demands of their tyrannical leader, Hirth (Eric Portman), or risk the summary execution that ends the hopes of Vogel (Niall MacGinnis) to join the Hutterites.

The process of Vogel's integration into the Hutterite community is expressed musically in Vaughan Williams's score. The Hutterite group is introduced on screen by Anna (Glynis Johns), who sings the German folk tune 'Lasst uns das Kindlein wiegen' ('Let us cradle the child') as she pushes stuffing into a scarecrow at the edge of a wheat field. Kennedy notes that the tune is 'then treated orchestrally in the style of one of VW's [sic] hymn-tune preludes' (2004, 6). In contrast to the duplicity of the Nazi group, Anna represents the straightforward simplicity and honesty of the Hutterite community. As the melody of her song enters the nondiegetic track while she speaks of the Hutterites, it becomes more broadly associated with the wider community. This impression is bolstered by the spontaneous singing heard after the evening meal, which the Nazis question only to be told the people sing because they like to. This confirmation of communal singing as an activity that binds together the Hutterite group supports the notion that Anna would have learnt her song from within the community and thus extends its representational compass to the wider group. Community cohesion and co-operation is further expressed in the montage sequence that depicts the Hutterites working together to harvest and thresh the wheat, and these shots additionally foreground both the productive and sustaining nature of the land, and the closeness of the community to it. The sequence positions Vogel, the baker, as the final link in the chain of labour. It is Vogel who makes the first contact with Anna, and who subsequently feels protective of her and sympathetic to the ethos of the community. Having agreed to return to join the group after spending the remainder of the war in internment, Vogel's complete integration into the Hutterite group is demonstrated as he whistles the tune of Anna's song in the bakery while he prepares dough and slides into the oven a cake he has made to celebrate Anna's birthday. The reawakening of Vogel's gentle humanity may be cut short, but nonetheless the narrative element of a character who is brought to a deeper appreciation of the land and the qualities it can confer is one that recurs in films that foreground landscape, and one in which music plays a key role.

In addition to the visual emphasis that a film can give to the natural environment, Sitney (1993, 110) points out that in sound cinema, attention may be drawn to the landscape by verbal onscreen references to it. Spoken references to the landscape can conjure its image and call to mind the connotations it bears for the spectator even when it is not represented on screen. An example of this is found in the second film in this brief survey, *The Life and Death of Colonel Blimp*. In an extended soliloquy filmed in a long take in which the camera slowly moves into a closer framing of him, Theo (Anton Walbrook) explains to the immigration officer his reasons for wishing to return to England after the death of his English wife Edith (Deborah Kerr):

> And very foolishly I remembered the English countryside, the gardens, the green lawns, the weedy rivers and the trees she loved so much. And a great desire came over me to come back to my wife's country.

A great deal of meaning is contained in these two sentences. Theo's memory of Edith is expressed through her love of the English countryside. Higson (1995, 44) notes that the iconic image of the British landscape, of gently rolling hills and cultivated fields, is most typical of southern England. Higson describes how, 'through processes of displacement and condensation', this pastoral representation of one region of England is able to operate as an emotive shorthand symbol that not only comes to represent the whole of the British Isles but also carries notions of national identity and the associations that accrue to it. Edith's love of the countryside elevates her character because it suggests her appreciation for its natural beauty, but more importantly it aligns her with the qualities that the countryside symbolises, the sense of history, tradition, of life lived in harmony with nature.

The Life and Death of Colonel Blimp is the exception among these films, for the English countryside is referred to here without being shown on screen or represented in the musical score. Nevertheless, it is implicit in Theo's monologue that he is sympathetic to Edith's emotional response to the landscape and the qualities it represents, and in his expression of his love for Edith, his character is also elevated. Although Theo's speech unfolds without music, it is more usual for spoken onscreen references to landscape to draw attention to what is then made, or has been made, visible in the image, and for the spectator's reading of these scenes to be directed by the music that accompanies them. This process is made explicit in the third film under consideration, *A Canterbury Tale*. The narrative concerns three modern pilgrims who travel to Canterbury during the war: an American Army sergeant, a British Army sergeant, and a land girl, Alison (Sheila Sim).

In a key scene, Colpeper (Eric Portman), the magistrate and enthusiastic local historian, lectures the visiting troops on the history of the area. He is photographed almost in silhouette against the white light on the screen behind him. Pam Cook notes that one of cinematographer Erwin Hillier's favoured techniques to create a 'mysterious, Gothic ambience' was to shoot into the natural light and incorporate a 'swirling mist' (2002, 44). Here the effect is recreated in an interior setting using the powerful light from the projector, while the mist is supplied by the rising wisps of smoke from those in the audience. As the camera slowly moves in to a close-up of Colpeper, a strip of light illuminates his eyes as he urges the soldiers to walk the Pilgrims' Road and to contemplate their ancestors:

> Follow the old road, and as you walk, think of them and of the old England … And when you see the bluebells in the spring and the wild thyme, the broom and the heather, you're only seeing what their eyes saw. We ford the same rivers; the same birds are singing, and when you lie flat on your back, and rest, and watch the clouds sailing as I often do, you're so close to those other people that you can hear the thrumming of the hooves of their horses and the sound of the

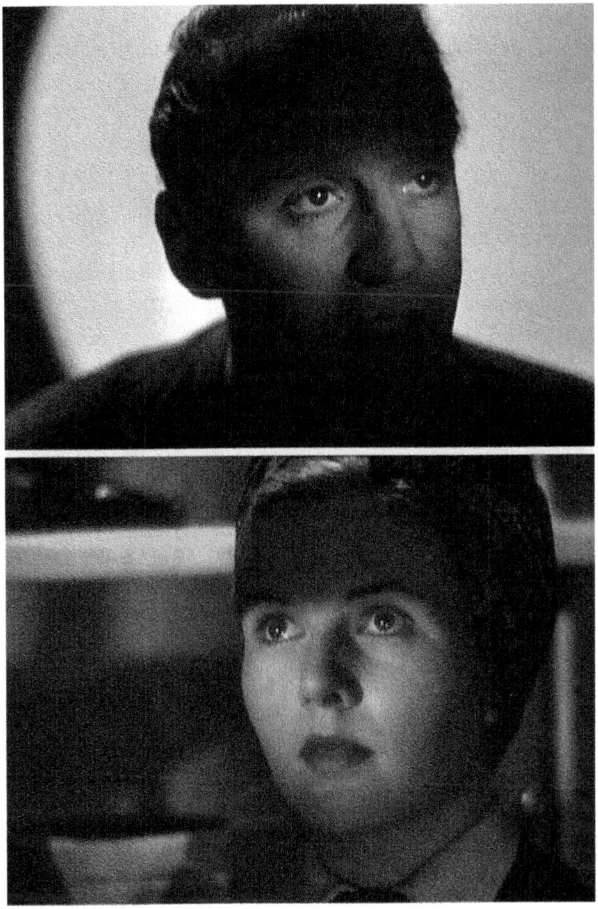

Fig. 3.2 Colpeper's speech (above) and Alison's rapt attention (below) in *A Canterbury Tale*

wheels on the road and their laughter and talk and the music of the instruments they carried.

The close-up shot of Colpeper is intercut with close-ups of Alison, and the two are equated as they share the same screen space, the same lighting of their eyes, and the same slow camera move (Fig. 3.2). Allan Gray's music cue begins after Colpeper mentions the wild thyme. The music lends his speech a lyrical quality, although as the image stays with Alison, who seems mesmerised by Colpeper, the music registers as an expression of her emotional response to his words. Later, two other musical themes return in a sequence that recalls Colpeper's lecture. The first is associated with the Pilgrim's Road and specifically with Alison's recollection of a holiday she had spent camped on the road with her fiancé. The music is first heard as she tells the publican about this holiday, and it subsequently returns to accompany scenes of Alison's horse-drawn journey through the countryside. This theme, brightly scored and optimistic, is heard prominently as Alison walks the Pilgrim's Road alone in the sunshine, before it gives way to choral singing as she sees Canterbury Cathedral in the distance. The choir forms a brief mystical bridge between the music that recalls Colpeper's instruction to walk the old road, and the second theme, of music associated with the earlier pilgrims. This second theme, introduced for shots of Chaucer's pilgrims in the film's prologue, together with the diegetic sound of their horses' hooves, music and laughter, then fills the soundtrack and represents what Alison hears in her mind (Fig. 3.3). This fulfils Colpeper's assurance that an appreciation of the natural landscape will foster a sense of the history that resides in it. Alison subsequently meets Colpeper, who confirms for her, and the cinema audience, that she hasn't imagined the music and voices, but that they come from within.

This sequence complicates Gorbman's theoretical division between music that brings us to a closer identification with a character in the narrative, and music that places us in contemplation of cinematic spectacle (1987, 68). Here, these effects are combined with a musical accompaniment that invites us both to identify with Alison by sharing her subjective emotional experience (we hear what she hears) and to enjoy the visual spectacle of the landscape.

The last film in this group, *The Loves of Joanna Godden*, similarly presents a combination of character identification and a deeper feeling for landscape. This occurs in a montage sequence in which Joanna (Googie Withers) is brought to appreciate the natural environment around her by Martin (Derek Bond). The film is set in the harsh and windswept landscape of the Romney Marshes. Martin admires the beauty of the light on the marsh, which Joanna dismisses as 'just a lot of flat fields'. Martin then draws attention explicitly to the music and sounds that accompany the shots in the montage when he tells her: 'try looking at it again, through my eyes – and listen to it, too'.

Fig. 3.3 Alison hearing the past in the Kent landscape of *A Canterbury Tale*

The film centres on the experience of Joanna, who inherits the family farm and is determined to run it as an independent woman in the male-dominated farming community. In the film's early scenes, Vaughan Williams's score closely matches the changing feelings Joanna reveals through her facial expressions in a moment-by-moment relationship, and the score is thus emphatically aligned with Joanna's subjectivity. This establishes the music's melodramatic role, so we are aware that it will act as a barometer of her emotions. This is confirmed when the image of Joanna, who in response to Martin's instruction gazes at the landscape, dissolves into a montage of shots of what she sees: a flying swan, the sea and pebble beach, sheep and fields of wheat. The camera repeatedly tilts upwards to emphasise the sense of space. On the soundtrack, the diegetic baaing of the sheep joins a pastoral oboe melody before it is taken up by the full orchestra to swell expansively with a surge that simultaneously suggests the rising romantic emotion and the visual opening out of the landscape before us. The image dissolves back to Joanna and Martin as he

Fig. 3.4 Appreciating the landscape in *The Loves of Joanna Godden*

tells her that 'things look very different when you've someone to share them with', and the sequence ends with their embrace (Fig. 3.4). Martin inspires Joanna to see and hear, and thus to feel, the beauty of the natural environment, and the film equates her newly found understanding with the awakening of her romantic feelings for him. Martin's opening instruction to listen is addressed to the cinema audience as well as to Joanna, and we are therefore primed to attend to the music and invited to engage with and understand her emotional experience.

In both *The Loves of Joanna Godden* and *A Canterbury Tale*, one character brings another to a deeper appreciation of the landscape by directing their attention to it. Although the process by which this is achieved remains the same, the difference in the music that accompanies these sequences guides the reading of them and expresses specific connotations for each landscape. The melodramatic mode adopted in *The Loves of Joanna Godden* ties the music to the emotional world of Joanna and her romantic awakening, whereas *A Canterbury Tale* uses its soundtrack to promote a broader mystical sense of the past residing in the present, of the continuing traditions and shared experiences that collapse the distance between the two. In each case, the sensitivity to landscape the character gains takes on a more profound meaning within the framework of the film. It signals for each character an emotional depth and capacity for feeling. For Joanna, it indicates a softening in contrast to the tough exterior she has presented since taking over the running of the farm, and, in the terms of the film, a more appropriate femininity. 'Why don't you stop trying to be a man?' Arthur (John McCallum) asks her, while a cuckoo calls insistently on the soundtrack to suggest her outsider status in the masculine farming community. For Alison, what Michael Powell (in Lazar 2003, 51) has described as the 'movement of sympathy, of understanding' between her and Colpeper, expressed in their shared connection to the past through landscape, provides a means for her to make peace with the loss of the fiancé she believes to have been killed in action. The Kent landscape holds a resonance for Alison through her memory of a caravanning holiday before the war, and Colpeper offers her the means both to access the closeness of the past and to recognise her own place within it. Aldred observes that, in *A Canterbury Tale*, the characters are privileged according to their closeness to the land, which is equated with their level of sensitivity to the past and its traditions (1987, 118). Alison's love of the landscape and its history is heightened by the richer experience of it that Colpeper opens up for her.

This process of enlightenment, of a deeper understanding gained through an appreciation in the landscape of qualities that are then expressed in the musical score, is explicit in *A Canterbury Tale* and *The Loves of Joanna Godden*. It is also clearly prefigured in the correlation between desirable qualities and a feeling for the natural environment that is made in *49th Parallel* and *The Life and Death of Colonel Blimp*. In each example, one character in the narrative—Anna, Edith, Colpeper, Martin—brings another—Vogel, Theo, Alison, Joanna—to a heightened awareness that enriches their life. There are, of course, variations in the films. In *The Life and Death of Colonel Blimp*, the reference is more oblique, understood rather than demonstrated, and *The Loves of Joanna Godden* lacks the contemporary wartime setting and time-frame that enhances the poignancy of the other films. Nevertheless, this element forms a common thread that runs between these films, and in three of the examples, music is a key element in the process.

This analysis of the ways that landscape imagery and music combine to create meaning suggests that the music has three effects. First, it indicates moments of spectacular visual pleasure in landscape scenes with expansive music at its highest volume as the Hutterites harvest the wheat, as Alison walks the Pilgrim's Road and as Joanna looks anew at the scenes around her. Second, it encourages us to identify with the characters by granting us access to their subjective experience. We see the landscape that they see, we hear what Alison hears in her mind, and we hear a musical representation of the emotions that are awakening in Joanna. Third, the music operates to identify the symbolic aspect of the landscape that is being evoked. For Vogel it is the gentle humanity of the Hutterite community living in harmony with nature; for Alison it is the sense of the past being present in the landscape as she hears the sounds of the ancient pilgrims. For Joanna it is the restoration of what the film sees as her natural femininity, as she finds herself falling in love with the man who has opened her eyes to the beauty around her. These meanings are not fixed and static, for the landscape offers a multivalent canvas of possible significations. Thus, the combination of landscape imagery and music in these films not only emphasises the presence of landscape as spectacle and visual pleasure, it also promotes character identification and exploits the particular connotative aspects that the landscape symbolises.

Landscapes That Resist the Rural Myth

I have so far explored cinematic landscape representations that romanticise their natural environments and employ music to highlight the positive symbolic connotations of the landscape. British films have also brought together music and landscape in ways that resist or subvert this process, and unsettle these idealised visions and restful scenes. I will explore three ways that this is achieved: a film may undermine the reassurance associated with the rural myth of the English countryside; it may focus on a more bleak British setting; or it may present the dangers of inhospitable foreign landscapes.

I noted earlier how pastoral music came to dominate British music in the years following the First World War, and it is perhaps unsurprising that the comforting reassurance of the pastoral idiom should again find expression in films made during, and immediately following, the Second World War. In this context, *Went the Day Well?* stands out for taking an alternative approach that engages with the visual tropes of the pastoral not to celebrate or idealise the associations these contains but in order to challenge the assumptions that they generate. The film presents the landscape as 'an emotional signifier of what the war was being fought for' (Geraghty 2000, 39), of what was at stake should the worst happen, and it is calculated to invoke the same national sentiment as Frank Newbould's contemporaneous recruitment poster, with its sunlit depiction of the South Downs and the slogan 'Your Britain – fight for it now'.[3] The film draws on deeply held feelings about the countryside, in particular its timeless continuity and resistance to change, in order to challenge the complacency of these notions. *Went the Day Well?* retains the power to shock through its juxtaposition of a tranquil rural setting with the violent actions both of the intruders and the village community.

Under the musical direction of Ernest Irving, William Walton's score for *Went the Day Well?* heightens the brutality of the events, which are rendered the more chilling for unfolding against the backdrop of village life. The stately march rhythm of Walton's title music, punctuated by soft drumrolls, now seems a prototype of the ceremonial music with which he would later become so associated, and this lends a retrospective familiarity to its stable forward momentum and calmly patriotic tone. A lyrical theme on harp and strings accompanies the first scenes of village life, although it is soon overwhelmed by the military march that enters with the soldiers who infiltrate the community. Walton's score subtly hints at the fact that the respected local squire, Wilsford (Leslie Banks), is a German agent through its use of the military march associated with the soldiers to accompany his first appearance rather than the gentle rustic tune associated with the other villagers (Swynnoe 2002, 153). The lyrical theme and its scoring are heard again as the Commander and Wilsford climb the hill to gain a strategic view of the location, and during a brief romantic interlude for the young couple who are soon to be married.

The most memorable uses of music, though, emphasise the violent acts perpetrated by the villagers. After Mrs Collins, the postmistress (Muriel George), throws pepper in the face of a German soldier, an orchestral swell builds quickly as she picks up an axe, lifts it above her head and brings it down on him. The music reaches a crashing climax as the axe hits its target and breaks off in an abrupt reverse sting that leaves a chilling silence broken only by Mrs Collins's unsteady breathing. The stinger registers as a shock for the audience, and here the musical device also takes the place of, and amplifies the effect of, a naturalistic sound effect. The expressionistic framing heightens its impact, with low-angle shots and an extreme close-up of Mrs Collins's face immediately following the blow (Fig. 3.5).

Fig. 3.5 The axe scene in *Went the Day Well?*

The shape of the musical phrase that accompanies the axe scene is echoed in a similar sequence later in the film, in which Nora (Valerie Taylor) shoots Wilsford, the traitorous squire. As she descends a staircase nursing a gun, the off-screen voices of Tom (Frank Lawton) and the land army girls are heard. They are oblivious to her intentions, and their chattering creates what Michel Chion has termed an 'anempathetic effect', whereby music or sound that is indifferent to the situation has the effect 'not of freezing emotion but rather of intensifying it' (1994, 8). Nora approaches Wilsford, accuses him of unbolting the latch to the barricaded window, and then shoots him. The musical swell begins after her first shot as he falls to the ground and it reaches its stinging climax as she fires two more shots. It ends suddenly to leave a moment's silence as Nora stumbles as though to faint. Wilkie Cooper's cinematography in this scene is equally expressionistic, with 'low key lighting, the cross-cutting between high and low angles and the brief use of slow motion as he falls dead' (Petrie 1996, 84).

These two sequences are united in employing the same musical shape, a similar expressionistic framing and cinematography, and in the shock they deliver to the audience. Most strikingly, these two brief sequences of spontaneous acts of violence convey both the horror of the situation and the emotional toll the actions extract from their unexpectedly feisty perpetrators. Penelope Houston (2012, 52) notes that the film retains a level of 'objectivity about the killings ... never lingering over the pain or the bodies'. Rather, I feel, these two scenes convey the pain not of those killed, but of those doing the killing. Through their carefully arranged shots, both scenes foreground and prioritise the experience of the women. The women's facial expressions demonstrate the horror they feel as they carry out the executions, and after each killing, the camera lingers on them to reveal the impact their actions have on them. These parallel scenes punctuate the narrative, the first occurring just after the halfway point in the film's running time and the second just before its end. The scene with Mrs Collins marks the first brutal act of defiance, while the scene with Nora marks the successful conclusion of the campaign it has set in motion. Although, as Houston notes, the latter scene is not the climax to the gun battle at the manor house, 'it feels like it' (2012, 53). Huntley (1948, 91) finds Walton's score musically 'less interesting' than his others from this period, although its impact is potent in these two scenes. The stark simplicity of the repeated musical stinger rings out in the context of the film's overall musical restraint, and its resistance of the pastoral mode, as a persuasive call-to-arms to contemporary audiences that more than fulfils its propaganda aims.

In wartime, the rural landscape is presented as the embodiment of what is being fought for, the myth of the timeless English countryside that reflects the 'unruffled harmony of its social order' (Cosgrove 1998, 262).[4] Higson (1995, 44) concurs that images with pastoral resonance foster a 'democratic myth of Englishness' through which hierarchical deference is reframed and naturalised into 'an ideology of community'. *Went the Day Well?* posits this social order as an enabling factor in the thwarted invasion, and Richards (1997, 101) finds at the heart of the film the radical suggestion that the 'old ruling class' may be unsound. The film challenges the hierarchical social order by showing how the concerns of the lower orders are disregarded by those above to the benefit of the disguised German invaders. Simon Heffer (2010) notes that the film's theme of resisting invasion was out of date even at the time of its production, given the reduced likelihood of that scenario once Hitler's forces were engaged in the invasion of the Soviet Union. The film's message, Heffer asserts, about 'forming a coherent modern society on principles that did not include automatic deference within a near feudal social order', is one that is aligned with the ethos of Ealing Studios, where the film was made (ibid.).

Nevertheless, in the introduction in which Charles (Mervyn Johns) addresses the audience directly and presents the main narrative as a central flashback, he describes life in the village 'as peaceful and quiet here then as it is now, even though there was a war on'. Thus he not only conveys a propagandist message by looking back from a victorious postwar period, but also implies that calm has returned to the village and life continues as before with its social order unchanged, an impression confirmed as Charles and the main theme return to bookend and close the film as the camera now reverses its journey and withdraws from the village. The idyllic version of rural England depicted in *Went the Day Well?* exploits the associations of its setting with stability and resilience. The audience is initially teased with the possibility of music used in a pastoral mode that romanticises the landscape, although the score makes its most memorable impact with the shock device, and horror film staple, of the loud musical stinger.

Elsewhere in British film culture the camera is turned on natural landscapes that do not conform to the reassuring rural idyll. One example is *The Long Memory*, in which the bleak landscape of the Thames estuary presents an unwelcoming environment for its inhabitants. Robert Hamer's film noir, which tells the story of a wrongly imprisoned man returning to exact revenge on those who framed him, highlights the importance of the terrain to the narrative by opening the film with a static shot of the mudflats behind the titles. Detritus litters the foreground, and the horizon line is high in the composition so that the sky occupies only the top third of the frame. This reverses the usual composition of landscape scenes, in which the expanse of sky suggests the openness of the landscape. William Alwyn's dark scoring conspires with this framing to suggest the oppressive nature of the location, and the desolation of the landscape expresses Davidson's (John Mills) alienation and social isolation. The music begins with a sombre fanfare before easing into a more gentle strain that is nonetheless cold-edged and lacking any lyrical warmth, with tremolo strings and bass chords that signal foreboding. After the titles the frame unfreezes and the camera pans across the mudflats to take in weather-beaten boats abandoned on the shore. Ian Johnson points out the way natural sounds are used to convey the film's 'joyless desolation', and how the last notes of the title music are mixed on the soundtrack with the 'mournful cry of the curlew' as the camera scans the scene (2005, 252). The landscape consistently expresses Davidson's self-destructive despair. In the film's final sequence Davidson is pursued across the mudflats by the man he has been convicted of murdering, trudging through the squelching mud until he falls and is held fast by it, powerless to free himself. The environment traps him, renders him a sitting target for the gun pointed in his direction. The English landscape, so often presented as a romanticised rural idyll, is depicted here as a challenging and hostile terrain, a trope that Geraghty find 'runs like a thin thread' through British films in the 1950s (2000, 53).

While some British terrains may be inhospitable and resistant to habitation, they rarely achieve the scale, drama and sheer overwhelming force of the Sublime elements of landscape. In his *Philosophical Enquiry into the Sublime and Beautiful* of 1757, Edmund Burke finds that certain aspects of nature—vastness, power, infinity—promote feelings of excitement that balance a sense of danger and delight to produce the 'strongest emotion which the mind is capable of feeling' (2015, 34). The experience of the Sublime suspends our reasoning, leaves the mind 'so entirely filled with its object, that it cannot entertain any other' and engenders feelings that are both threatening and at the same time thrilling (ibid., 47). In painting, Philip James De Loutherbourg (1740–1812) 'pioneered the idea of landscape itself taking over the role of protagonist' as the force of nature reminds man of his own impotence (Vaughan 1999, 227). In De Loutherbourg's *An Avalanche in the Alps* (1803), for example, the figures in the landscape verify the scale of the setting, just as the overhead shots in *Scott of the Antarctic* serve to underline the vastness of the blank terrain and the comparative insignificance of the figures in such surroundings. Although the British landscape endures fierce storms, the extreme life-threatening conditions that constitute our experience of the Sublime—earthquakes, avalanches, volcanoes—are more readily associated with foreign lands removed from the temperate climate of the British Isles. The Sublime is associated with the exotic and the 'other', and with the indifference of the natural world towards human concerns.

The Sublime may be experienced as the force of nature that overwhelms through its power, or through the scale of the landscape. These elements are brought to the fore in *Black Narcissus*. Sister Ruth (Kathleen Byron) rings the bell and her eagerness to look over the edge of the precipice introduces an effects shot that causes us to share the dizzying view straight down into the valley below (Fig. 3.6). Sister Philippa (Flora Robson) fails to respond to the bell, and as its chimes joins the soft musical underscoring to remind us of her oversight, she explains to Clodagh. 'I think you can see too far. I look out there and then I can't see the potato I'm planting,

Fig. 3.6 The edge of the precipice in *Black Narcissus*

and after a bit it doesn't seem to matter whether I plant it or not'—the clear air and the vistas the location offers bring home the insignificance of human existence. The experience of the Sublime 'subverts order ... [it] bypasses the rational mind and concentrates its force directly on the emotions' (Andrews 1999, 132). This occurs explicitly in *Black Narcissus*, where the repressed emotions of the nuns resurface to unsettle the increasingly fragile balance of their regulated lives, and the sound and image of the bell itself represents their attempts to impose and maintain their accustomed order upon their new location.

Although Brian Easdale's score grows briefly expansive as Sister Ruth opens the carved wooden doors to reveal the bell and the view to the mountains beyond when the nuns arrive at the palace, it is the emotional effect of the environment on the women that the music deftly charts. Easdale, who conducts his own score and is responsible for the whole soundscape of the film, resists the temptation to use music in a spectacular mode and as the camera takes in the precipitous high-angle view into the valley below, the music drops out to leave only the sound of the wind blowing. Much has been written about the sequence illustrating Sister Ruth's descent into madness, which Powell claimed had been shot and edited to fit a pre-composed music track in a reversal of the usual film music procedure (Powell 1986, 583–4).[5]

However, the sequence that precedes the one in which Ruth descends into madness demonstrates a melodramatic use of music that conveys both the force of emotions at play, and attributes them to the natural environment. The music starts softly as Sister Clodagh (Deborah Kerr) and Mr Dean (David Farrar) discuss the changes the palace has wrought on the nuns. She tells him of her returning memories of the man she might have married in Ireland. The music builds as the emotion rises in her voice, it ebbs and flows through her outpouring, marking the strength of her feelings and her restraint of them. The orchestral surges increase and decrease, as waves of emotion that flood the scene and then are reigned in. The music reaches a peak of volume and intensity as Clodagh expresses her frustration at the effects of the natural environment: 'I couldn't stop the wind from blowing and the air from being clear as crystal and I couldn't hide the mountain'. Or rather, it reaches a climax of volume and intensity, with brass flourishes, *after* her line of dialogue. Here, for the second time in the scene, the music continues to rise after she has finished speaking, as though her voice has released a wave of emotion that exceeds what she is able to say. It adopts a melodramatic mode—it acts as an unspoken expression of the emotion that she has unleashed but must also hold back. The effect is of a well of feeling simmering under the surface, simultaneously both articulated and repressed, for the music carries the emotion beyond the intensity of the words and suggests an avalanche of feeling that threatens to burst through if not held in check. Powell recalls that there had been discussion over whether or not the scene was necessary, and he concludes that the words are needed and the challenge was to find 'the balance between the words, the action and the music' (Powell 1991).

The exotic environment and heady altitude of the convent in *Black Narcissus* prompt the melodramatic return of unwelcome memories and repressed emotions that destabilise the order of nuns. The threat of the extreme location in the more masculine adventure of *The Four Feathers* (Zoltan Korda, 1939), however, lies squarely in the physical, rather than in the emotional challenges they present to their protagonists. The sequence in which Durrance (Ralph Richardson) is blinded by the sun provides an example. Miklós Rózsa's music starts with a gentle sting when Durrance spots something in the desert and climbs a jebel for a better view. The camera initially holds its position and as Durrance moves away from it towards the jebel he is dwarfed by the rocky mountain. The scale of the setting is further amplified in the next shot of his ascent by being filmed from below. At the peak of the jebel, shot from a low angle, Durrance drops his handkerchief, and as he bends over to pick it up the hat falls from his head. The camera follows the descent of the hat, marking its narrative importance as an item that might have offered protection from the sun, and the Eastern inflection in Rózsa's score becomes prominent as it matches the action. The image of the scorching sun is repeatedly cut into the sequence. The Eastern shading in the music returns for a point-of-view shot that demonstrates Durrance's blurred view of the ground below, and is again to the fore as he stumbles when he tries to retrieve his hat and loses consciousness. Durrance's subsequent blindness and collapse are associated musically with the dangers posed by the exotic location, dangers that primarily imperil his physical well-being. Here the Western orchestral sound succumbs to the Eastern inflection, as Rózsa mirrors musically the onscreen situation of the Westerner overwhelmed by the extreme climate of the foreign land. The music draws attention to the outsider status of the British troops and their vulnerability in an unfamiliar and unforgiving natural environment.

The films considered in this chapter variously present the landscape in one of three ways: as an idealised environment accompanied by music in a pastoral idiom; as a bleak location that subverts these ideas; or as an overwhelming experience of the Sublime. All of the films adopt audiovisual strategies that emphasise the presence of landscape and highlight its effects on their characters, whether they embrace or resist the rural myth of the countryside. The British countryside occupies a deeply held symbolic importance in the nation's cultural psyche as an enduring locus of tradition, tranquillity, and community values. In times of conflict, its further associations with resilience imbue the iconic landscape with the heightened emotional resonance of a shared national symbol of resistance (Richards 1997, 145). This attachment was mobilised and reaffirmed by British films during the Second World War in order to draw the country together and to promote a sense of shared purpose and nationhood in support of the war effort. It is appropriate that the deeper connotations of landscape imagery should be expressed in music of a pastoral character, music that evokes, romanticises and celebrates these qualities. Pastoral modes of expression formed one of the stylistic cornerstones in the revival of a recognisably national music, and it is therefore fitting that Ralph

Vaughan Williams, a key figure in that movement, should act as such a clear link between it and the landscape representations in 1940s British cinema. When joined on screen by scenes of the idyllic and iconic landscape, music that evokes the feelings associated with the pastoral vision makes it possible for these films to amplify the spectacle of landscape, to represent the subjectivity of their characters and to make clear the symbolic aspects that are called into play. Moreover, the clear invitation to engage with the characters' subjective experience, and to identify with it, allows these films to promote and reinforce a cultural sense of a shared national identity with a hitherto untapped power.

In the next chapter, I focus my exploration of pastoral music on one particular aspect of it as I look more closely at British film scores that engage with folk song traditions. As we shall see, folk song brings into play some of the associations of music in a pastoral idiom and adds its own refinement of their meanings. Rather than a step away from the pastoral idiom, then, scores that incorporate folk song demonstrate how broader pastoral effects may gain cumulative power when they are combined with the specific connotations of folk song traditions. In addition, they illustrate the fluid nature of the boundaries between my categorisations and the nimble ability of film music to dance effortlessly across them and to accumulate a greater representational power in the process.

Notes

1. William Vaughan reports that in the late eighteenth and early nineteenth century more than a third of works exhibited at the Royal Academy were landscape scenes, a vogue supported by numerous prints and publications (1999, 183).
2. The feminist cultural geographer Gillian Rose also explores these associations in her critique of the 'phallocentrism of the geographic gaze', and engages with Mulvey's arguments in *Feminism and Geography*, Cambridge: Polity Press (1993), pp. 87–104.
3. The imagery of Frank Newbould's 1942 recruitment poster of the South Downs is echoed in the poster for *Went the Day Well?*, both in its distant view of the village nestled among trees in the valley, and in its warmly idealised palette of muted natural ochres. The film poster strikes a strong contrast between the monochrome depictions of the villagers wielding arms on the left of the image and the warm pastel earth tones of the village seen from afar, and therefore sets up visually the opposition at the heart of the film. The cover of the most recent Blu-ray disc release of the film (Studio Canal's

OPTBD2066 in 2011) takes as its main image the village scene from the original poster. Newbould's poster is available to view online in the collections of the Imperial War Museum: https://www.iwm.org.uk/collections/item/object/20289.

4. In this respect landscape imagery, in its evocation of a stable and unchanging way of life, also promulgates a deeply conservative ideology in which the inequalities handed down from feudalism are presented as a natural state of affairs and the hierarchical social order is maintained. Gifford describes this as the 'double edge of the critique against avarice'—a discourse (such as *A Canterbury Tale*) that criticises wealth and material values also works to maintain the status quo by implying that others 'should not aspire to them' (1999, 52).
5. Composer Brian Easdale recalls this differently, stating 'it was all done to the film and I had to synchronise the music … all done after the film', Easdale, Brian (1984) Interview with R.S. (unidentified), Emeric Pressburger papers, BFI Special Collections, EPR/16/4.

References

Aldred, Nanette. 1987. *A Canterbury Tale*: Powell and Pressburger's Film Fantasies of Britain. In *The Neo-Romantic Imagination in Britain, 1935–55*, ed. David Mellor, 118–122. London: Lund Humphries in association with the Barbican Art Gallery.

Andrews, Malcolm. 1999. *Landscape and Western Art*. Oxford: Oxford University Press.

Burke, Edmund. 2015. In *A Philosophical Enquiry into the Sublime and Beautiful*, ed. Paul Guyer. Oxford: Oxford University Press.

Chew, Geoffrey. 2001. Pastoral. In *The New Grove Dictionary of Music and Musicians*, ed. Stanley Sadie, vol. 19, 217–224. London: Macmillan.

Chion, Michel. 1994. *Audio-Vision: Sound on Screen*. Trans. Claudia Gorbman. New York: Columbia University Press.

———. 2009. *Film, A Sound Art*. Trans. Claudia Gorbman. New York: Columbia University Press.

Cook, Pam. 2002. *I Know Where I'm Going*. London: British Film Institute.

Cosgrove, Denis. 1998. *Social Formation and Symbolic Landscape*. Madison: University of Wisconsin Press.

Dyja, Eddie, ed. 1999. *BFI Film and Television Handbook*. London: British Film Institute.

Eisler, Hanns, and Theodor Adorno. 1994. *Composing for the Films*. London: Athlone Press.

Fowler, Catherine, and Gillian Helfield, eds. 2006. *Representing the Rural: Space, Place and Identity in Films About the Land*. Detroit: Wayne State University Press.

Geraghty, Christine. 2000. *British Cinema in the Fifties: Gender, Genre and the 'New Look'*. London: Routledge.

Gifford, Terry. 1999. *Pastoral: The New Critical Idiom*. London: Routledge.

Gorbman, Claudia. 1987. *Unheard Melodies: Narrative Film Music*. London: British Film Institute.

Harper, Sue. 2010. The Ownership of Woods and Water: Landscapes in British Cinema, 1930–1960. In *Cinema and Landscape*, ed. Graeme Harper and Jonathan Rayner, 149–159. Bristol/Chicago: Intellect.

Harper, Graeme, and Jonathan Rayner, eds. 2010. *Cinema and Landscape*. Bristol/Chicago: Intellect.

Heffer, Simon. 2010. *The Essay – British Cinema of the 1940s, Episode 1: Went the Day Well?* BBC Radio 3, originally broadcast: 13 September.

Higson, Andrew. 1995. *Waving the Flag: Constructing a National Cinema in Britain*. Oxford: Clarendon Press.

———. 2006. A Green and Pleasant Land: Rural Spaces and British Cinema. In *Representing the Rural: Space, Place and Identity in Films About the Land*, ed. Catherine Fowler and Gillian Helfield, 240–255. Detroit: Wayne State University Press.

Hoskins, W.G. 1985. *The Making of the English Landscape*. London: Penguin.

Houston, Penelope. 2012. *Went the Day Well?* London: British Film Institute/ Palgrave Macmillan.

Howes, Frank. 1966. *The English Musical Renaissance*. London: Secker & Warburg.

Hughes, Meirion, and Robert Stradling. 2001. *The English Musical Renaissance, 1840–1940: Constructing a National Music*. Manchester/New York: Manchester University Press.

Huntley, John. 1948. British Film Music. *The Penguin Film Review* 6: 91–96.

Johnson, Ian. 2005. *William Alwyn, The Art of Film Music*. Woodbridge: The Boydell Press.

Kalinak, Kathryn. 1992. *Settling the Score: Music and the Classical Hollywood Film*. Madison: University of Wisconsin Press.

Kennedy, Michael. 2004. Booklet Notes to 'The Film Music of Ralph Vaughan Williams, Volume 2', Chandos CD CHAN 10529(3).

Kohl, Stephan. 2006. Rural England: An Invention of the Motor Industries? In *Landscape and Englishness*, ed. Robert Burden and Stephan Kohl, 185–202. Amsterdam/New York: Editions Rodopi.

Lazar, David, ed. 2003. *Michael Powell Interviews*. Jackson: University Press of Mississippi.

Lefebvre, Martin. 2006. Between Setting and Landscape in the Cinema. In *Landscape and Film*, ed. Martin Lefebvre, 19–60. New York/Abingdon: Routledge.

Mellers, Wilfrid. 1989. *Vaughan Williams and the Vision of Albion*. London: Barrie & Jenkins.

Mulvey, Laura. 1975. Visual Pleasure and Narrative Cinema. *Screen* 16 (3): 6–18.

Petrie, Duncan. 1996. *The British Cinematographer*. London: British Film Institute.

Powell, Michael. 1986. *A Life in Movies*. London: Heinemann. Reprinted 2000: Faber & Faber.

———. 1991. *Black Narcissus* Commentary Track on Network Blu-ray 7957001.

Pugh, Simon, ed. 1990. *Reading Landscape: Country-City-Capital*. Manchester: Manchester University Press.

Rawsthorne, Alan. 1975. The Celluloid Plays a Tune. In *Twenty British Composers*, ed. Peter Dickinson, 30–36. London: J & W Chester.

Richards, Jeffrey. 1997. *Films and British National Identity: From Dickens to Dad's Army*. Manchester: Manchester University Press.

Saylor, Eric. 2008. 'It's Not Lambkins Frisking At All': English Pastoral Music and the Great War. *The Musical Quarterly* 91 (1–2): 39–59.

———. 2017. *English Pastoral Music: From Arcadia to Utopia, 1900–1955*. Urbana: University of Illinois Press.

Sitney, P. Adams. 1993. Landscape in the Cinema: The Rhythms of the World and the Camera. In *Landscape, Natural Beauty and the Arts*, ed. Salim Kemal and Ivan Gaskell, 103–126. Cambridge: Cambridge University Press.

Stradling, Robert. 1998. England's Glory: Sensibilities of Place in English Music, 1900–1950. In *The Place of Music*, ed. Andrew Leyshon, David Matless, and George Revill, 176–196. New York: Guilford Press.

Swynnoe, Jan G. 2002. *The Best Years of British Film Music, 1936–1958*. Woodbridge: Boydell Press.

Thumim, Janet. 1991. The "Popular", Cash and Culture in the Postwar British Cinema Industry. *Screen* 32 (3): 245–271.

Trend, Michael. 1985. *The Music Makers: Heirs and Rebels of the English Musical Renaissance, Edward Elgar to Benjamin Britten*. London: Weidenfeld & Nicolson.

Vaughan, William. 1999. *British Painting: The Golden Age from Hogarth to Turner*. London: Thames & Hudson.

Vaughan Williams, Ralph. 1963. *National Music and Other Essays*. London: Oxford University Press.

CHAPTER 4

Folk Song: National and Regional Music

The rediscovery of folk song traditions was of central importance for the composers associated with the English Musical Renaissance in their quest to construct a national style of musical composition. They were influenced by British music of earlier periods, and indigenous folk songs supplied a rich seam of inspiration and prompted a renewed interest in the form. For Charles Villiers Stanford, who with Hubert Parry led the teaching of composition at the Royal College of Music, folk song held 'a special importance in any national scene', and his commitment was shared by Alexander Mackenzie at the Royal Academy of Music (Hughes and Stradling 2001, 32, 39). These founders of the Renaissance held a broader view of folk song than that later prescribed by a key figure in the revival movement, the folk song collector and enthusiast Cecil Sharp. For them it encompassed national songs, whereas Sharp took a more restrictive and ideological approach and limited his scope to those created 'by the common people, in contradistinction to the song ... which has been composed by the educated' (1907, 3). The traditional folk song met the desire for an accessible style of music, and as with other music in a pastoral idiom, folk song is frequently combined with landscape imagery in British film culture. In certain respects, folk song invokes similar associations to those aroused by other pastoral music, although with a different emphasis. Whereas pastoral music holds among its associations an inclusive ideal of a shared national identity, folk song promotes a greater sense of regional specificity and brings a closer focus on the communities living in the locations depicted

P. Mazey, *British Film Music*, Palgrave Studies in Audio-Visual Culture, https://doi.org/10.1007/978-3-030-33550-2_4

and their traditional ways. In this chapter I will consider the connotations of folk song in the scores of British films. I will explore in particular the correlation between folk song in documentary films and in feature films, and show how this is emblematic of a documentary impulse in films of this era.

Folk Song, Landscape, and Documentary

The melodic and accessible quality of folk song makes it ideal for inclusion in a film score, where by its nature it brings into play three significant connotations—it is communal, it is national or regional, and it is a traditional historic practice. First, it is created by the community rather than the individual. Folk song is transmitted orally through generation upon generation of singers, and the character it derives from being passed on in this way is of primary connotative importance in film, for, by this oral process, it sheds individual attachment. For Cecil Sharp, oral transmission ensures that folk song is communal in two respects: it is 'communal in authorship, and communal in that it reflects the mind of the community' (1907, 15). Folk song represents the community, and this invests it with its second major connotation, a close connection to the nation or region of its origin. The third major connotation of folk song stems from its roots as an ancient practice, a historic remnant of traditional ways.

These three connotative aspects combine to generate further associations, the most evident being the connection between folk song and the natural environment, and the use of folk song therefore brings into play the cultural associations discussed in the previous chapter in relation to pastoral music. Folk song connotes traditional closely knit communities and thus tends to produce an impression of archaic, pre-modern rural life. The link between folk song and rural life connects it to a further element that characterises the English Musical Renaissance, the desire for a musical idiom that expresses a feeling for landscape. As with other pastoral music, folk song is frequently combined with landscape imagery on screen in a way that reinforces and naturalises the correlation between the two. This bolsters its ability to conjure the notion of a largely rural community, and of traditional lives lived in a close relationship with the land. In British cinema scores, folk song operates as a bonding element between communities and their natural environments. The association of a community with a tradition of folk song emphasises both its tightly knit nature and its closeness to the land, and this holds true for both documentary and feature films of this period.

However, a clear divergence occurs between the use of English folk song and Celtic folk song. Whereas both evoke ideas of national or regional identity and a sense of community cohesion, Celtic folk song tends to promote a sense of difference to the cinema-going audience. This perception is perhaps most pronounced in films that use folk song to accompany depictions of more isolated Celtic communities and thereby imply an archaic practice not shared by the urban audience, whose cinema-going itself suggests a level of modernity not enjoyed by those depicted on screen. Irrespective of whether the audience may be familiar with the folk tunes used, their national or regional qualities have the effect of portraying the represented communities as 'other' to the intended audience of the film. What is important here is not that the folk song itself should be identifiable, but that it should be identifiable *as* folk song. In documentary films, as in feature films, the use of English folk song brings a different emphasis that enlists the song as a guarantor of tradition and history without compromising the modernity of the community by suggesting that folk song is an ongoing practice.

The short documentary *The Dim Little Island* (Humphrey Jennings, 1948) illustrates this point. Designed as a morale booster in the days of postwar austerity, the film is built upon the commentaries of four eminent men who provide positive messages about the state of the arts, nature and industry. Vaughan Williams's music, from his 'Five Variants of Dives and Lazarus', begins softly with landscape images and commentary by the naturalist James Fisher, who outlines the interest, beauty and pleasure to be found in the wild environment. A vocal rendition of 'Dives and Lazarus' introduces Vaughan Williams's own commentary, joined on screen by a series of slow pans where each image dissolves into the next—a rocky escarpment, a summer cloudscape, a reed bed. The singer gives way to Vaughan Williams's arrangement for strings and harp as the composer begins his instructive commentary:

> Listen to that tune – it is one of our English folk tunes. I knew it first when I was quite a small boy, but I realised even then that here was something not only very beautiful, but which had a special appeal to me as an Englishman. It dates from a time when people of necessity made their own music.

The historical reference is joined on screen by an engraving of an Elizabethan scene in which a woman plays a duet on the harpsichord with a lutenist, followed by an artfully arranged shot of a lute beside a leaded light window. The composer goes on to relate and celebrate the levels of contemporary musical activity in the country. In three sentences, Vaughan Williams encapsulates the connotations of folk music: the 'special appeal' of its national flavour; the communal aspect of its production; and its historic tradition that offers a sense of continuity with the past. The commentary's direct appeal reminds us that folk song is part of our heritage, and its place on the soundtrack to accompany scenes of the landscape binds the natural environment into this equation and merges it with ideas of history, music, and national identity.

English folk song, highlighted as historic, is presented as part of a tradition that can revitalise and inspire contemporary musical culture, rather than as an enduring practice within our communities. As such, it is infused with a strain of nostalgia, an echo of an earlier and simpler time. The infrequent and isolated uses of English folk songs in films during this era reflect these connotations, and attach them to individuals rather than to a wider community. The character of the mudlark Jackson (Michael Martin Harvey) in *The Long Memory*, for instance, sings to himself the English folk song 'Searching for Lambs' ('As I went out one May morning' – a song collected by Cecil Sharp and included in his 1916 volume *One Hundred English Folk Songs*). The song's pastoral evocation strikes a sharp contrast with the bleakness of the surroundings and marks Jackson as a harmlessly eccentric outsider. English folk song is used not to mark a closely knit community but a single character living an isolated existence apart from the wider society, while its archaic connection suggests that Jackson is out of time and something of a misfit. Other uses of English folk song are similarly fleeting instances, and none imply a continuing tradition.[1] English folk song is not employed as a significant structural element of the score in the way that Celtic folk song is used in films that represent communities outside of England.

In contrast to the occasional use of English folk tunes, films set in parts of the British Isles outside of England tend to employ folk song in a more sustained manner and to forge a more integrated relationship between the music, the communities, and their environment. Documentary films frequently build their scores entirely on folk song, with the effect that folk song becomes a means of expressing regional difference and distinction from the intended audience. Richard Addinsell's score for the documentary short *Ulster* (Ralph Keene, 1941) operates in this way. The music incorporates both the Londonderry Air and the Irish or Scottish folk song 'I Know Where I'm Going'. The Londonderry Air (the tune set as 'Danny Boy') connects the score specifically with Northern Ireland, and in this film it is used in a quasi-diegetic way, post-synchronised onto shots of a violinist in a market town. When the image cuts from the bustling town to a pan across the natural landscape, the soundtrack changes to a woman singing 'I Know Where I'm Going', and the tune continues in the underscore as the narrator resumes his commentary to accompany images of farmworkers tending their fields. It is notable that the woman's song begins at the point when the scene alters to show the rural landscape. This audiovisual match creates the impression that the voice and the song somehow emanate from the natural environment, that the natural environment gives rise to them. The folk song is emphatically associated with the landscape scene as though embedded within it. In *Ulster*, the vocal rendition of 'I Know Where I'm Going' returns to accompany shots of a young girl leading a single goat towards the farm buildings. This scene bears a remarkable likeness in tone and effect to the shots of the young woman leading Highland cattle in Powell and Pressburger's *I Know Where I'm Going!* (1945). The latter scenes are accompanied by wordless female voices intoning a theme 'derived from the music for the Curse of Moy Castle' (Donnelly 2008, 226). In both sequences, the young girl is entirely at ease in her work and environment, and the distance between her experience and that of the cinema audience (and their onscreen proxy, Joan (Wendy Hiller), in *I Know Where I'm Going!*) is accentuated.[2]

Folk song is used again to link the community with the natural environment in *The Silent Village*, Humphrey Jennings's 1943 documentary filmed in the Welsh mining village of Cwmgiedd. A landscape view fills the frame as on the soundtrack an unaccompanied male voice choir sings 'Men of Harlech'.[3] As in *The Dim Little Island* and *Ulster*, the folk tune begins with the establishing shot of the landscape as though to imply that the music inheres in the natural environment and emanates from it. The folk song continues through scenes of the miners returning to their homes, to find tables laid for tea and wives and children waiting. The sequence and the song end with a distant shot of the village within the landscape. The scenes are bookended between views of the wider landscape setting, and in this way the community is visually and aurally enfolded into the landscape.

The folk songs heard in *The Silent Village* represent the community, although there is no suggestion that they are sung by the men we see on screen. This technique of not synchronising the music directly has the effect of associating it with the entire community, regardless of its diegetic origin. Richard Dyer notes that uncertainty about whether music is entirely diegetic or nondiegetic may result when an environment is presented as 'utterly pervaded by music'. Dyer finds that music which bears this indeterminate nature expresses 'a kind of fantasy of collectivity through music that transcends the individuals producing the sound' (2010, 96). This liberal approach to synchronisation and its resulting diegetic instability is a recurring feature in folk song scores in both documentary subjects and narrative feature films. The resistance to associating the music directly with the characters we see, and thereby disassociating it from the wider unseen community, foregrounds the communal character of the folk song and exploits its ability to hold the entire community in its representational embrace. In both documentary subjects and narrative feature films, this less rigid synchronisation between music and image operates as a means to express community cohesion, and it is an area of clear structural commonality between the two filmmaking disciplines.

The British documentary movement had a profound impact upon British cinema during the 1940s, and met a desire both in critical discourse and among audiences for films that aspired to a more recognisable representation of reality. Writing in 1947, John Huntley notes that the British documentary movement had only exerted a 'very mild and occasional' influence on feature film production during the 1930s. With the onset of the Second World War, however, the 'desire for realism and fact' became a major influence in British cinema (1947, 106). The Ministry of Information's growing awareness of the propaganda potential of cinema in support of the war effort dovetailed with audience tastes which, in increasingly uncertain times, were moving to favour films that reflected their own lives and experiences. This blending of 'documentary integrity and … fictional warmth' (Durgnat 2011, 150) yields a category of cinema that is variously referred to as 'semi-documentary', 'fictional documentary', or 'story documentary'.

The documentary leanings of British cinema in the 1940s were welcomed not only by the popular audience but also by contemporary journalistic critics. The critics saw in the documentary tendency a means to encourage an indigenous cinema of quality that was both serious and socially aware, and clearly positioned in opposition to what was regarded as the frivolous escapism of Hollywood. John Ellis has analysed the critical discourse of the 1940s and identified the recurring elements in films praised by the critics for their 'quality'. These include both the 'surface' realism of settings and backgrounds, and the 'narrative' realism of plausible stories. In addition, authenticity is required in the portrayal of working class lives and female desire, with a stress on humanist values and the use of a 'convincing emotional register similar to that of real life' (1978, 32). Although these documentary elements were lauded in the 1940s, Michael Powell's first personal film, *The Edge of the World* (1937) is exemplary in anticipating many of the features that would later be highly valued. Significantly, for his first real 'auteur' project, Powell adds a further marker of authenticity by using folk song as the basis of its musical score. Taking *The Edge of the World* as a key example, I would like to compare the way it uses folk song with two other films that share similar settings and narrative concerns: Robert Flaherty's documentary *Man of Aran* (1934) and the fictional feature *The Brothers* (David MacDonald, 1947).

Films that base their scores on folk song tend to have a narrative focus upon isolated communities in the more remote reaches of the British Isles and beyond, frequently island communities that face challenges presented by the natural environment and the elements. The films emphasise the natural environment, and contain location shots of the landscape that act as a documentary element, a guarantor of the veracity of the setting. Sue Harper points out that producers favoured studio production and disliked location shooting as it placed filmmakers 'beyond the control of their paymasters' (2010, 150). With conditions less easily controlled than in the studio, location shooting is more complicated, more time-consuming, and more costly than studio work. The additional inconvenience presented by location shooting is, for the filmmakers who use it extensively, a measure of the significance they accord to landscape and to achieving an authentic sense of place. *The Edge of the World* is a prime example. The film was shot almost wholly on location on the Scottish island of Foula, in difficult circumstances which Powell has related both in the first volume of his autobiography (1986) and in a book of some length first published in 1938 entirely dedicated to the enterprise.[4]

The director is clear about his intentions, stating that after 'editors, cutters, producers, sound-recorders, composers, and critics had done their worst and their best, the grim outline of the island still dominated the picture. That is how I wanted it' (1990, 161). Powell took pride in the fact that, with the exception of some pick-up shots and close-ups filmed in the studio, 'by and large', the film had been completed on the island. 'I had a dream', he writes grandly, 'and the dream was of the Hebrides' (1986, 257, 225). Foula, in the Shetlands, eventually stood in for the Hebridean St Kilda, and Powell writes of the island as a protagonist in the adventure of the film's making just as it acts as a protagonist in the drama of the film's narrative: the island presented 'such an unwelcoming face to the intruder ... she wanted to be loved, but wouldn't make the first move. And goodness me, how difficult she made it for us' (1986, 254).

Powell embraced location shooting as a realist element, although he was less enamoured of the work of the documentary movement. He was repeatedly unequivocal in declaring his dislike of documentary (in Lazar 2003, 46, 78), of not getting on with the documentary movement, of documentaries being for 'disappointed feature film-makers or out-of-work poets' (1986, 532, 241). In spite of this, when Powell explained his ideas for *The Edge of the World* in the early stages of its conception, it drew comparisons with *Man of Aran* (1934), Robert Flaherty's depiction of the remote Aran islanders' struggle for survival against the elements (Fig. 4.1). Powell found Flaherty 'a lovely man', and the two discussed and disagreed

Fig. 4.1 'Waves and seaweed and pretty pictures' in *Man of Aran*

on the approach to Powell's film. The documentary-maker regretted that Powell had not filmed the actual evacuation of St Kilda, the event which inspired the film. Flaherty's stance appears in retrospect somewhat ironic, given his own penchant for recreation, not to say falsification, in his documentary films. Powell envisioned his film as a drama about people, and dismissed *Man of Aran* for its lack of a story—it was just 'a lot of waves and seaweed and pretty pictures' which had taken Flaherty six months to edit and still 'wasn't any good' (1986, 237, 241; Christie 1978, 23). For Powell, location shooting offers visual grandeur and spectacle, but in common with the film's other documentary elements—including its folk song score—its purpose is to serve and give force to the drama of the narrative.

The combination of location filming and the factual basis of the story clearly positioned *The Edge of the World* in the realm of documentary for many commentators, in spite of its melodramatic elements. This may be read either as an endorsement of the film's emotional authenticity, or an acceptance of the leeway granted to the makers of documentaries in respect of the presentation of 'actuality'. In many respects, the film anticipates the semi-documentary form favoured in the 'quality' 1940s film, and confirms Ellis's conclusion that the documentary may only attain the 'spirit of the real' if it stresses human values and adopts 'the procedures of the fictional narrative' (1978, 33–34). The film's strong aura of authenticity is fortified not only by exterior location filming, but also through its use of genuine interiors, such as those of the croft and the church, which, much to Powell's satisfaction, were 'so obviously the real thing' (1990, 272). This might explain the readiness of the documentary makers to overlook the film's rich melodrama in order to claim it for their school. Durgnat, for example, includes *The Edge of the World* in a list of contemporary documentaries, and discusses it in this context without identifying its odd-man-out status (2011, 145). The documentary makers wielded considerable critical influence at the time, although Powell 'resented and disputed' the 'annexation' of his film in this way (Barr 2005, 8–9).

It is perhaps unsurprising that comparisons should be drawn between *Man of Aran* and *The Edge of the World* given their common theme of remote island communities struggling for survival in inhospitable and unforgiving environments. Both films foreground the sublime elements of the landscape—the overwhelming power of raging storms and the threat to the protagonists' survival. Both films frame their characters within the landscape so as to accentuate their vulnerability and their nobility, and both exploit the visual possibilities afforded by their locations. Additionally, the films share an ethnographic quality of presenting the lives and cultures of communities outside the experience of, and in many ways alien to, those of the cinema-going audience. This is part of their appeal, and both films employ folk song in their musical scores in a way that accentuates the 'otherness' of the communities depicted, and that vouches for the authenticity of these depictions. Folk song is genuine—it exists as a musical form in the real world. In contrast to original music composed for a film score, indigenous folk song brings a potent charge of authenticity, an assurance of documentary realism, to the films that employ it. The incorporation of folk song into a film soundtrack operates as an indicator of veracity for the film, but more importantly it provides deeper levels of meaning. Eisler and Adorno regard folk song ineffective as a means to evoke a sense of place, as it is all 'grounded on a limited number of elementary rhythmic formulas', or, put simply, it all sounds the same (1994, 14). Their error lies in the assumption that the usefulness of folk song is determined by its ability to arouse in the audience a recollection of an existing association between it and a specific location. They overlook the fact that folk song has the effect of authenticating the location it depicts regardless of whether it is actually authentic.

The score for *Man of Aran* was provided by John Greenwood, who had studied composition with Charles Villiers Stanford at the Royal College of Music. It is credited in the film's titles as being 'based on the original Irish folk songs of the Aran Islands'. This signals that the documentary aspirations of the film are to be reflected in its musical score, although no actual singing is shown in the film, or heard on its soundtrack. The film's musical director, Louis Levy, notes that the singing voices of the Aran women have 'the same inflections and curious quarter-tones as those of the Chinese' (1948, 124). The connotative value of folk song here is not in its evocation of the Aran Islands, for the connection between music and location would not necessarily be an automatic response in the wider audience, although we would have no reason to question its validity. More to the point is that the Aran islanders' songs, which Levy writes can go on for half an hour, are really 'age-old stories' (1948, 124). In tracing the origins of folk song, Cecil Sharp identifies the use of rhyme, rhythm and metre as 'aids to memory' by story-telling natives in different parts of the world and concludes that folk song 'either preceded the folk-tale, or was coincident with it' (1907, 5). The folk song tradition of the islanders therefore speaks for the timeless and unchanging history of these communities. The tradition, it is suggested, of songs and music handed down from generation to generation, continues unaltered in these island communities. Folk song connotes both the sense of an ongoing shared historical tradition and of the social cohesion of a closely knit community.

The implication of a continuing folk song tradition places the community depicted firmly in a bygone era for the cinema audience. Sharp's mission to popularise English folk song rests upon his claim that it is an evolving form that has developed through, and therefore expresses, feelings and tastes that are communal rather than individual. While he chides those who would see the practice of collecting folk song as mere archaism, Sharp confirms that the tradition of folk-singing, as he understands it, ended with the generation born prior to 1840 (1907, 119). Folk song therefore speaks of a tradition that has died out, and of a time earlier than our own. For *Man of Aran*, it is the notion of a community of such remoteness that it is caught in an earlier time that is conveyed by weaving these tunes into the film's score and by announcing the fact in the opening credits.

The strategies adopted by Flaherty project an inaccurate version of life on the Aran Islands—one that is more primitive, untouched by any hint of progress or modernity. The film's inter-titles proclaim the unchanging continuity of life—'For a thousand years Man of Aran has searched such crevices for soil'—while Flaherty averts his camera's gaze from the existing farms in favour of staging the hunt of a basking shark. Levy reveals that these old methods had long since died out, and the filming made use of 'old, rusted harpoons, dormant on shelves in the huts for many years' (1948, 124). An inter-title describes the gentle sharks as 'monsters' and the soundtrack (the music ends abruptly in a reverse sting when the shark is first sighted) and editing conspire to create a false sense of drama and danger. Flaherty was later criticised when the extent of the film's construction, misrepresentation, and recreation of archaic practices became clear (McLoone 2005, 46–7).

The soundtrack of *Man of Aran* contributes to the misleading implication that the archaic methods it depicts are ongoing. Levy reports that after the filming, the islanders were brought to the Gainsborough studios in Islington 'to post-synchronize dialogue, sound-effects and music' (1948, 123). The result is a very loosely-synchronised sound montage. The images register as silent footage, an impression accentuated by the use of inter-titles, while the added soundtrack of music and sound effects is inconsistently applied. There is no synchronised dialogue, instead a track of recorded speech accompanies some sequences, although it is used 'wild' and never matches up directly with what is on screen. This highlights the artifice of the process, and the overt lack of technical sophistication in the sound montage may have been seen as an appropriate reflection of the primitive way of life depicted. The closest synchronisation comes with the scene of the man breaking rocks, as the shots of his hammer blows are cut to match the heavy beats of the music in a manner reminiscent of the eponymous hero's forging song in Wagner's *Siegfried.* McLoone notes that the low-angle framing and fast montage-style editing accentuates his 'physical strength and determination' and 'works to heroicise the Man and to give an epic dimension to his rather mundane tasks' (2005, 47). This impression of a magnified and noble stature is supported by the musical allusion to Wagner's heroic simpleton. Other sequences in the film unfold without musical accompaniment. Music drops out of the sequence that depicts the hunt of the basking shark and is replaced by post-dubbed sound effects, while long passages of the film remain unscored.

The Edge of the World, on the other hand, contains a lot of music for a film of its period. Relatively few sequences forego underscoring, and even dialogue scenes are accompanied by soft and atmospheric background music. Only occasionally does the music come into close synchronisation with the images, at such key dramatic moments as the cliff race. In stating that 'images are everything' in his films, with words and music used to 'distil emotion', Powell describes *The Edge of the World* as 'essentially' a silent film (1986, 168). Flaherty seeks truth by harking back to the Soviet filmmakers, whose fast-cutting montage editing he apes in a bid to inject drama where none exists. By contrast, Powell's ambitious vision aligns him most closely with F. W. Murnau, in that both directors employ elaborate technical effects to create a sophisticated visual poetry in which artistry always remains subordinate to feeling. At the time, C. A. Lejeune commended Powell for his use of the 'tricks of the trade – double exposures, ghost figures, narrative fade-outs, super-impositions of sound', always in the service of the narrative (1937, 10).

As if reaching back to the days of the silent film, Powell took to the island a portable wind-up gramophone and played records during the filming. He mentions taking recordings of both Smetana's *Moldau* and Bax's *Tintagel*, and describes the latter as 'eerie, mystic music that seems to me the very essence of islands and the sea' (quoted in Lazar 2003, 4). Powell kept this fact from the composer W. L. (Bill) Williamson, who was to orchestrate the songs recorded by the women of the Glasgow Orpheus Choir under the direction of Hugh Roberton, and to write additional music for the film (1986, 258). Powell's understanding of the importance of music is evident in his pre-recording of songs that could then be integrated into the fabric of the film rather than merely applied later, 'like the rich glazing on a ham' (1986, 582). An example of this integration occurs in the montage sequence that celebrates the birth of Ruth's (Belle Chrystall) baby and welcomes the newborn into the community. The music and singing heard in this segment is associated with the diegetic by the image of John (Grant Sutherland) playing the lullaby on his violin (although the women whose voices we hear are not shown), before an optical effect through which it segues into the faster music for the evening's dancing and celebration. The lullaby's initial similarity to the film's background music raises the question of whether it is occurring on the soundtrack only or in the world of the film. The resolution through the image of John fiddling connects the music that accompanies the film nondiegetically to the music heard diegetically within it. This casts an air of authenticity over all of the film's nondiegetic music. It proffers a guarantee that this music belongs to the world of the film and thereby masks the reality of the addition of much of it at a later stage in the filmmaking process.

The effectiveness of the folk songs sung by the women's chorus in *The Edge of the World* may be measured against similar music in a film that shares many of its elements, David MacDonald's *The Brothers* (1947), based on the 1932 novel by L. A. G. Strong. The decade that separates the release of *The Brothers* from that of *The Edge of the World* is a significant one for British film culture. The later film stands at a further remove both from the influence of the audiovisual experimentation that characterised the British documentary movement in the 1930s and from the silent cinema aesthetic embraced by Powell. Both films are set on remote Scottish islands and depict communities with their own traditions and ways of life. Both begin with shots of the landscape filmed from the sea, and the island settings are emphasised by this opening journey, as the spectator is transported to the location. Both also introduce a chorus of women's voices to accompany these opening journey scenes, and this connects the voices with the islands and imbues the environment with a sense of mysticism and exoticism.

However, whereas for Powell this establishes a link that will be built upon coherently as the film progresses, MacDonald only returns to it for one further scene, and as this parallels an equivalent scene in the earlier film, it is possible to compare the two. The films both include contests, challenges of male strength and athletic ability, presented as traditions whereby disputes between opposing views may be resolved, and in both cases these occur between the families of the main protagonists. The cliff race in *The Edge of the World* and the boat race in *The Brothers* both end in the death of one of the participants, and lead directly to sequences that depict their funerals. Both include similar scenes of the body being carried on oars to the burial site by the men of the community while the women remain at home. Both sequences are scored with unaccompanied women's voices, and yet they create quite different effects owing to the way the music is combined with the images.

The sequence in the earlier film opens with a single female voice and a shot of shafts of sunlight on the sea filmed from the island. The solo voice is joined by a chorus of women's voices as views of the landscape are intercut with closer shots of raindrops falling on water and grasses blowing in the wind before the funeral procession begins. The shots of the procession are composed with a visual flair: these are filmed first from below, then from the side showing only the legs of the men carrying the body, then from the front as the procession approaches and moves over the camera, then from behind as the men walk away (Fig. 4.2). The images maintain a

Fig. 4.2 The funeral sequence in *The Edge of the World*

division of screen space along the diagonal line from the bottom left hand to the top right hand corner, and on the soundtrack the diegetic trudging of the men's feet joins the women's song. The song ends in the graveyard and after a brief pause the tune resumes in the orchestra to close the scene. Powell credits the 'wonderfully moving' women's voices for endowing the sequence with 'the true note of tragedy' (1986, 258). The cinematography lends the images an ethereal mistiness that captures both the steady rainfall and the sense of numbing grief felt throughout the community.

By contrast, in *The Brothers* the weather is dry and the images are clear. The sequence begins inside the croft as the body is carried down the stairs, scored with the women's voices while the women are seen on screen. As the scene moves outside the voices are replaced on the soundtrack by bagpipes, and on screen two pipers lead the procession as the men are filmed in the middle distance walking away from the camera (Fig. 4.3). The scene returns to the interior and the women, and the chorus resumes. Some of the women in the background are swaying and appear to be singing,

Fig. 4.3 The funeral sequence in *The Brothers*

although the track is not synchronised and the singing is faded out to make way for the bagpipes as the scene dissolves back to the procession arriving at the graveyard. The picture fades to black and then opens on a view of the sea as the orchestra offers a closing flourish of the bagpipe tune. Overall, the impression is one of detached distance when set against the engaging strategy employed by Powell to place the spectator in the heart of the scene, close enough to witness the exchange of looks between the mourners at the graveside, and those between the lovers who will be parted by the bereavement.

The Scottish composer Cedric Thorpe Davie provided the score for *The Brothers*. He had studied at the Royal Scottish Academy of Music (RSAM) in Glasgow, and later at the Royal Academy of Music and the Royal College of Music, where he studied under Vaughan Williams and Gordon Jacob. Thorpe Davie returned to Scotland to teach at the RSAM, and later founded the department of music at St. Andrew's University (Lindsay 2001, 430). Although Thorpe Davie was knowledgeable about Scottish music, no claim to folk song 'authenticity' is made, and no choir identified, in the credits of *The Brothers*. The repeated alternation between the women's chorus and the bagpipes breaks up the flow of the sequence and fragments both pieces of music in contrast to Powell's approach to allow the music its measure and to structure the visual images accordingly. The comparison affords a contrast between a sequence that prioritises the music and uses the images to compound its effect and one in which music is applied afterwards in order to confirm the images it accompanies. When set alongside the characters' tartan shawls and sashes, the music in the later film's funeral sequence struggles to rise above the level of a generalised aural shorthand for 'Scottishness'. It is perhaps ironic that in *The Brothers*, with its Scottish director and composer, the spectator should be more conscious both of occupying the perspective of an outsider looking in, and of the constructed nature of what is presented, than in *The Edge of the World*. Although *The Brothers* includes much footage shot on location, its reliance on back projection and studio mock-ups introduces a sense of artifice not found in the earlier film. The contrasts between location filming and studio work are more noticeable, and therefore more jarring, in *The Brothers* than in *The Edge of the World*. The problem of the artificial note this strikes illustrates the importance of landscape and location to this group of films, whose narratives are built upon the very insularity of their island communities. Powell, who disliked simulated exterior scenes, ensures a greater sense of documentary reality through his extensive location filming (1992, 79).

Although it is not directly analogous, a funeral sequence from a third film deserves to be mentioned alongside those in *The Edge of the World* and *The Brothers.* It occurs in *The Silver Darlings* (Clarence Elder, 1947), a film based on Neil M. Gunn's 1941 novel about Scottish fishing communities in the 1850s. In a short sequence that runs for less than a minute of screen time, the community gathers to mourn the unnamed victim of a cholera epidemic. Led by the priest, and accompanied only by the flat metallic tone of a slowly-rung funeral bell, the people sing a mournful song at the home of the departed (Fig. 4.4). Although the sequence does not begin with an establishing shot accompanied by the voices, the soundtrack of the song bleeds back over the close of the previous scene. Clifton Parker composed the score for the film, although Robert King is credited with supervising the 'Hebridean Songs and Music'. The scene is filmed to suggest that the singing is diegetic although the images are not closely synchronised with the music. The song is allowed to continue

Fig. 4.4 The funeral sequence in *The Silver Darlings*

without fragmentation and it combines with the images in a bond that inscribes the image track with the sense of taking place in real time. One of the mourners sets fire to the croft by lighting its thatched roof, and the voices rise in intensity as the flames fill the screen. The musical conclusion of the song is paralleled in the image, which adjusts to a more distant shot of the burning straw roof in the early evening light, and confirms visually that we are moving away from the scene.

The song of mourning continues without interruption on the soundtrack, so the solemnity of the lament is not compromised. As a consequence, the scene is quietly moving, even though the deceased is an unknown representative of the community rather than a familiar character. In common with that in *The Edge of the World*, the music that accompanies the funeral sequence in *The Silver Darlings* is permitted to unfold to its own musical logic, and it is the more effective for being allowed to retain its simple plangent line.

The Edge of the World offers an additional charge of documentary reality by dramatising the real evacuation of St Kilda, an event that carries a potent symbolism of 'the destruction of community, the violent uprooting of tradition, the victory of modernity' (Richards 1997, 203). Powell exploits the resonance of these themes by framing the drama within an extended flashback, an explicitly nostalgic device. The flashback emphasises the fact that the drama occurs in the past, that we are taking a backward look at a community that is already broken up, a traditional way of island life that is no more. Ian Christie (in Powell 1990, xiv) notes that the dissolution of the island community in *The Edge of the World* anticipates 'the collapse of the Himalayan convent' at Mopu in *Black Narcissus*, and the two films may also be equated in the way they introduce the gentle melancholy of remembrance aurally in their flashback sequences. In the earlier film, Andrew Gray (Niall MacGinnis) explains to the visitors to the now-deserted island what they might have seen and heard ten years before on the Sabbath day. At the words 'the bell would be ringing', the bell enters the soundtrack and its ghostly image is superimposed onto the bell tower over the two pieces of frayed rope that would once have held it in place and are now all that remains. The image dissolves into the past and the transition is complete.

In *Black Narcissus*, Clodagh's (Deborah Kerr) flashbacks to memories of Ireland and her romance are ushered in by soft choral singing, by the barking of a dog, and by the singing of 'Lullay, Mine Liking', which Edith Rickert identifies as an English carol of the fifteenth century (1928, 66).

Powell describes it as 'an Edwardian carol' and notes that Brian Easdale composed new music for its use in *Black Narcissus* (Powell 1991). The flashback segments present a rich, romanticised vision when set against the austerity of the convent, a distinction marked aurally as the excitement of the hunt, the building choral chanting, the steady momentum of the horses' hooves and the baying of the hounds in Ireland evaporate at the close of the flashback to leave the hollow sound of a single dog barking in Mopu. Clodagh's evident pleasure in their remembrance—she finds herself smiling in the chapel as she emerges from her reverie—signals her yearning for a time that has passed. Visually, her image within her memory dissolves into her present-day image as she returns to herself in the same way the image of the bell dissolves to confirm the temporal shift in the earlier film.

Folk Song and Documentary Satire

Films that take on the guise of documentary by employing its methods and approaches not only knowingly send up the conventions of documentary, they also stake a claim to its aura of authenticity. In its introductory scenes, *Black Narcissus* adopts the tone of a travelogue in the anthropological shots that accompany Mr Dean's (David Farrar) voiceover narration of his letter to the Mother Superior in which he describes the people of Mopu.[5] Whereas Andrew Moor acknowledges the 'travelogue feel' of the Canadian location footage in *49th Parallel* (along with an echo of Flaherty's *Nanook of the North* (1922), which had also been filmed in the Hudson Bay area), here he detects in Dean's voiceover a near parody of '1940s Griersonian paternalism' (2005, 49, 191). Location filming evokes an aura of documentary and casts a concomitant aura of authenticity upon these scenes. For all Powell's stated disdain of pure documentary, he sought a grainy, ragged feel in *49th Parallel*, as if aspiring to a documentary realism, and discussed with cameraman Frederick Young how to give the images a rougher texture, as if they had been 'snatched ... out of the war' (quoted in Lazar 2003, 114). The appropriation of further elements associated with documentary, such as voiceover narration, bolsters this impression and it remains undiminished by the suspicion of an element of parody.

Elements that gently satirise the documentary movement are a recurring feature in the films of Powell and Pressburger, and these are evident as much in their use of sound as images. Christie (in Powell 1990, xii) points out Powell's citing of the unlikely survival of Peter (David Niven) after he jumps from the burning bomber without a parachute in *A Matter of Life and Death* (1946) as a 'deliberate snook cocked' at the movement, in addition to the tongue-in-cheek omniscient narration that opens the film ('This is the universe – big, isn't it?'). The target of the parody is more specific in the introductory narration of *A Canterbury Tale*. Esmond Knight's recitation of the rhyming couplets (in the style of Chaucer) is rhythmically freer than the strict metre applied to W. H. Auden's iconic verses for *Night Mail* (Harry Watt, 1936)—'Here is the Night Mail, crossing the border, bringing the cheque and the postal order'. If the reference is not clear when Knight raises his voice to be heard over the sound of the tanks in imitation of the commentator on the earlier film, who has to shout to be heard over the sound of the train, it becomes so when the train enters the landscape at the words 'Gone are the ring of hooves, the creak of wheel, down in the valley runs our road of steel'.

A more explicit parody of *Night Mail*'s combination of sound and image is contained in *I Know Where I'm Going!*, in the montage sequence depicting Joan's dream as she repeats the mail train's overnight journey from England to Scotland. The sequence incorporates the traditional songs 'I Know Where I'm Going' and 'Loch Lomond' ('You'll Take the High Road'), as well as a reprise of the dance music already heard in the restaurant scene, together with voice and sound effects in a rich aural and visual mix. The shots of the model bells used behind the titles of *A Canterbury Tale* appear here as a reversed out background for Joan's dream of her marriage ceremony. *Night Mail* is referenced specifically in shots of the train wheels matched rhythmically by the repeated phrase 'Everything's arranged' on the soundtrack, as well as in shots of the (model) train speeding through hills playfully clad in tartan (Fig. 4.5).

Pam Cook (2002, 33) notes the temptation to read into these scenes a 'deconstruction of stereotypes', a presentation of Scotland 'as a fictional invention that offers an escape route from contemporary urban values' in the manner of Lerner and Loewe's musical *Brigadoon*. However, Joan's reverie of Scotland serves a further purpose in the story world of *I Know Where I'm Going!*. Joan's dreams are presented as the fanciful imaginings of an Englishwoman who has not crossed the northern border before, underlined by the use of 'Loch Lomond', perhaps the most recognisable musical marker for Scotland. By positioning the subsequent narrative in contrast to the montage of Joan's dreams, the filmmakers invite us to accept the greater reality of the delays and hindrances to Joan's progress,

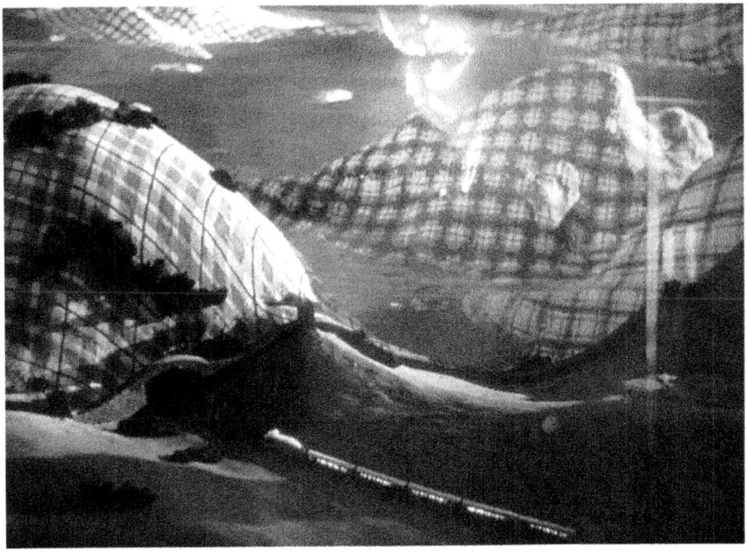

Fig. 4.5 A fantasy of Scotland in *I Know Where I'm Going!*

along with the events accompanying them. In this way the film seeks to authenticate its own fantasy of Scotland by juxtaposing it with a more extreme version of that fantasy.

Powell and Pressburger's representation of Scotland in *I Know Where I'm Going!* exemplifies a construction of the country that Colin McArthur describes as the 'Scottish Discursive Unconscious'. Within this way of thinking, Scotland is seen as broadly 'highland, wild, "feminine", close to nature' and possesses mystical and magical properties that enable it 'to enchant and transform' visiting strangers. Furthermore, so pervasive are these ideas across all the cultural forms that feed into the construction that even Scots themselves 'live within it' (McArthur 2003, 12, 77). In many respects, the Scottish Discursive Unconscious is the Celtic equivalent of the rural myth of the English countryside, expressed in the pastoral forms of music and image explored in the previous chapter. Both concepts align rural landscapes with the values of a stable history, tradition and community that resist the threat of encroaching modernity; both invest the natural landscape with mystical, romantic and restorative powers; and both are hegemonic in their operation. Additionally, in their cinematic guises, both are directed primarily at urban audiences and reflect the movement of retreat and return that is intrinsic to the pastoral form, wherein a journey undertaken by the city-dweller to the countryside provides both an escape from the pressures of, and yields insights into, urban life (Gifford 1999, 81).

Although the rural myth of the English countryside and the Scottish Discursive Unconscious can be equated in many respects, the representation of Scotland in these films foregrounds its difference to other parts of Britain, and particularly to England. Its 'otherness' is highlighted through the encounters of the visitors with the local communities. Richards (1997, 191) finds in *Whisky Galore!* (Alexander Mackendrick, 1949), that it is not specifically the English, but rather 'bureaucrats, officials, Whitehall', embodied by the character of Captain Waggett (Basil Radford), who are the targets of the satire. This is offset by the English Sergeant Odd (Bruce Seton), who is welcomed by the islanders and integrated into the community (in the same way that Joan is integrated into the community in *I Know Where I'm Going!*, while Bellinger and his friends are not).

Whisky Galore! begins with a parody of documentary films in its scene-setting commentary, delivered by an uncredited Finlay Currie. The tongue-in-cheek tone of the narration ('to the west there is nothing, except America') extends to its introduction of the islanders as 'happy people, with few and simple pleasures' as a stream of young children emerge from a cottage. The parody acknowledges the anthropological aspect of the glimpse the film affords into the lives of the remote community, and McArthur points out that the 'stereotypical images' of the fisherman and his wife are accompanied by 'characteristically inane music' (2003, 35). Ernest Irving's score for *Whisky Galore!* is credited as being 'based on old Scottish tunes' and played by the Philharmonia Orchestra. McArthur finds in the use of the classical orchestra a certain alienating effect that results from a lack of fit between the music and its orchestration, and in which he discerns the 'assertion of [an] unconscious middle-class discourse' (2003, 34, 43). Given the ubiquity of the western orchestral sound in cinema scoring of the period, it is unlikely to have struck contemporary spectators as the imposition of a middle-class way of seeing and hearing the world. Perhaps more importantly, the standard orchestral texture of much of the music enables a smoother incorporation of Scottish tunes with music more typical of a comedy film. Kate Daubney (2006, 63) notes the prominence of 'distinctively Scottish melodies' in *Whisky Galore!*'s opening music, and McArthur (2003, 35) notes the use of the 'Scotch Snap' (a musical rhythm in which a short note falls quickly before a longer one) throughout. As the film progresses the energy and

Fig. 4.6 Images illustrate music in the mouth-music sequence in *Whisky Galore!*

jig-like bounce of much of the nondiegetic music maintains the feel of Scottish folk music.

This energy is particularly apparent in scenes that depict the islanders operating together as a group, for example, in the salvage of the cases from the stricken vessel, and in the urgency of the music that accompanies the montage sequences in which news spreads through the community, first of the whisky, and then of the arrival of the Customs and Excise officer. Equally jaunty music accompanies the montage sequence in which the whisky is hidden, with fast percussive effects matching the briskness of the editing and suggesting the clinking sound of the bottles.

The social cohesion of the islanders, and their celebration of renewed supplies of whisky, is also expressed through two sequences that incorporate diegetic music. The first of these, the mouth-music (‘*port a beul*’) sequence, immediately follows Captain Waggett announcing to his wife that he suspects all of the islanders, and in reiteration of their collective action—‘all of them!’. An unaccompanied solo voice begins which is then joined by further voices until a wordless choral effect is achieved, in a representation of the coming together of the whole (male) community. The images correspond to the voices, showing first one, then two, and then increasing numbers of islanders singing and swaying while enjoying the whisky (Fig. 4.6). The images, although not directly synchronised to the music, cohere with its logic. As the voices fade from the soundtrack, the numbers depicted on screen decrease to leave only one, in a satisfying visual arc built along musical lines. The tune the men have been vocalising is taken up by the orchestra to accompany a montage of landscape scenes of the island that carries the narrative through to the next day. The second sequence that illustrates the community coming together through music (and whisky) is the depiction of the *réiteach*, the pre-wedding celebration where the islanders dance to diegetic music played on the bagpipes, which is then taken up and augmented by the nondiegetic orchestra. Mark Brownrigg (2007, 322) notes that the orchestra 'imitates the drone of the pipes, and captures perfectly the excitement and delight' of the gathering. The shift from the diegetic to the nondiegetic sphere operates as a subtle means to engage the audience to participate in, rather than merely view, the enjoyment of the event. As instances where the group is 'identified collectively' through music, these scenes are unique in the cycle of Ealing comedies (Daubney 2006, 62), and it is significant that it is a remote island community with the suggestion of its own musical traditions that is thus depicted.

Other music in the film closely matches onscreen action in a practice known as 'Mickey-Mousing', a technique particularly associated with animation and comedy (Manvell and Huntley 1975, 91). An example of this is the music that accompanies Waggett as he hops through the surf to find the whisky hidden in a cave. At other times the music points up the satire by punctuating the action or dialogue with mock-seriousness, as in the solemn chords that accompany George (Gordon Jackson) as he returns home to confront his overbearing mother. In these instances, the music is more generic and aligned with the incidental music Irving recalls providing for the earlier comedy films of Gracie Fields, George Formby, Will Hay and Tommy Trinder (1959, 145).

The combination of folk song and location shooting produces a persuasive sense of documentary authenticity. Christine Geraghty (2000, 52) notes the film's 'documentary approach' in the way it creates 'a sense of people drawing their skills and purpose from an understanding of what it means to live in that spectacular landscape'. The documentary realism remarked upon is all the more notable for its mention in connection with a comedy film, and reveals the extent to which location shooting may be interpreted as a documentary element. It is also a reflection of the film's musical score, and the extent to which authentic, or at any rate authentic-sounding, folk song is able to confer a further level of 'documentary' realism upon the film. In its mouth-music sequence, and to a lesser extent in the scenes of the *réiteach, Whisky Galore!* privileges the music and arranges its images accordingly in the same way that the musical logic of the vocal laments accompanying the funeral sequences in *The Edge of the World* and *The Silver Darlings* are permitted to unfold without fragmentation. These sequences are authenticated by their use of music as a structuring device, in alignment with the way that music is used in their real-life equivalents. In each case, the music, evocative of the island communities and freed from subordination to the image track, guarantees both its own veracity and that of the images it accompanies. Rather than weakening this verisimilitude, the less rigid alignment between the songs and their assumed diegetic sources on screen instead intensifies it. The music, untroubled by the requirement to adhere minutely to the diegetic scene, pervades the environment and its community with its atmosphere.

Scores entirely built on folk song similarly create an aura of cohesion based on the suggestion of shared musical traditions that validate the representations of the communities they depict, and at the same time necessarily mark them as 'other' to the majority of the films' audiences. In turn, this highlights the ethnographic element of the depiction and further enhances the documentary feel of these films. Scores structured on folk song therefore lend more of a documentary aspect to a film than scores in the more customary symphonic idiom that merely incorporate ethnic musical markers to conjure local colour as a separate element from their structuring form. Donnelly describes the film music technique of 'taking certain musical aspects and using them as an essence', a 'shorthand' that is then used in a manner 'that foregrounds them as an effect within a musical fabric that is not premised upon such ethnic musical language'. In this way, the ethnic markers intentionally become 'stylistic decoration' rather than intrinsic to the music (2008, 222). The extent to which a film's score employs folk song as a structuring element, rather than as a shorthand marker, determines the level of documentary authenticity it contributes to the film. Folk song forms an aural counterpart to the documentary realism assured by extensive location shooting, and the technical skill with which studio shooting is integrated into the film in order to prevent the artifice from disturbing the spectator's suspension of disbelief. For instance, the frequency and obviousness of the studio inserts in *The Brothers* works against the creation of a coherent sense of place, and this is compounded rather than mediated by the conventionality of the score. In contrast, the elegant integration between music and image in the mouth-music sequence in *Whisky Galore!* facilitates its effective incorporation into the film, although it was filmed later at Ealing and inserted 'under Charles Crichton's re-editing' (McArthur 2003, 49).

When folk song is employed as a structuring element in a score, it reverses the conventional thinking that the way to create a sense of documentary reality is to use as little nondiegetic music as possible. Charles Barr (2003, 64) notes the paradox that documentary films are often quite liberal in their use of music, while feature films that aim for a documentary feel tend to resist its use. Nevertheless, feature films that aspire to a level of documentary realism in depictions of specific communities tend to employ folk song as a means to particularise a community within its environment. Folk song is used to score scenes of ritual and ceremony—funerals, public gatherings, and celebrations—where the music would be part of the ritual in the lives of the community, and it acts as an authenticating element. By drawing upon indigenous folk song traditions, the filmmakers align their narrative features with the aesthetics of documentary, and adopt the freer interplay between music and image found in the documentary movement. This freedom allows folk song to retain its own musical form and logic, and enables it to lend a greater sense of actuality than music which is fragmented and cut to fit the needs of the image. The clear correlation between the use of folk song in documentary films and its use in feature films allows us to see not only that folk song acts as a strong marker of authenticity in both, but also to appreciate the profound influence of the documentary movement and its aesthetic ideals upon much of British feature film production.

Scores that draw upon folk song usually accompany representations of cultures other than that of the primary target audience. Jeffrey Richards has written of the fabrication of a Celtic identity for the non-English parts of the United Kingdom, based upon elements of Romanticism (wild landscapes, music and song, and the supernatural) and formulated in opposition to the 'perceived qualities' of the English. Thus Scotland, Wales and Ireland become associated with an ancient heritage of music, song, and poetry, although these traditions may be much later inventions and constructions. This was the case with James MacPherson's fabrication of the Ossianic poems, published in 1765 and fraudulently claimed to be translations of ancient Gaelic texts (Richards 1997, 8, 178–9). Cecil Sharp, in language that is problematic for the modern reader, writes of 'the English race' and describes folk songs as their 'race-products' (1907, 136). The concept of folk song is bound up with debates about nationalism and class, and it continues to arouse controversy (Pegg 2001, 63). In this respect, Sharp's insistence on the purity of rural artisans and labourers for their lack of musical cultivation and tutoring cannot escape an air of primitivism, of a member of a dominant class observing and recording the activities of members of a class less privileged, and in hindsight this casts a somewhat uncomfortable shadow over the project. The folk song collectors have been criticised for bringing 'bourgeois values' to the area, specifically for being 'pro-nationalistic, anti-urban, middle class' (de Val 2000, 344–5). A residue of unease lingers in the way that folk song is used in films to connote not only authenticity of place but also to suggest the otherness and exoticism of communities less developed, more remote from the modern world than the cinema-going audience.

This is explicit in the combination of image and music found in *The Four Feathers* (Zoltan Korda, 1939) in a sequence that depicts boats on the Nile being hauled upstream by groups of men. For the montage that records the arduous work and the progress of the barges, Miklós Rózsa had wished to use a 'traditional boatman's song'. The composer employs a 'primitive Sudanese melody' that he had found while researching in the British Museum, 'accompanied by percussive African rhythms' (Rózsa 1982, 72). Rózsa imagined the boatmen 'calling to each other in a kind of antiphony' from either side of the river. Arabic words, transcribed phonetically into English, are sung by two male choruses placed 'in opposite corners' of the recording studio (ibid.). The chanting of the men begins as an establishing shot pans along the river before the image dissolves to a view of the native workers. The work song fills the soundtrack to accompany Osmond Borradaile's location shooting and it adds its own measure of authenticity to the scene. The song is not synchronised directly with the screen, and it is joined on the soundtrack by the shouts of the men and the whip cracks of those in charge, with the effect that it conveys an impression of emanating from the location and the entire cohort of native workers. In employing the same technique to combine music and image, this film shares the anthropological perspective of the outsider looking in found in many of the depictions of communities with folk song traditions. The culture of the islanders in *Man of Aran* is thus presented as equally different and 'other' to the audience as that of the Sudanese boatmen in *The Four Feathers*.

Whereas film music generally draws upon the style and character of other musical forms, films that structure their scores on folk song employ examples of genuine pre-existing music to authenticate their representations of communities and locations. The composers associated with the English Musical Renaissance recognised in folk song a particularly national form of musical expression. Ralph Vaughan Williams regarded it as 'a manifestation' of national music. National music, he wrote, 'is not necessarily folk-song; on the other hand folk-song is, by nature, necessarily national' (1963, 62). This national quality marks the British films that integrate folk song into their scores with a strong national or regional inflection. The use of folk song in films echoes its use in concert music and reflects a shared impulse in the desire of the composers and the filmmakers to employ a style of music with a national character.

The pastoral atmosphere conjured by folk song often creates a merging in the cinematic consciousness between communities and the landscapes they inhabit, where one seems almost to arise as a consequence of the other. In many of the films considered in this chapter, folk song is heard in choral arrangements that foreground its communal nature and call into play the wider associations of choral sonorities. This interplay between musical categories illustrates the fluid nature of the borders between them and the ease with which music crosses them. In the process of this drift across styles, the music accrues a cumulative power as it calls upon the expressive potential of its combined elements. Under the broad umbrella of a pastoral aesthetic, each style brings its own palette of associations to deepen the effects it creates in its cinematic context. Although a cultural preoccupation with the natural environment and natural elements are still prominent, a differently nuanced relationship emerges when choral voices unrelated to folk song are employed, and this is the central concern of the next chapter.

Notes

1. English folk songs are also heard in *Love Story* (Leslie Arliss, 1944) ['The Miller of Dee'], *Sea of Sand* (Guy Green, 1958) ['Greensleeves'], *Tawny Pipit* (Bernard Miles, Charles Saunders, 1944) ['O, Waly, Waly'], and *The Upturned Glass* (Lawrence Huntington, 1947) ['Madam, Will You Walk']. None of these films suggest that folk song is a continuing tradition for their characters.
2. The similarity between these scenes raises the intriguing question of whether the filmmakers were familiar with this documentary short. Powell attributes the film's title to being that of 'the little Irish song' to the suggestion of his Irish wife Frankie Reidy (1986, 460), although he would have known

Addinsell as the composer for the hurriedly made *The Lion Has Wings* (Powell et al., 1939). In 1940, the same year as *Ulster*, Richard Addinsell provided the music for Powell and Pressburger's *Contraband*, although this had been the subject of a disagreement between the filmmakers. Accounts of the incident vary. According to Powell, Pressburger had assumed that the commission would go to his Hungarian compatriot Miklós Rózsa, the composer on both *The Spy in Black* (Powell, 1939) and *The Thief of Bagdad* (Powell et al., 1940), and had told him as much (1986, 341). Powell regarded Addinsell as 'the *crème de la crème*', felt that 'it was time to give an English composer a chance', and was resolute in spite of an 'understandable coolness' between the filmmakers over the matter (1986, 341). Rózsa tells a different version, in which Powell agreed to him composing the score, and then changed his mind. Rózsa regarded it as a 'simple act of bloody-mindedness' (Macdonald 1994, 163), which may help to explain Rózsa's later dismissal of Addinsell as 'a dilettante' (quoted in Brown 1994, 278).

3. Later in *The Silent Village* the male voices return with the Welsh folk song 'All Through the Night' ('Ar Hyd Y Nos'). This song is also heard in *Tawny Pipit* (Bernard Miles, Charles Saunders, 1944), in *The Captive Heart* (Basil Dearden, 1946), where it is sung by the male voice choir organised by the Welsh character Dai Evans (Mervyn Johns), and in the Welsh-set *The Happiness of Three Women* (Maurice Elvey, 1954). The latter film also features 'Sosban Fach' (Little Saucepan), a Welsh folk song also sung by Welsh train passengers in *The Halfway House* (Basil Dearden, 1944).
4. The impact of the experience on Powell is evident in his short documentary *Return to the Edge of the World* (1978), which charts his return to Foula forty-two years later. Powell is accompanied by his wife Frankie (both had appeared in the opening scenes of the film), John Laurie, who played a key role in the film, and Sydney Streeter, who worked on this film and other Powell and Pressburger titles as production manager and assistant director. The documentary includes scoring by Brian Easdale rather than reusing the film's music. It is included as a special feature on the film's BFI Blu-ray and DVD release (BFIB1030).
5. Brian Easdale also incorporates into his scoring a traditional Nepalese folk song, suggested as diegetic as Clodagh and Mr Dean visit the Holy Man, which adds a further layer of documentary authenticity (BFI Music Cue Collection, MUS-126).

References

Barr, Charles. 2003. The National Health: Pat Jackson's *White Corridors*. In *British Cinema of the 1950s: A Celebration*, ed. Ian Mackillop and Neil Sinyard, 64–73. Manchester/New York: Manchester University Press.

———. 2005. Hitchcock and Powell: Two Directions for British Cinema. *Screen* 46 (1): 5–13.

Brown, Royal S. 1994. *Overtones and Undertones: Reading Film Music*. Berkeley: University of California Press.

Brownrigg, Mark. 2007. Hearing Place: Film Music, Geography and Ethnicity. *International Journal of Media and Cultural Politics* 3 (3): 307–323.

Christie, Ian, ed. 1978. *Powell, Pressburger and Others*. London: British Film Institute.

Cook, Pam. 2002. *I Know Where I'm Going!* London: British Film Institute.

Daubney, Kate. 2006. Music as a Satirical Device in the Ealing Comedies. In *European Film Music*, ed. Miguel Mera and David Burnand, 60–72. Aldershot: Ashgate.

de Val, Dorothy. 2000. The Transformed Village: Lucy Broadwood and Folksong. In *Music and British Culture, 1785–1914*, ed. Christina Bashford and Leanne Langley, 341–366. Oxford: Oxford University Press.

Donnelly, K.J. 2008. *I Know Where I'm Going!* Hearing Germanic Music in the Scottish Isles. In *Destination London: German-Speaking Emigrés and British Cinema, 1925–1950*, ed. Tim Bergfelder and Christian Cargnelli, 220–229. New York/Oxford: Berghahn Books.

Durgnat, Raymond. 2011. *A Mirror for England: British Movies from Austerity to Affluence*. London: British Film Institute.

Dyer, Richard. 2010. *Nino Rota: Music, Film and Feeling*. London: British Film Institute.

Eisler, Hanns, and Theodor Adorno. 1994. *Composing for the Films*. London: Athlone Press.

Ellis, John. 1978. Art, Culture and Quality: Terms for a Cinema in the Forties and Seventies. *Screen* 19 (3): 9–50.

Geraghty, Christine. 2000. *British Cinema in the Fifties: Gender, Genre and the 'New Look'*. London: Routledge.

Gifford, Terry. 1999. *Pastoral: The New Critical Idiom*. London: Routledge.

Harper, Sue. 2010. The Ownership of Woods and Water: Landscapes in British Cinema, 1930–1960. In *Cinema and Landscape*, ed. Graeme Harper and Jonathan Rayner, 149–159. Bristol/Chicago: Intellect.

Hughes, Meirion, and Robert Stradling. 2001. *The English Musical Renaissance, 1840–1940: Constructing a National Music*. Manchester/New York: Manchester University Press.

Huntley, John. 1947. *British Film Music*. London: Skelton Robinson.

Irving, Ernest. 1959. *Cue for Music*. London: Dobson Books.

Lazar, David, ed. 2003. *Michael Powell Interviews*. Jackson: University Press of Mississippi.

Lejeune, C.A. 1937. The Edge of the World. *The Schoolmaster and Woman Teacher's Chronicle*, 23 September. Reprinted in Booklet Notes for BFI Blu-ray BFIB1030.

Levy, Louis. 1948. *Music for the Movies*. London: Sampson Low.

Lindsay, Maurice. 2001. Cedric Thorpe Davie. In *The New Grove Dictionary of Music and Musicians*, ed. Stanley Sadie, vol. 25, 430. London: Macmillan.

Macdonald, Kevin. 1994. *Emeric Pressburger*. London: Faber & Faber.

Manvell, Roger, and John Huntley. 1975. *The Technique of Film Music*. London: Focal Press.

McArthur, Colin. 2003. *Whisky Galore! & The Maggie*. London/New York: IB Tauris.

McLoone, Martin. 2005. Man of Aran. In *The Cinema of Britain and Ireland*, ed. Brian McFarlane, 41–51. London: Wallflower Press.

Moor, Andrew. 2005. *Powell & Pressburger: A Cinema of Magic Spaces*. London: I. B. Tauris.

Pegg, Carole. 2001. Folk Song. In *The New Grove Dictionary of Music and Musicians*, ed. Stanley Sadie, vol. 9, 63–67. London: Macmillan.

Powell, Michael. 1986. *A Life in Movies*. London: Heinemann. Reprinted 2000, London: Faber & Faber.

———. 1990. *Edge of the World: The Making of a Film*. London: Faber & Faber.

———. 1991. *Black Narcissus*. Commentary Track on Network Blu-ray 7957001.

———. 1992. *Million Dollar Movie*. London: Heinemann.

Richards, Jeffrey. 1997. *Films and British National Identity: From Dickens to Dad's Army*. Manchester: Manchester University Press.

Rickert, Edith. 1928. *Ancient English Christmas Carols, 1400–1700*. London: Chatto & Windus.

Rózsa, Miklós. 1982. *Double Life: The Autobiography of Miklós Rózsa*. Tunbridge Wells: The Baton Press.

Sharp, Cecil J. 1907. *English Folk-Song, Some Conclusions*. London: Novello.

Vaughan Williams, Ralph. 1963. *National Music and Other Essays*. London: Oxford University Press.

CHAPTER 5

Choral Music: Christian and Pantheistic Mysticism

Choral voices are a recurring element in the scores of British films, where they conjure a range of connotations. Films can use choral music to harness a religious feeling that arises from it being historically enmeshed with traditions of Christian worship, as a means of expressing and enlivening liturgical texts. Choral music can also promote broader ideas of mysticism and otherworldliness when voices are set in a pastoral idiom that links them with the natural environment and evokes its associations. Whenever choral sonorities are heard, the origin of choral singing as an activity bound up with religious services resonates through them and colours them with a deeply spiritual hue. The choral repertoire reflects these aims and origins, chiefly comprising settings of biblical subjects and spiritual journeys that embody a sense of uplift. With these historical antecedents, choral voices sail in a sea of connotation, bathed in a spray of religious and spiritual association. These are brought into play when choral voices are heard in British films, to which we might add further ideas—of tradition, history, and stability—that arise from the established nature of the institutions of the church.

The choral tradition in England reaches back to the church music of William Byrd in the sixteenth century and the secular English cantata founded by Henry Purcell in the seventeenth century. The following century brought a new form of English oratorio introduced by Handel. In contrast to opera, this gave prominence to the chorus, which through its connection with the church guaranteed the form's respectability (Young

P. Mazey, *British Film Music*, Palgrave Studies in Audio-Visual Culture, https://doi.org/10.1007/978-3-030-33550-2_5

1962, 105). The eighteenth century also saw the establishment of the major choral societies and festivals; the Three Choirs Festival in 1715 and the Birmingham Festival in 1784, while the last quarter of the nineteenth century 'witnessed a revolution in choral music' with the founding of new festivals and societies (McGuire 2013, 122). In the nineteenth century, choral societies flourished among urban industrial communities and attained 'high technical excellence' (Young 1962, 191). As well as being a locus of musical activity outside of the capital, the festivals premiered new choral works. At their height, the festivals commissioned 'some 200 choral pieces' from English composers between the 1870s and 1910, before a decline that Charles Reid attributes to the joint effects of the First World War and the growth of gramophone recordings and radio broadcasts (1963, 266).[1] In spite of this, the festivals continued to commission new works, and parallels can be drawn with the system in the British film industry of commissioning scores from individual composers. Both disciplines provide a market for a composer's output and both require the musician to work within a range of constraints. Composers with experience of writing for voices, most notably Ralph Vaughan Williams, Brian Easdale, and William Walton, exploit the expressive potential of these in their film scores. The central concern of this chapter is to analyse these choral voices and to uncover the multiple levels of meaning they evoke. The chapter begins with simple cases of the isolated use of pre-existing diegetic choral music and it progresses to the more complex and integrated employment of choral sonorities.

Choral Voices, the Church, and Mystical Elements

In their most straightforward guise, choral voices can be introduced onto the soundtrack of a film to suggest their diegetic presence within the narrative. The association of choral voices with the church is frequently supported by instruments with a comparable historical association, notably the organ. Both are contained in an isolated use of choral voices in *Pygmalion* (1938). Higgins (Leslie Howard) and Pickering (Scott Sunderland) meet in front of St Paul's Church in Covent Garden, and Higgins boasts that in three months he could teach Eliza (Wendy Hiller) to speak well enough to pass her off as a duchess. The diegetic sound of the (unseen) church organ begins as he mentions the 'noble architecture of these columns' and it continues in the underscore. When Eliza tries to sell him a flower, claiming that she is short for her lodgings, Higgins accuses her of lying as she had previously offered to change half a crown. Eliza loses her temper and kicks the basket towards him. As he turns to leave with Pickering, choral voices emanate from the church to stop him in his tracks. Looking heavenwards, Higgins comments that it is a reminder to be charitable and drops a stream of coins into Eliza's flower basket. The diegetic music and voices support the cause-and-effect logic of the narrative, as the generosity they motivate enables Eliza to request from Higgins the teaching he had boasted of. Here the musical effect is an isolated one.

More extended uses of diegetic choral voices tend to accompany scenes of religious rituals or ceremonies. An example occurs in *The Queen of Spades* (Thorold Dickinson, 1949), an adaptation of Alexander Pushkin's short story, in a sequence that depicts the funeral of the old Countess (Edith Evans). With a visual iconography of painted pillars, richly decorated walls and candlelight, this sequence also bolsters the atmosphere of its location by drawing upon the historic traditions of Russian music in the choral singing, particularly the use of deep male voices, and the chiming of bells. The film's cue sheet lists the choral entry simply as a traditional piece for 'Russian Choir' by an unknown composer.[2] This adds an authentic element to accompany the Russian atmosphere created by the orchestral textures of Georges Auric's score. The scene begins with the image of a bell that fills the screen and sounds a deep toll on the soundtrack. It is joined by a choir, unseen although suggested as diegetic, who sing a lament as first Lizaveta (Yvonne Mitchell) and then other mourners approach the coffin to pay their respects while Herman (Anton Walbrook) looks on. When Herman approaches the coffin the bass voice dominates before the singing pauses to leave silence. This is broken by Herman's cry when he believes he sees the lifeless Countess open her eyes, a dramatic moment amplified by being synchronised with the fermata in the music. The choral voices resume as Herman stumbles away. The film juxtaposes the decorum of the religious ritual with the debauchery associated with the other vocal elements in the film, the authentic gypsy songs sung by Maroussia Dimitrevitch that accompany scenes of the soldiers' drunken gambling in the tavern.

The musical contrast between the solemnity of the choral music and the sensual abandon of the gypsy songs in *The Queen of Spades* is also to the fore in the Gainsborough melodrama *Madonna of the Seven Moons* (Arthur Crabtree, 1944). In this film, the opposition is both more emphatically made and more narratively significant. Phyllis Calvert plays a dual role as the film's central character, a woman whose childhood trauma causes her to alternate between two distinct personas; the respectable wife and mother Maddalena, and her alter ego the free-spirited gypsy Rosanna. Hans May's score is dominated by a tango theme associated with Rosanna; it plays on her musical box, her lover Nino (Stewart Granger) hums it in the street and serenades Rosanna with a vocal rendition. The 'Rosanna' theme floods the nondiegetic score. It is heard twelve times in the film and it takes a central narrative role as the diegetic catalyst for Maddalena's change of persona. Maddalena hears a gardener whistling the 'Rosanna' tune, and its effect on her is expressed in a powerful nondiegetic orchestral restatement of the theme as she rushes to her *prie-dieu*. Her prayers are accompanied by nondiegetic organ music that accentuates the potency of the religious imagery that surrounds her as she seeks to restore herself. Donnelly (1997, 163) finds the organ only 'loosely associated with the Maddalena character'. I find a stronger connection, subsequently heightened by the addition of choral voices, which set up an opposition between the church music that represents Maddalena and the tango that represents her immersion in the persona of Rosanna. For in addition to signalling the two sides of her persona, these musical oppositions act diegetically during the narrative to confirm or unbalance her persona. Each operates as an antidote to the effects of the other.

Organ music, suggested as diegetic, is heard in the first scenes of the film as Maddalena prepares to leave the convent to marry. It is augmented by, and then gives way to, the orchestral strains that accompany a transitional sequence that uses the image of Maddalena's prayer book both to emphasise her unchanging devotion and to indicate the passage of time between the prologue and the central section of the film. The prayer book, the cross she wears, the Christian imagery in her room and the suggestion in her name of Mary Magdalene,[3] all strengthen the alignment of the Maddalena persona with the religious association conveyed by the organ and the choral music. Once Maddalena's personality has crossed over to her incarnation as Rosanna, it is organ and choral music that threatens to return her to being Maddalena. As Rosanna stands before the columns of a church, organ music is heard from inside. The organ is joined by choral singing that rises in volume to immobilise Rosanna as she makes to leave. Rosanna's fixed expression cuts to reveal the (suggested) diegetic source of the singing—a procession of choir boys and monks crossing the piazza to enter the church. The organ music fills the soundtrack and Rosanna stands as though spellbound, desperately grips Jimmy (Peter Murray-Hill) and begs him to hold her up and not to let her kneel. In common with the example from *Pygmalion*, while the organ calmly enters the soundtrack as a background diegetic element, it is the entrance of the choral voices that causes Rosanna to react.

At a later point in *Madonna of the Seven Moons*, Rosanna attends a carnival that brings together the film's narrative strands. She sees a cross on a banner carried aloft in the carnival procession, and the image superimposes her wide-eyed expression onto the frame of her memory of the earlier church procession. The choral music is briefly uppermost on the soundtrack and the reflection of the white cross is visible in the dark areas of Rosanna's eyes (Fig. 5.1). Rosanna's memory seems to draw her back to the church. As she wanders the streets, the reduced sounds of the carnival indicate that she is moving away from it, and it is replaced by choral strains as she approaches the church. The choral singing, sounding acoustically appropriate with a resonant echo effect, again fills the soundtrack as Rosanna kneels before the open doors of the church and crosses herself in a moment of complete alignment between music and image. Here the

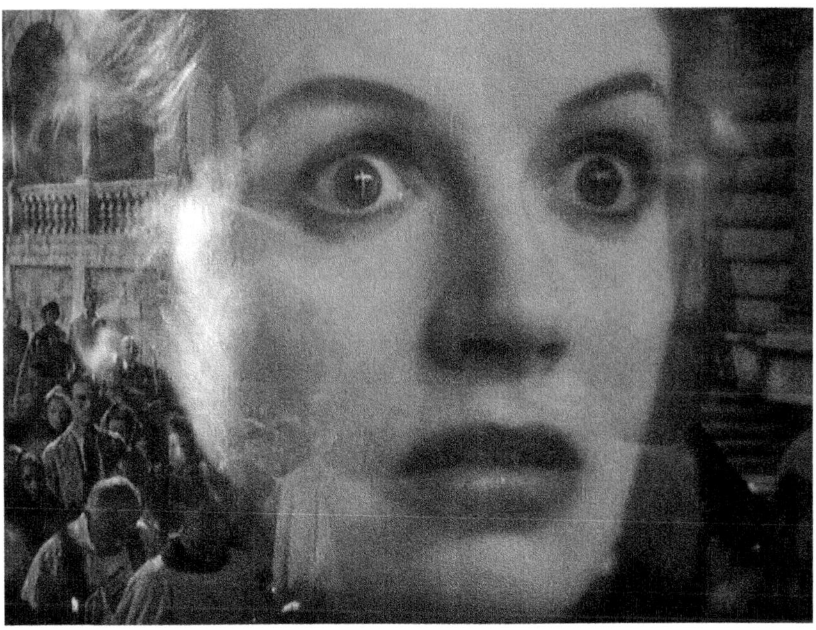

Fig. 5.1 Rosanna affected by choral music in *Madonna of the Seven Moons*

diegetic choral singing takes the role of nondiegetic music in expressing Rosanna's emotions and her subjective experience, and indicating her total immersion in the music that she hears. The choral elements here are in all probability inserted from an existing recording as no choral forces are credited in the film, and their effects might have been equally well achieved with any number of similar choral works. The choral voices act in a generic way to conjure a mood of religiosity when set against Rosanna's tango theme. The central opposition between the personas of Maddalena and Rosanna, delineated musically in the juxtaposition of the choral music and the tango theme, is introduced in the opening titles, which appear on the image of a church interior with a church candle burning in the foreground to the accompaniment of the 'Rosanna' theme. As the film draws to a close, the organ music returns as Maddalena receives the last rites with both the cross and the rose that Nino has thrown to her on her breast. The organ, nondiegetic for only the second time, takes up the 'Rosanna' theme and musically unites her two sides and resolves the musical-visual conflict that had been introduced at the outset.

Madonna of the Seven Moons employs choral voices that incant a liturgical text within the film's diegetic world, which ties them to a specifically religious ritual. The short documentary *Message from Canterbury* (George Hoellering, 1944) similarly includes diegetic choral music, and features works by Henry Purcell, Thomas Tallis and Orlando Gibbons. The choral music accompanies rural landscapes and agricultural scenes, and shots of the cathedral taken through apple orchards are intercut with interior shots of the cathedral and the singing choristers. With its pastoral imagery, *Message from Canterbury* frequently recalls *A Canterbury Tale* (Powell and Pressburger, 1944), while a close alignment is evident in a shot from the cathedral tower to the city, in distant shots of the cathedral accompanied by choral singing, and in scenes of the cathedral amidst the rubble of its war-torn surroundings. Both films additionally emphasise the history of the city by opening with quotations from Chaucer.

However, whereas the documentary employs diegetic choral pieces, and confirms this with scenes of them being performed, *A Canterbury Tale* introduces nondiegetic choral voices as a recurring motif that repeatedly expresses a more mysterious and ethereal mysticism. Allan Gray's choral theme is first heard in the introductory section that follows the film's title sequence. The image of the view from the bell tower of Canterbury Cathedral dissolves to that of a manuscript bearing the prologue of Chaucer's *Canterbury Tales.* At the same time, the muscular orchestral force of the title music and the chiming bells that combine with it melts into the lighter strains of a choir, which the accompanying imagery suggests is 'heavenly'. Chaucer's words are narrated in voiceover on the soundtrack and as the image of the text dissolves to an early illustrated map of England, bells softly rejoin the choir. The camera moves to a closer view of the map. The voiceover describes people's desire to make pilgrimages, and the image follows the road to Canterbury, which is represented pictorially with the cathedral prominent in its design. The line drawing of Canterbury on the map dissolves to a line drawing of Chaucer's pilgrims, and a further dissolve brings us to the footage of the pilgrims that opens the main body of the film. The choral theme, associated with Canterbury Cathedral and Chaucer's pilgrims, is heard on four further occasions. On each subsequent hearing, the choral voices are visually associated with Canterbury Cathedral and, through their audiovisual link with the cathedral and the earlier pilgrims, the voices evoke both a mystical continuity with the past and a sense of divine intervention in the lives of the characters, and particularly that of the central character Alison (Sheila Sim).

Significantly, Gray's choral voices sing without words. This has the effect of shifting the spiritual element away from a strictly Christian or religious meaning. Removing the words of a liturgical text severs the connection of the voices to a specifically religious atmosphere and instead promotes the sense of a more generalised spiritual or numinous feeling. Wordless choral singing retains the association between massed voices and an ethereal higher force, and yet releases them from the anchor of a narrow set of religious beliefs. The wordless chorus encompasses a broader spectrum of spiritual feeling that suggests, if not exactly a divine intervention that implies a predetermined outcome, then certainly the sense of characters' fates being guided by otherworldly forces.

The first recurrence of the choral theme in *A Canterbury Tale* comes after an hour and a quarter of the film's running time. During the sequence discussed in detail in the third chapter, the choral voices are heard when Alison sees Canterbury Cathedral in the distance as she walks the Pilgrim's Road. A moment later, she hears the sounds and music of the earlier pilgrims, in a repeat of the order in which they were heard in the film's prologue. The choral theme returns when the modern-day pilgrims travel with Colpeper on the train to Canterbury. Peter (Dennis Price) states his intention to inform the authorities that Colpeper (Eric Portman) is the 'glueman', who has been attacking local girls, and the latter responds that 'there are higher courts than the local bench of magistrates'. Colpeper gazes out of the train window, and, from his point of view in the moving train, Canterbury Cathedral is glimpsed in the distance. The choir ushers the music onto the soundtrack with a greater force and the bells and theme from the title sequence ring out as the train approaches its destination.

The choral theme recurs for a third time when Alison receives the news that her fiancé, whom she had thought lost in combat, is alive. The choral voices are heard as she takes in the news and rushes to open the windows of the caravan in the garage where it is being stored. The camera holds and focuses on the image of the cathedral seen in the distance through the grimy garage windows. The final restatement of the choral theme closes the film. The sound of the organ in the cathedral played by Peter and the congregation singing 'Onward Christian Soldiers' dissolves into the sound of bells ringing, matched by the image of the bells. The choral theme adds a final flourish at high volume to accompany two shots of the cathedral from a distance. The first is a closer image and the second a repeat of Alison's view of it from the hill above, which affirms that she is central to the narrative. This montage suggests that we are taking our leave of the location, it bookends the film with a reprise of the music and images of the film's prologue, and it reverses the opening journey that transported us, with the modern-day pilgrims, to Canterbury.

A Canterbury Tale closes with an extended montage of sound and image, a segment of practically dialogue-free audiovisual narration that looks forward to Michael Powell's later experimentation with the 'composed film'. In Powell's concept of the composed film, the music is composed first and the images edited accordingly, an arrangement that allows music to be 'the master' (1986, 583). Andrew Moor likens *A Canterbury Tale* to the documentary films of Humphrey Jennings, in particular to *Listen to Britain* (1942), and finds in both a utopian vision expressed through an 'air of mystical religiosity' (2005, 110, 116). The two films are further aligned in the way that both prioritise sound and music, and in the optimistic and uplifting renditions of 'Rule Britannia' and 'Onward Christian Soldiers', bells and choir that close *Listen to Britain* and *A Canterbury Tale* respectively (ibid., 115). Powell recalls that he and Pressburger worked 'very closely with the composer' on mixing the sound for the film, and made 'little adjustments' and 'discoveries' at this final stage. The director, pleased with the film's closing sequence, considered Allan Gray's montage of the hymn, music and bells a 'triumph of sound and imagination' (1986, 457, 448).

The recurring choral theme in *A Canterbury Tale* blurs the border between diegetic and nondiegetic music. The association of the choral effect with the image of the cathedral initially implies a diegetic source for the sound, for choral singing and the peal of bells do emanate from cathedrals, and the bells are identified as diegetic. However, the distance of the characters from the cathedral when the choral voices are heard, combined with the clarity and volume of the choral cue and the fact that it is wordless, confirms it on each recurrence as a nondiegetic presence. Rather than reproducing the sound that the characters hear, the choral theme instead signals a mystical happening that is visually associated with Canterbury Cathedral. At these moments, the 'historical symbol' of the cathedral becomes a 'sign of transcendence' (Moor 2005, 116). In this way, the film works to break down the distinction between the Christian religious symbol of the cathedral and a more inclusive and pervading sense of otherworldly mysticism. This blending of Christian and more broadly spiritual elements in a way that aligns them and operates to collapse the distance between them is a recurring aspect in films that include wordless choral music on their soundtracks.

In Olivier's *Henry V* (1944), William Walton employs a wordless chorus in both the diegetic and nondiegetic planes in ways that engage with the film's complex spatial and temporal strategy. Temporally, *Henry V* offers a vibrant interplay between the time of the historical events depicted, the time of the play's performance at the Globe Theatre and, significantly, elements that reflect the time of the film's production. Hubert Clifford acknowledges the three time periods as 'an awkward problem for the composer', for which Walton drew on authentic musical sources skilfully woven into a coherent whole expressed 'in terms of his own musical mind' (1944, 173). In addition to these temporal layers, Anthony Davies notes that the 'spatial detail in the frame' seems to refuse to identify itself as either entirely 'theatrical stylization' or 'cinematic realism', and this enables the visuals to 'take on the credibility of the cinema without losing the consciousness of theatre' (1988, 30). Davies cites the example of the opening panoramic shots over the model of Elizabethan London. While not overtly staking a claim to realism, these images nevertheless attain a 'realistic dimension' by adopting a style of aerial photography that recalls its use in wartime newsreels particularly to demonstrate the effects of war (ibid.). At the same time, the model's clear reference to Claes Visscher's panoramic engraving of London from 1616 lays claim to a level of historical authenticity, notwithstanding the engraving's inaccuracies.

The pan along the Thames in the opening scene of the film is joined on the soundtrack by the orchestra and a wordless chorus intoning Walton's 'glorious ode, or paean' (Palmer 1990, 6), a piece that steadily builds to a climax of great intensity. Here, Palmer notes, Olivier invokes 'the heroic defence of the city against the Luftwaffe, indeed of the whole of our cultural heritage' (ibid.). Palmer describes the theme as a 'fanfare-like motif … over a rock-steady pentatonic basso ostinato' and notes that it recurs 'whenever patriotic or national values are being discussed or national pride evoked' (1972, 250). This, however, is the only time that the theme is joined by the wordless chorus, the only time that deeper male voices are used wordlessly, and the only time that the wordless chorus is used as a wholly nondiegetic sonority within the film. Each time we subsequently hear a wordless chorus, its diegetic source is confirmed by the onscreen choirboys. Following the Battle of Agincourt, the scene returns to the French Court to the accompaniment of Walton's re-working of selections from Canteloube's pastoral *Chants d'Auvergne* folk songs, with the 'apple-cheeked timbres of girls' and boys' voices' (Palmer 1990, 12). The choirboys act as a transitional continuity element both visually and aurally. The diegetic choral singing of the boys at the French Court (of the bridal song, or epithalamion, drawn from Canteloube's *L'Antouèno*) is replaced by the diegetic choral singing of the boys at the Globe Theatre as the scene returns to its starting point at the film's conclusion. These scenes are thus differentiated from the nondiegetic wordless voices that launch the film.

The opening choral music creates a different effect and its single use suggests a clearer purpose. As in *A Canterbury Tale*, its wordless nature frees it from a religious specificity while retaining a sense of otherworldliness that imbues the scene with a sense of wonder. This draws us into and encourages us to engage with the world of the film. In a similar fashion to the entreaty of the Chorus—'On your imaginary forces work'—this introductory choral accompaniment casts an ethereal spell that prompts us to accept that we have travelled back in time to 1600. From 1600, the Chorus will carry us back still further to the time of the action, although that journey will have the benefit of explanatory words and the entrance of nondiegetic music into the space of the Globe to spur the change of scene and beseech us to use our thoughts to send the characters 'jumping o'er times'. The spiritual association of the opening wordless chorus conjures the sense that the ghosts of the past are beckoning us back to the earlier time, and it prepares us for the fluid temporality in which the film revels.

Henry V draws to a close with pealing bells and a wordless chorus joining the orchestra as Henry and Katherine (Renée Asherson) march ceremoniously to the thrones and the scene returns to the performance at the Globe Theatre. The Chorus declaims his epilogue and the wordless chorus resumes as the choirboys and theatre orchestra are seen on screen. The camera pulls back to reveal the Globe flag being lowered, signalling the end of the performance, and the image returns to the model of London as the music calms and slows. The flute roulade that had accompanied the floating playbill at the beginning of the film returns to accompany the entrance of the dancing paper that carries the end title credits. The credits roll to a stirring reprise of the 'Agincourt Song' for orchestra and chorus. Geduld (1973, 64) notes that Walton's version of this traditional song 'recasts the simple, original tune into an almost timeless paean' and highlights the propaganda message of this 'song of thanksgiving and triumph that is meant to belong to 1945 [sic] as much as to 1415'. For Geduld, this triumphal ending bears comparison 'functionally and stylistically' with the uplifting 'Hallelujah' that closes *Belshazzar's Feast*, Walton's 1931 oratorio (ibid.). The experience from the concert hall that Walton brings to his film score is pointed out by Clifford. Judged 'by purely musical standards', he opines, 'the best in this score nears comparison with Walton's own output for the concert platform' (1944, 173).

Walton's experience of the concert hall is also evident in the similarly uplifting choral finale that ends his score for Paul Czinner's film of *As You Like It* (1936), the only use of choral voices in the film. This aligns Walton's score with orchestral concert works that employ a chorus to provide a final flourish, for example, the wordless female voices that close 'Neptune', the final movement of Gustav Holst's *The Planets* (1920). The power of such a choral ending is not diminished by its brevity, for, as Reid notes, 'it colours in retrospect the score as a whole' (1963, 279). In respect of film music, Manvell and Huntley report that choral voices are 'commonly used … to give an effect of emotional "uplift"' (1975, 159). The chorus is used in this way in the closing scene of *Things To Come*. The space gun has launched the rocket and the young couple begin their journey through the starry sky as their fathers watch from an observatory. Cabal (Raymond Massey), enthused with the prospect of discovering new lands, grandly declaims to the more circumspect Passworthy (Edward Chapman): 'For man no rest and no ending. He must go on, conquest beyond conquest … All the universe, or nothing … Which shall it be, Passworthy, which shall it be?'. The noble strains of Arthur Bliss's epilogue rise to underscore his question. The image cuts to a close-up of Cabal in profile, and as he repeats 'which shall it be?', the sound of his voice is muted and replaced by a chorus of voices echoing his words. Cabal's profile fades to leave only the image of the stars in the night sky as the choral voices continue to reiterate the question and accompany the final orchestral climax. This brings the film to an uplifting close, the joyful voices rising positively and hopefully to counteract the air of general pessimism that has preceded them. The nondiegetic choral voices lift the mood of the film's denouement and inject an optimistic message into its closing moments.

A similar sense of hope and uplift is injected into the last scenes of *The Halfway House* (Basil Dearden, 1944) by a wordless female choir. In common with the examples above, it is only heard in the film's concluding scenes. The 'Halfway House' of the film's title is an inn in the Welsh countryside where a diverse group of visitors meet and find their lives changed in some way. The hotel is revealed to have been destroyed in a bombing raid exactly one year earlier, and the visitors have experienced a mystical time-slip reminiscent of those in J. B. Priestley's 'time' plays. The film reaches a climax with the recurrence of the air raid on the date of its anniversary. Lord Berners provides blasting dramatic music to accompany a montage of shots depicting the inn's destruction, interspersed with superimposed close-up shots of the hotel's visitors, each of whom describes how their brief sojourn at the hotel has transformed, refreshed and revitalised their lives. Each visitor in turn walks away through the burning wreckage of the building. The last words are spoken by the terminally ill conductor David Davies (Esmond Knight), the character whose story had opened the film. In voiceover he narrates Psalm 23 ('The Lord is my shepherd'), and as the familiar words end, the music quickly swells and rises in volume to a stirring climax. As the music becomes expansive the camera moves up from the ghostly innkeepers Rhys and Gwyneth (Mervyn and Glynis Johns), who stand amid the fiery ruins. The image dissolves to a model shot of the blazing inn and the wordless chorus of women's voices enters the soundtrack. A further dissolve reveals the present-day ruin of the inn and then a slow pan across the natural landscape is accompanied by the wordless choral finale. Philip Lane notes that the score instructs the voices to be treated 'as part of the orchestra and not too prominent except towards the end', although, given that the voices are 'pretty forward throughout', the music director Ernest Irving 'or the engineers' must have felt differently (2008, 14). Lane suggests that, as 'the singers had only to perform a three-minute piece', it may have seemed wasteful for their presence not to be foregrounded (ibid.).[4] Both this film and *Things To Come* are notably understated in limiting the use of their choral forces. In *The Halfway House*, particularly, it may have been tempting to introduce wordless choral voices during moments of uncanny happenings. Choral voices would not have seemed out of place when, for instance, the spectral innkeepers are revealed neither to appear reflected in mirrors, nor to cast a shadow. The film's resistance to the use of choral sonorities to accompany these moments demonstrates musical restraint.

The Halfway House, in common with *A Canterbury Tale*, employs a wordless choir in a way that draws on its historical association with the church and organised religion, and then broadens its connotation to represent a sense of divine mysticism that encompasses but is not limited to a Christian faith. The film's narrative has the feel of a parable, or perhaps it would be more accurate to say multiple parables, built as it is upon multiple narratives of transformed lives. In this respect, it is aligned with the cycle of portmanteau films produced at Ealing during this period, two of which, *Dead of Night* (1945) and *Train of Events* (1949) included contributions from Basil Dearden, the director of *The Halfway House*. This film's mysticism embraces events that may be regarded as occult, and that conjure supernatural elements regarded as inimical to religious doctrine, notably the ghostly innkeepers and the séance.[5] These elements act as a counterbalance to the Christian undertones in the film and mingle with them to present a broader sense of mysticism. The use of Psalm 23 is immediately followed by the wordless choir, which has the effect of diluting its religious specificity and presenting a more pantheistic and inclusive spirituality.

It is significant that the choral voices that bring *The Halfway House* to its conclusion are accompanied on screen by a slow pan across the Welsh landscape, a configuration that suggests the same retreating movement as the distant views that close *A Canterbury Tale*, and similarly associates the natural environment with mystical properties. Burton and O'Sullivan equate *The Halfway House* with *A Canterbury Tale* in the way that both films present their landscapes 'picturesquely … as soothing and regenerative spaces' (2009, 62). The observation is apposite, for choral voices that accompany landscape imagery act to celebrate the natural environment and to imbue it with an aura of mystical potential.

Choral Voices and Natural Forces

As we have seen, wordless choral voices can invest the sequences that include them with a sense of mysticism and wonder. Wordless choral effects are a recurring aural presence in films that emphasise the natural environment and its effect on their characters. P. Adams Sitney notes that the introduction of sound into cinema gives landscape a voice. The inclusion of natural sounds expands the 'auditory environment … beyond the visible frame' and thus vitalises landscape images (1993, 110). This effect is heightened by music, and wordless choral singing frequently amplifies the mystical or spiritual elements in the natural landscape in British cinema. Jumeau-Lafond (1997, 266) notes the recurring use of the wordless chorus to 'endow nature with a sacred quality' in the art music of French composers and such British composers as Frederick Delius and Ralph Vaughan Williams.[6] In a film score, wordless choral singing used in this way can also imbue our understanding of a character's subjectivity with a particularly heightened poetic feeling. Wordless voices suggest both a presence and an absence: the presence from which the voices emanate and the intangible and ethereal nature of unseen and indistinct beings.

The otherworldliness of disembodied voices can create an aura of temporal distance, of the past and of memory. When Andrew Gray (Niall MacGinnis) surveys the deserted and ruined cottages on his return to the island in *The Edge of the World*, the women's wordless singing evokes the ghosts of the past. In a double-exposure, spectral images of the former islanders file past him as his memories fill the screen. The disembodied voices do not emanate from the ghostly figures, although they are amalgamated with them in the frame of Andrew's memory to present a potent nostalgic vision through which we are drawn back in time towards the film's central flashback narrative (Fig. 5.2).

Choral voices similarly act as ghostly echoes of the past in *Black Narcissus*, and remind us of how much this film shares with Powell's first personal project. In the introductory montage prompted by Mr Dean's letter to the nuns, as he narrates in voiceover that Ayah lives at the palace with the 'ghosts of bygone days', a chorus of women's voices sings her name and at the same moment the camera takes in the frayed curtains flapping in the wind and the wind chimes sounding at the window. These are joined on the soundtrack by distant cries of 'Ayah' as the camera pans across the faded wall paintings of the old General's concubines. Moments later, the women's voices return accompanied by the sound of the wind

Fig. 5.2 Wordless voices and spectral images in *The Edge of the World*

blowing and the image of dry leaves rustling around the stone steps. The music forges a connection between the spirits of the earlier occupants of the 'House of Women' at Mopu and the wind that blows 'seven days a week' and accordingly affords the ghosts of the past a constant place in the present. Furthermore, the association of the wind with the women's voices casts both as 'signifiers of female sexuality' (Street 2005, 34), and their equation as natural forces by contrast implies that the chaste existence of the nuns is unnatural. The unceasing elemental power of the wind influences the atmosphere at the summit and is a continual reminder of the challenge the nuns face as they attempt to impose order upon it, an exercise whose futility Sister Clodagh (Deborah Kerr) acknowledges when she tells Dean 'I couldn't stop the wind from blowing or the air from being clear as crystal'.

The association of the choral voices with the ghosts of the women and both with the wind has the additional effect of anthropomorphising the wind. The wind is endowed with a human voice and this further imbues it with an aura of intention. This is explicit in the scene in which Sister Ruth

(Kathleen Byron) applies red lipstick and sits with Sister Clodagh. The chorus is heard on the soundtrack, and its connection to the women is reinforced by the images of the murals intercut with those of the candle burning down to indicate the passage of time. The choral chanting reaches a climax (and the sexual metaphor is appropriate) as Sister Ruth's madness erupts into action as if to suggest the uninhibited sexuality of the women of the past bursting through and overwhelming the repressive restraint of the present order. In the climactic moments, Ruth runs along the palace corridor and brushes away the covering that has been placed over the sensual statuary in a symbolic representation of the spirits of the palace's earlier occupants reasserting their control and undermining the order that the nuns have sought to impose on the location. The pulse and volume of Brian Easdale's choir steadily and inexorably increase in a way that recalls Vaughan Williams's suite for solo viola, small (wordless) chorus and small orchestra, *Flos Campi* (1925), a celebration of earthly love in which each section is prefaced by a quotation from the Song of Solomon. Vaughan Williams adopts a pastoral idiom, employing long melodic lines with an improvised feel. Easdale creates a similarly sensuous atmosphere and both pieces build towards a final consummation. However, Easdale's voices are denied the ecstatic and transcendent musical release granted to those of Vaughan Williams. Instead, Easdale points up Sister Ruth's frustration by using a hauntingly yearning melody to accompany her exploration of Dean's home, which sharpens in contrast the violence of his rejection of her and the closing off of the hope that her passion will be requited. Easdale's chorus is firmly associated with the ghosts of the past and the wind that always blows in *Black Narcissus*, with the result that we are made aware of the haunting by aural as well as visual means. The circular association between the wind, the women and the choral voices infuses each element with the aura of the other two, so that the presence of one evokes the presence of all three.

The effect of the swelling choral chanting in the climactic sequence of *Black Narcissus* is paralleled in the 'Death Pack' sections of Brian Easdale's score for Powell and Pressburger's *Gone to Earth* (1950). The vocalising is again wordless, or virtually wordless; the words 'Tally Ho' are incorporated into the sounds that indicate the eerie presence of the ghostly hunters. The choral voices introduce two key sequences that frame the film's narrative arc. The film's heroine, Hazel Woodus (Jennifer Jones), is a child of nature whose belief in the folkloric superstitions passed down to her by her gypsy mother enables the men who desire her to take advantage of her innocence. As in Mary Webb's source novel of 1917, Hazel is equated with Foxy, the wild fox she cares for, while Reddin (David Farrar), the squire who seduces her away from her gentle but unpassionate husband, with the ghostly Black Huntsman and his spectral hounds. Easdale's main theme is heard prominently throughout the film, frequently on horns that accentuate its connection to hunting, to Reddin and to Hazel's superstitious beliefs, to the extent that the motif comes to represent fate. Specifically it represents Hazel's fate as Reddin's quarry and endows it with an aura of tragic predestination.

The sense of predestination, the working of fate towards an unavoidable outcome, is also expressed through the use of the wordless choral voices in the opening and closing sequences of the film. The opening segment presages Hazel's end, hunted down by the fox hounds and riders. Easdale's main theme sounds on horns while the camera slowly pans across the landscape at dusk. Out on the hill, Hazel picks up Foxy, pauses as she hears the hunting horns, and looks up to see the darkening sky and the spindly trees silhouetted against it. She breaks into a run, and her flight is intercut with shots of other animals—a rabbit, a mouse, a hen and its chicks, a sheep and a lamb—fleeing the pack as the cries of the hunters and the baying hounds usher the urgent orchestral accompaniment onto the soundtrack. The hunters' cries become more organised into wordless vocal chanting in a steady insistent rhythm that grows increasingly agitated and urgent as it builds to a fevered climax, until with a scream Hazel rushes into the cottage and shuts the door behind her. At this point, the sounds quickly fade, the main theme is heard more distantly on the horns and Hazel sees a calmer sunset landscape as she looks out through the cottage window. The hunters are not seen on screen and remain a purely aural presence, which posits them as part of Hazel's subjective experience.

The opening scenes prioritise Hazel's subjectivity, and align the audience with her point of view. The music provides the sense of a pathetic fallacy where Hazel's experience is expressed in the natural elements as the skies darken and the choral chanting seems to chase her to the cottage door. The scene is Pressburger's creation. Its closest parallel in Mary Webb's novel is a description of Hazel being woken in the night by Foxy's bark and suspecting the vixen may have scented the 'death pack':

> It was said that the death pack, phantom hounds of a bad squire … scoured the country on dark stormy nights. Harm was for the house past which it streamed, death for those that heard it give tongue (1979, 17)

The fatalistic premonition of the film's tragic end contained in this opening sequence is also suggested visually. Natacha Thiéry (2005, 233) notes that, as in *Black Narcissus* and *The Red Shoes* (Powell and Pressburger, 1948), the death of the female character in *Gone to Earth* is visually anticipated in the early part of the film. When Hazel enters the cottage she is framed, holding Foxy, in the outline of the coffin her father is working on, thus she is marked with 'the seal of death' (ibid., 238) (Fig. 5.3). Not only does this presage her death, but the wooden frame of the coffin provides a visual parallel to the rotted timbers around the disused mine-shaft down which Hazel will plunge to her death while fleeing with Foxy from the hunters and hounds at the end of the film.

Death, Thiéry finds, lingers as a 'vaguely felt presentiment ... hidden in the images' of the Romantic landscape, in the 'twilight effects, red and orange skies streaked with clouds, dark and twisted tree trunks' (2005, 234). I would contend that while the presentiment of death may hover in the visual shadows, its presence is signalled consistently and forcefully in

Fig. 5.3 Hazel's fate anticipated visually in *Gone to Earth*

the film's musical score. This occurs not only through the choral effect that accompanies the 'death pack', but also prominently through Easdale's main motif, heard at least fifteen times in the film, frequently on the horns that evoke the mythical hunters and equate them with Reddin as he pursues Hazel. In observing that the film 'is like a hunt, with Hazel as the prey', Thiéry (ibid., 231) encapsulates the narrative energy of the film but overlooks Easdale's contribution to it. The saturated palette of Christopher Challis's striking landscapes visually renders Mary Webb's richly evocative descriptions:

> The red light from the west stained her ... The small clouds that went westward took each in its turn the prevailing colour, and vanished, dipped in blood (Webb 1979, 14)

In the same way, the unashamedly poetic style of Webb's prose demands the bold melodramatic force of Easdale's score, which matches the intensity of its expression, and seems to draw its inspiration directly from the pages of the novel, as in this description of Hunter's Spinney:

> Here the Black Huntsman stalled his steed, and the death-pack coming to its precincts, ceased into the hill. Here, in November twilights, when the dumb birds cowered in the dark pines, you might hear from the summit a horn blown very clearly, with tuneful devilry, and a scattered sound of deep barking like the noise of sawing timber, and then the blood-curdling tumult of the pack at feeding time (Webb 1979, 67)

In Easdale's score, a 'horn blown very clearly' forms the main recurring motif, and the choral chanting that aurally depicts the baying 'sound of deep barking' builds to a 'blood-curdling tumult' in Hazel's flight to the cottage and again in the final moments of the film. Easdale supplies a musical analogue to Webb's heightened poetic language.

The wordless chorus returns to the soundtrack as a threatening element when Hazel again finds and picks up Foxy in the closing sequence of the film, the shots intercut with those of the hounds and the hunters seeking a kill. The opening scenes are evoked visually in the repeated use of shots of a rabbit and mouse at this point, confirming the sense of predestination contained in the opening scene. The music is tremulous with mounting drumbeats and the voices now form a more brooding, rumbling presence before they begin to chant under the building orchestral swell. Once

Hazel starts to run, the music drops out to leave only the diegetic sounds of the hunt, the horns, the baying of the hounds and the thrum of the horses' hooves. Following this expression of musical restraint, the orchestra returns only briefly to build quickly with the chanting chorus as Hazel, the pack at her heels and the huntsmen imploring her to drop the vixen, falls into the gaping shaft.

Brian Easdale's use of the chorus in *Gone to Earth* to represent the relentless momentum of the hunt is prefigured in the 'Hunting Song' that he composed for the hunting scenes contained in Sister Clodagh's flashback memories of Ireland in *Black Narcissus*. Sarah Street notes the parallel in the combination of landscapes and natural sounds in both films (2012, 159), and they may also be equated in their use of a wordless chanting chorus to express an inexorable and potently surging drive towards a tragic fate. Powell provided Easdale with 'pages of detailed notes' on his musical requirements for *Gone to Earth*, and the composer responded with a highly effective score (Lane 2011, 11), although the complications of co-production with David Selznick and the controversy of its afterlife have tended to overshadow the merits of the film and to dominate the discourse surrounding it.

Other films use wordless choral effects as a means to imbue elemental forces with a less specific personification that nevertheless strongly suggests a mystical or spiritual enactment of intention. In *I Know Where I'm Going!*, for instance, at the point where Joan's travel schedule is blown from her hand into the sea, Allan Gray introduces a wordless women's chorus that takes over the soundtrack from the male voiceover reciting the itinerary. The male voice quickly fades as though easily overpowered by the natural forces represented by the women's voices, which conspire to arrest Joan's progress. The elemental power personified in the female voices silences the voice of male authority and ends the illusion that Joan is in control of her journey or the destiny that it symbolises. Perhaps through a primal connection between the fecundity of the land and that of women, and ancient notions of 'Mother Earth' and 'Mother Nature', natural forces are most frequently associated with the feminine in this group of films.

A wordless female chorus similarly embodies the sea in Vaughan Williams's score for *The Loves of Joanna Godden*. As in *I Know Where I'm Going!*, the voices enter the soundtrack when the elemental forces they personify exert their influence over the characters. Joanna (Googie Withers) is troubled as she tries to relax on the beach at Dungeness while

Fig. 5.4 The drowning sequence in *The Loves of Joanna Godden*

Martin (Derek Bond) swims. The female chorus enters softly to accompany a close-up of Joanna sleepily laying her head on the pebbles (Fig. 5.4). She wakes to realise that Martin is not there. Loud orchestral blasts match her action as she rises to a sitting position and they express her agitation as she fears the worst. As Martin's discarded towel is revealed bobbing in the shallow waves, the women's voices return more insistently as if to suggest that the sea itself is taunting Joanna with its success at having widowed her, and, reading more deeply, that she is being punished by natural forces for transgressing her 'natural' place as a woman. The wordless voices endow the sea with a sense of intention, in a reflection of the poetic and Romantic formulation whereby those who have drowned are said to have been 'taken' by the sea.

The association of women's voices with elemental forces draws further resonance from its connection to female spirits in folklore, such as the Sirens of Greek mythology, the Wilis of Slavic folklore and the Valkyries of Norse legend. The many regional variants of the Wilis feed into wider cultural forms, from the eponymous water nymph in Dvořák's opera *Rusalka*, to *Giselle* in Adam's ballet and Puccini's first opera, the one-act

Le Villi. In the latter two examples the Wilis are the spirits of maidens who, having died of broken hearts, take their revenge on unfaithful men by dancing them to death. The Valkyries of Norse mythology, the female figures who decide who will live and die in battle and attend to the needs of the fallen in the afterlife, perhaps gain their widest cultural currency through Wagner's retelling of these myths in *Der Ring des Nibelungen*. In film culture, a Valkyrie figure is explicitly conjured in Eisenstein's *Alexander Nevsky* (1938). In the calm following the battle on the ice, an off-screen mezzo-soprano sings Prokofiev's lament for the fallen Russian warriors:

> He who fell for Rus in noble death,
> His dead eyes will I kiss, his cold brow caress.
> And to him, brave lad, who remained alive,
> I shall be a true and loving wife

While the camera pans over the fallen soldiers, Olga (Vera Ivashova) wanders among them with a flaming torch while the men variously call out 'Maria', 'Izyaslava', 'Nastasia', 'Sister mine'. In this way, the disembodied voice represents all of the women loved by the men and her voice is cast as the one they hear in their last moments of life. Through her presence, Olga is associated with the sentiments expressed in the lament, although it is not suggested that she is the singer, and therefore the solo voice retains a universality that speaks to all of the men on the battlefield.

Although not wordless, the plangent quality of Prokofiev's battlefield lament in *Alexander Nevsky* connects it to the Irish keen, a wailing vocalised outpouring of grief sung by funeral mourners. In his score for *Captain Boycott* (Frank Launder, 1947), William Alwyn adapts a keening melody that he had noted on a trip to Ireland to research local music for the film (Johnson 2005, 165). The film's titles appear in front of a succession of dissolving shots showing the progress of a horse-drawn mail coach through the spectacular Irish landscape. Alwyn accompanies the sequence with the keening melody for solo soprano, performed by an uncredited Joan Cross (ibid., 168). The keening voice returns briefly in the latter part of the film, first to accompany shots of women witnessing the destruction of a cottage, and then to suggest a diegetic presence as a funeral procession passes through the town. In the title sequence, though, the voice creates an effect similar to the use of folk song (examples of which Alwyn also collected and used in the score[7]) in its suggestion of the people's connection to the land and to the spectacular mountain scenery.

The wordless keening melody echoes the solo soprano heard in Vaughan Williams's *Pastoral Symphony* (1921), a work inspired by the composer's recollection of his wartime experience at Écoivres and 'a wonderful Corot-like landscape in the sunset' (Vaughan Williams 1964, 121). Here the soprano vocalises without words. For Wilfrid Mellers (1989, 92), this 'angelic messenger' bears a poignant promise of rebirth, while for Hugh Ottaway (1972, 25) she signifies an 'essential bond of blessedness between Man and Nature'. Vaughan Williams's use of the female voice is a recurring element in both his film music and his concert work, and can be seen as a thread that unites these passages in terms of their effect. Kennedy notes the strong impression made across the composer's output by the '"vocal" use of instruments', and conversely, of voices used (with particular reference to *Flos Campi*) as 'instrumental colouring', revealing Vaughan Williams's 'preoccupation with sonorities' (1980, 171, 211). Mellers highlights the 'mysterious, erotic-ethereal' sonority created in the combination of viola and solo flute in *Flos Campi*, and the way the strings recall their use in the *Pastoral Symphony*, as 'sighing winds or supernatural creatures' which can also be heard anthropomorphically as 'equivalents to human misery or despair' (1989, 108). These techniques are evident again in the one-act opera *Riders to the Sea* (1925), where they 'emulate wild wind and surging sea', and are used to devastating effect in the *Sinfonia Antartica*, Vaughan Williams's re-working of his music for *Scott of the Antarctic* (ibid.). Ottaway similarly finds precedents in *Riders to the Sea* for the atmospheric techniques employed by Vaughan Williams for the *Scott* music (notably the keening voices, wind machine, and certain orchestral textures), as well as the common theme of 'Man versus Nature, with Man bravely accepting his loss of the battle'. Never before, Ottaway notes, had Vaughan Williams 'written so atmospherically' (1972, 50). Kennedy concurs that the music for *Scott of the Antarctic* reveals an 'enlargement of [the composer's] vocabulary' that encompasses the virtuosic handling of the large orchestra in *The Loves of Joanna Godden*, and is hinted at in the desolate music that accompanies the outbreak of foot and mouth disease in that film (1980, 359).

Kennedy points out that writing music for films seems to have rekindled in the composer the opulence of his earlier orchestral style, now 'matured by experience' (1980, 279). Vaughan Williams had also gained experience of the practical side of the film industry, and, before agreeing to accept the commission for *Scott of the Antarctic*, he requested a conference to ensure his 'very definite ideas' about the music would accord with those of the filmmakers (reprinted in Cobbe 2002, 415). At Ernest Irving's suggestion, he negotiated a number of conditions concerning how the music would be used in conjunction with dialogue and sound effects (Irving 1959, 175–6). When concern was expressed over the inclusion of the wordless soprano voices, Irving explained to Vaughan Williams in humorous verses that reference both the English soprano Margaret (Mabel) Ritchie,[8] and C. A. Lejeune, the film critic of *The Observer* throughout this period:

> Miss Mabel Ritchie's off-stage tune
> Besides annoying Miss Lejeune
> Would cover, blur, confine and fog
> Our most expensive dialogue …

Ursula Vaughan Williams reports that the composer insisted upon the inclusion of the soprano (and small female chorus), and eventually 'converted Irving who in turn converted the authorities' (1964, 279).

In *Scott of the Antarctic*, the music represents the environment, and positions it as a significant character in the narrative. The bleak and inhospitable location is echoed in the wind machine while the mystical vocalising of the wordless soprano brings to Scott's journey the sense of a spiritual quest. Irving notes Vaughan Williams's 'predilection for the human voice', and that in addition to writing songs, oratorios and operas, the composer 'frequently uses it symphonically, without words, just as he employs other reed instruments in the orchestra' (1948, 145). In his programme note for the *Sinfonia Antartica*, Vaughan Williams notes the 'women's voices used orchestrally' (reprinted in Manning 2008, 371). The wordless singing of the soprano that conveys the notion of the polar expedition as a spiritual journey for Scott reflects a preoccupation with this theme that runs through much of Vaughan Williams's work.[9] The female voice, at once elemental and ethereal, is also presented as a siren-like call to the men that draws them away from their wives and summons them back to the Antarctic wastes. The soprano personifies the lure of the frozen continent, and imbues it with a mystical aura of knowing intention. The film begins as Scott leaves the Antarctic, and John Mills narrates Scott's diary entry in voiceover: 'I leave behind a whole continent, vast, mysterious, inhospitable, and still … unknown'. The music that incorporates the wordless female voices begins on his last word and ushers in a montage of still images of the terrain and film of powdery snow blowing in waves over the

Fig. 5.5 Wordless voices and frozen landscapes in *Scott of the Antarctic*

frozen plains (Fig. 5.5). This opening sequence was unusual in being expanded and edited by the filmmakers to accommodate Vaughan Williams's music once they realised how effectively it brought the images to life (Huntley in Oliver 1999, 161). The wordless female voices return briefly but emphatically to the soundtrack to accompany the wind that blows into the tent when Captain Oates (Derek Bond) sacrifices himself with the words 'I am just going outside and may be some time', and again finally when the ill-fated expedition is lost. Each recurrence attests to the wordless vocalising as the siren call of the frozen environment.

Irving (1948, 145) acknowledges the soprano voice as the 'siren-lure of the Antarctic', and this allusion is reiterated in the film by Kathleen Scott (Diana Churchill), when she tells her husband 'You knew the Antarctic long before you knew me. I always knew you'd go back and I'm not the least jealous'. This recalls the speech made by Celia Johnson in *In Which We Serve* (Noel Coward, David Lean, 1942), in which she refers to the ship as a rival for her husband's attention, and is one of the subtle ways the later film adopts something of the spirit of a war film. *Scott of the Antarctic* bears a narrative similarity to war films that detail the selection and training of an expert group for a particular mission, such as *Against the Wind* (Charles Crichton, 1948) and *The Cockleshell Heroes* (José Ferrer, 1955). Frend had first considered the idea of the film in 1939, although he recognised that its story of heroic failure would be 'more acceptable in peacetime than in wartime' (1948, 137). *Scott of the Antarctic* is further aligned with the British war film in its adoption of a documentary aesthetic. The film visually recreates a number of Herbert Ponting's famous photographs of the original expedition and his documentary film *The Great White Silence* (1924), and it aspires to a level of documentary authenticity by including instruments and other items from the expedition as set decoration (James 1948, 44). Charles Frend stresses the semi-documentary style of the film and feels that Scott's diary provided the opportunity to use his voice as a commentary to 'link episodes and bridge transitions' and to tell the story 'from Scott's viewpoint' (1948, 140–1). However, the film does not question that viewpoint, or Scott's motives, as Barr points out, it dutifully recreates the expedition, 're-enacting but not analysing its failure' (1977, 79). Insofar as the musical score represents the environment, it may share this 'tact which avoids intruding into "personal" feeling' (ibid.), although it simultaneously compromises it by inscribing a spiritual symbolism to the expedition.

While the music foregrounds the adverse conditions of the environment, it also presents the elements as challenges to be overcome by the expedition. The orchestral elements that create the desolate sound world are identified by Ottaway as, in addition to harp and strings, the 'hard, icy glitter of piano and xylophone; the more silvery tone of glockenspiel and celesta; the luminous, watery quality of the vibraphone' (1972, 50). Ursula Vaughan Williams recalled that the composer was excited by the challenge to invent

> musical equivalents for the physical sensations of ice, of wind blowing over the great, uninhabited desolation, of stubborn and impassable ridges of black and ice-covered rock (1964, 279)

Vaughan Williams also provided music for the two women in the film, Scott and Wilson's wives Kathleen and Oriana, although this is only heard fleetingly in the film and held at a very low volume on the soundtrack. Moreover, when the men recall their wives at the end of the film, the montage sequence that illustrates their recollections is unscored. In this way, the emotional centre of the film remains Scott and his single-minded quest, and the score fulfils Irving's wish for the music to 'bring to the screen the hidden and spiritual illustration into which the camera, however ably directed, is unable to peer' (1948, 144). Whereas Vaughan Williams's score for *The Loves of Joanna Godden* mirrors Joanna's emotional state and filters its pastoral celebrations through her experience of the landscape, there is a clear gender divide between the emotional subjectivity it expresses and that which in *Scott of the Antarctic* is diffused into the overarching sense of a spiritual journey for its protagonist. The later film resists the use of music in a melodramatic mode, and thereby avoids the suggestion of uncontained emotional excess and maintains an 'appropriate' masculine restraint towards any overt display of feeling. The men's emotions are registered through their understatement and self-control, the depth of their emotions expressed through the recognition of the effort of their containment. In a way that is characteristic of the representation of Englishness in British cinema of this era, 'feeling is expressed in what is not said or done' (Dyer 1994, 17).

In *Scott of the Antarctic*, the women's wordless vocalising is heard fleetingly on only three occasions, and yet it leaves a memorable impression. The potent effect of choral voices may belie the restraint with which they are introduced onto a film's soundtrack. This restraint is apparent in instances of choral voices joining the film's final fanfare in an uplifting manner, as noted in *Things To Come* and *The Halfway House*, although the wordless nondiegetic chorus is used equally sparingly in *I Know Where I'm Going!* and *The Loves of Joanna Godden*. The additional expense and complication of including choral voices for these brief moments indicates the value placed upon their expressive possibilities by the composers and music directors responsible.

A clear pattern of division emerges in the use of choral voices and in the effects they create in British cinema of this period. Choral voices are either employed as a category of pre-existing music, introduced diegetically for their religious connotations, or they vocalise wordlessly on the nondiegetic soundtrack. It is in the latter incarnation that choral forces find their boldest expression—as a musical sonority that suggests the workings of an otherworldly power, the presence of ancestral spirits, or one that personifies natural forces and endows them with an aura of mystical intention. Young (1962, 55) suggests that choral music is distinctive in its 'natural contiguity to words'. Indeed, in its original context of religious worship the music is the means to deliver the message of the words, which are of paramount importance. When they are absent, Reid (1963, 275) mourns the lack of words, and finds the wordless choral voices in Delius's *A Song to the High Hills* and *A Mass of Life* 'an evasion of the voice's grand function … to articulate thought'. However, removing choral voices from a religious setting divests them of any liturgical obligation and consequently liberates their broader expressive potential.

Wordless choral voices are found most frequently in the scores of classically trained composers, those whose compositions outside of the film industry include choral or vocal works; Arthur Bliss, Lord Berners, William Walton, and with most consistency, Ralph Vaughan Williams and Brian Easdale. The scoring of choral music represents an area of intersection between a composer's work for the film studios and that for the concert hall. Vaughan Williams provides the clearest example, for his use of wordless voices as an orchestral sonority equates his film music stylistically with his broader musical output. Perhaps more than any other British composer of the period, Vaughan Williams's music forms an integrated whole that sees no alteration in style between film and concert work. This is most evident in the adaptation of his film score for *Scott of the Antarctic* into his seventh symphony, the *Sinfonia Antartica*. Vaughan Williams's programme note to the symphony states that the work was 'suggested' by the film score, and that some of the themes were 'derived from my incidental music to that film' (reprinted in Manning 2008, 371). The composer sought to play down the close connection between the score and the symphony, perhaps out of a concern for the critical disapprobation that might greet any music deemed overly programmatic. In a letter to his publisher, Alan Frank, in May 1952 Vaughan Williams expresses concern that the symphony might be thought 'a mere bit of carpentry', and adds candidly 'which, as a matter of fact, it largely is; but don't tell anybody this' (reprinted in Cobbe 2002, 499).

A comparable relationship between film music and concert music may be found in the case of William Walton, whose film scores, notably those for Olivier's Shakespeare films, were adapted for performance in the concert hall. In his music for *Henry V*, and in the suite adapted from it, Walton embraces the principle of drawing on music of earlier periods in order to create an atmosphere of continuity with the past, together with a sense of national feeling, highly appropriate to the propaganda mission of the film. Walton demonstrates the technical ability to absorb music from multiple sources and to blend it into a coherent entity. With a fresh and modern musical voice, he encompasses the sonorities and styles of earlier musical periods without the whole striking a note of artifice. The composer was outspoken, though, in his disdain for the folk song school. 'There's no overwhelming reason', he stated in 1942, 'that modern English music should chew a straw, wear a smock-frock, and travel by stage-coach. Folk-tunes … are all the same' (quoted in Lloyd 2001, 263). Nevertheless, he adopts a method not dissimilar to composers who drew inspiration from earlier modes in order to weave these influences into a contemporary musical framework. In a similar way to folk song, choral voices may register as an element of archaism, harking back to an earlier time and promoting notions of stability and reassurance arising from their links to a national musical heritage.

There is a remarkable unity of purpose in how these films employ their wordless choruses. A distinction, perhaps only a subtle one, may be drawn between the wordless choral voices of Vaughan Williams, which personify and represent natural forces, and those of Brian Easdale, which associate the voices of ancestral and mythical forces with natural forces and bring them into choral expression. Both use wordless voices systematically to evoke mystical feelings and to connect them with natural forces and the natural environment, and in so doing create a strong sense of place and, in giving voice to the location, emphasise its role as a character in the narrative. In this way, both composers adapt a musical form with a heritage of spiritual representation and use it to foreground an existing cultural sensitivity to the natural environment and landscape. Choral voices may illustrate the workings of mystical elements, they may represent those elements for characters in the narrative, or they may seek to reproduce the feeling of an otherworldly presence for the audience. In addition, they are able to inscribe upon the narratives they accompany an epic dimension, a suggestion not only of stoicism, of an elevated nobility of feeling for characters or themes, but also by evoking a mystical presence they suggest a sense of predestination, of events unfolding according to a pre-ordained plan. Fatalism and notions of predestination are also aroused by some of the examples explored in the next chapter, where we take a step away from music in a pastoral idiom to consider the varied use of the march in British film culture. The march may be primarily associated with the war film, where its stable rhythm provides stirring and memorable thematic material, although as we shall see, other genres exploit the range of connotations available to its diverse styles.

Notes

1. The choral societies and the choral festivals nurtured the tradition of choral music in Britain, and led to the commissioning of works that are now mainstays of the choral repertoire. Hubert Parry's *Scenes from Prometheus Unbound* was premiered in 1880, and followed in 1887 by *Blest Pair of Sirens*. Elgar's *Dream of Gerontius* (1900) was written for the Birmingham Festival, as were the two completed oratorios of the composer's planned trilogy: *The Apostles* and *The Kingdom*. Vaughan Williams's choral *Sea Symphony* was first performed at the Leeds Festival in 1910; Walton's *Belshazzar's Feast* in 1931 again in Leeds. In more recent times, Young (1962, 278) identifies a strand of '"ethical" cantata' in which modern music seeks to address contemporary matters; into this category may be placed Vaughan Williams's *Dona Nobis Pacem* (1936), Michael Tippett's *A Child of Our Time* (1944) and Britten's *War Requiem* (1962).
2. British Film Institute Special Collections, Music Cue Sheet MUS-1140.
3. The reference in the name 'Maddalena' to the redeemed sinner Mary Magdalene is appropriate given the character's dual personality and the constant danger of her slipping back to her less respectable side.
4. Lane also suggests the probability of one of the singers being Irving's wife, who would later perform a similar vocal role on the soundtrack of *Scott of the Antarctic* (2008, 13).
5. Lord Berners composed a waltz to accompany the séance scene, and it is played on the piano diegetically by Davies (Esmond Knight) during the sequence. Used in truncated form in the film, Berners titled it *Valse* and published the whole piece as part of his complete piano works (Lane 2008, 13). The use of a waltz for the séance invites comparison with the shimmering waltz theme that Richard Addinsell provides for the ghostly Elvira in *Blithe Spirit* (David Lean, 1945), herself summoned back to an earthly plane by the séance in Lean's film.
6. Jumeau-Lafond writes: '"silent" voices are often used to illustrate those privileged moments in the score which endow nature with a sacred quality' ('des voix "silencieuses" pour illustrer un moment privilégié de la partition, et où s'exprime une sacralisation de la nature que l'on rencontrera bien souvent', 1997, 266, my translation).
7. The music cue sheet for *Captain Boycott* includes 'God Save Ireland', 'The Girl I Left Behind Me', 'The Heights of Alma', 'Cruiskeen Lawn' and other Irish melodies and dances arranged by William Alwyn (Music Cue Sheet MUS-195, BFI Special Collections).
8. Margaret Ritchie originated roles in the Benjamin Britten operas *The Rape of Lucretia* (1946) and *Albert Herring* (1947) and appeared as the soprano Adelina Patti in *Pink String and Sealing Wax* (Robert Hamer, 1945).

9. The theme of a spiritual journey is found in the composer's settings of the poems of Walt Whitman in the song for chorus and orchestra *Toward the Unknown Region* (1907) and the *Sea Symphony* (1910), and in his fascination with John Bunyan's *The Pilgrim's Progress*. Vaughan Williams produced incidental music for a stage performance of Bunyan's allegorical work in 1906, as well as a one-act pastoral *The Shepherds of the Delectable Mountains* in 1922, before completing his own operatic adaptation in 1949, first performed at Covent Garden in 1951. Ottaway notes the 'borrowings' from the Bunyan music that are to be found in the composer's Fifth Symphony (1972, 35–6). Eric Saylor (2013, 171–4) details Vaughan Williams's settings of Bunyan, and Grimley notes a connection with the *Pastoral Symphony* (2008, 172).

References

Barr, Charles. 1977. *Ealing Studios*. London: Cameron & Tayleur in association with David & Charles.

Burton, Alan, and Tim O'Sullivan. 2009. *The Cinema of Basil Dearden and Michael Relph*. Edinburgh: Edinburgh University Press.

Clifford, Hubert. 1944. Walton's Henry V Music. *Tempo* 9: 173–174.

Cobbe, Hugh, ed. 2002. *Letters of Ralph Vaughan Williams, 1895–1958*. Oxford: Oxford University Press.

Davies, Anthony. 1988. *Filming Shakespeare's Plays: The Adaptations of Laurence Olivier, Orson Welles, Peter Brook and Akira Kurosawa*. Cambridge: Cambridge University Press.

Donnelly, K.J. 1997. Wicked Sounds and Magic Melodies: Music in 1940s Gainsborough Melodrama. In *Gainsborough Pictures*, ed. Pam Cook, 155–169. London/Washington: Cassell.

Dyer, Richard. 1994. Feeling English. *Sight & Sound* 4 (3): 16–19.

Frend, Charles. 1948. Introduction to the Scott Film. In *Scott of the Antarctic: The Film and Its Production*, ed. David James, 136–142. Neasden: Convoy Publications.

Geduld, Harry M. 1973. *Filmguide to Henry V*. Bloomington: Indiana University Press.

Grimley, Daniel M. 2008. Music, Ice, and the Geometry of Fear: Vaughan Williams's *Sinfonia Antarctic*. *The Musical Quarterly* 91 (1–2): 116–150.

Irving, Ernest. 1948. The Music – An Interim Report. In *Scott of the Antarctic: The Film and Its Production*, ed. David James, 144–146. Neasden: Convoy Publications.

———. 1959. *Cue for Music*. London: Dobson Books.

James, David. 1948. *Scott of the Antarctic: The Film and Its Production*. Neasden: Convoy Publications.

Johnson, Ian. 2005. *William Alwyn, The Art of Film Music*. Woodbridge: The Boydell Press.

Jumeau-Lafond, Jean-David. 1997. Le chœur sans paroles ou les voix du sublime. *Revue de musicology* T. 83e (2e): 263–279.

Kennedy, Michael. 1980. *The Works of Ralph Vaughan Williams*. London: Oxford University Press.

Lane, Philip. 2008. Booklet Notes to 'The Film Music of Constant Lambert and Lord Berners', Chandos CD CHAN 10459.

———. 2011. Booklet Notes to 'The Film Music of Brian Easdale', Chandos CD CHAN 10636.

Lloyd, Stephen. 2001. *William Walton: Muse of Fire*. Woodbridge: Boydell Press.

Manning, David, ed. 2008. *Vaughan Williams on Music*. Oxford: Oxford University Press.

Manvell, Roger, and John Huntley. 1975. *The Technique of Film Music*. London: Focal Press.

McGuire, Charles Edward. 2013. Large Choral Works, and the British Festival Tradition. In *The Cambridge Companion to Vaughan Williams*, ed. Alain Frogley and Aidan J. Thomson, 121–135. Cambridge: Cambridge University Press.

Mellers, Wilfrid. 1989. *Vaughan Williams and the Vision of Albion*. London: Barrie & Jenkins.

Moor, Andrew. 2005. *Powell & Pressburger: A Cinema of Magic Spaces*. London: I. B. Tauris.

Oliver, Michael, ed. 1999. *Settling the Score: A Journey Through the Music of the Twentieth Century*. London: Faber & Faber.

Ottaway, Hugh. 1972. *Vaughan Williams Symphonies*. London: BBC Publications.

Palmer, Christopher. 1972. Walton's Film Music. *The Musical Times* 113 (1549): 249–252.

———. 1990. Booklet Notes to 'William Walton: Henry V', Chandos CD CHAN 10437 X.

Powell, Michael. 1986. *A Life in Movies*. London: Heinemann. Reprinted 2000: Faber & Faber.

Reid, Charles. 1963. Britain from Stanford to Vaughan Williams. In *Choral Music*, ed. Arthur Jacobs, 266–285. Harmondsworth: Penguin.

Saylor, Eric. 2013. Music for Stage and Film. In *The Cambridge Companion to Vaughan Williams*, ed. Alain Frogley and Aidan J. Thomson, 157–178. Cambridge: Cambridge University Press.

Sitney, P. Adams. 1993. Landscape in the Cinema: The Rhythms of the World and the Camera. In *Landscape, Natural Beauty and the Arts*, ed. Salim Kemal and Ivan Gaskell, 103–126. Cambridge: Cambridge University Press.

Street, Sarah. 2005. *Black Narcissus*. London: I. B. Tauris.

———. 2012. *Colour Films in Britain: The Negotiation of Innovation 1900–55*. London: British Film Institute & Palgrave Macmillan.

Thiéry, Natacha. 2005. That Obscure Subject of Desire: Powell's Women, 1945–50. In *The Cinema of Michael Powell: International Perspectives on an English Film-Maker*, ed. Ian Christie and Andrew Moor, 224–238. London: British Film Institute.

Vaughan Williams, Ursula. 1964. *R.V.W. A Biography of Ralph Vaughan Williams*. London: Oxford University Press.

Webb, Mary. 1979. *Gone to Earth*. London: Virago.

Young, Percy M. 1962. *The Choral Tradition*. London: Hutchinson.

CHAPTER 6

The March: Military and Ceremonial Music

In British cinema, music in a rhythm suggestive of marching infuses films with a military flavour, a sense of collective action and a potent charge of patriotism. The composers working in the British industry exploit these connotations to provide stirring march themes that are often employed in a restrained manner that inflects the films with a deeper British resonance. While the effects created by march themes vary according to their orchestration, tempo and character, they are united in drawing upon a rich heritage of British military and ceremonial music.

The lineage of the march themes composed for British films can be traced back to the popular marches played by British military bands. The military bands had a substantial impact upon musical culture in Britain, and this reverberates through British art music and thereby through British film music. The first noted regimental bands were small groups, established by officers in the elite London regiments in the late eighteenth century, and were staffed by professional musicians working on a freelance basis (Herbert and Barlow 2013, 6). In a parallel to the musicians who were later employed in the British film industry, these professional players would combine their work for the regiments with seats in theatre orchestras and other musical activities. By the beginning of the nineteenth century, the burgeoning popularity of military bands led to an increase in both their size and number, and brought with it a growing demand for musicians. This expansion of musical activity generated a greater demand

P. Mazey, *British Film Music*, Palgrave Studies in Audio-Visual Culture, https://doi.org/10.1007/978-3-030-33550-2_6

for wind and brass instruments, for which the military was the largest customer.

In addition, the refinement of the valve system for brass instruments and the improvement of key systems for woodwind instruments that occurred in the first half of the nineteenth century were prompted by the needs of the military bands (Farmer 1950, 44–45). These ameliorations brought benefits to amateur musicians, those who played in brass bands for example, through the economies of scale achieved with industrial production methods as well as the fact that the instruments were 'generally more efficient and easier to learn' (Herbert and Barlow 2013, 2). In the second half of the nineteenth century the military bands became increasingly standardised and professional, and the establishment of the Royal Military School of Music, at Kneller Hall in Twickenham in 1857, marks a key stage in this process. Through this evolution and development of the military bands, 'the idiom of military music ... became embedded in the British musical consciousness' (ibid., 6).

In the second half of the nineteenth century, military bands and military music took an increasingly important role in ceremonial state events, and this was to alter the way they were perceived. While military music was 'genuinely admired as a form of cultural patriotism', it was its use in ceremony and grand ritual that marked it out as a separate and 'essentially functional species' (ibid., 216). The establishment recognised the power of military music in state ceremonials, as a means of bolstering the 'imperial image of the British monarchy at a time when its real political power was in decline' (ibid., 225–6). Thus, military music engendered patriotism and loyalty on a wide scale in the same way that the specific marches adopted by individual regiments fostered a sense of shared identity and loyalty at a more local level. The tunes adopted by the individual regiments were sometimes especially composed by the bandmasters. More often, though, in a situation unique to the British Army, they were 'arrangements of folk songs associated with the counties and districts to which the regiments were linked' (Murray 2001, 687). The broader repertoire of the military bands was wide-ranging, and its intersections with art music often took an oblique rather than a direct form. At both public concerts and private events in the officers' mess, the military band was not confined to playing military music, and programmes included 'popular overtures, marches, some dance music and operatic transcriptions' (Herbert and Barlow 2013, 235). The military bands' influence on art music lay less in the composition of new music designed for them, and more in their role in originating and popularising the march as a musical genre, which 'contributed to a style that was seen as quintessentially British' (ibid., 13).

This style is perhaps most associated with Edward Elgar, whose music is suffused with marches. The *Pomp and Circumstance Marches* are the best-known, although Jerrold Northrop Moore notes that it is the slow march—'the march of reflection, nostalgia, elegy even'—that spreads its character through Elgar's large-scale works, the symphonies and oratorios (2004, 13). Elgar embraces the march both in compositions with a particularly military flavour or ceremonial purpose and those without. The unity of his approach highlights the same practice in concert composers working in the film industry, whose use of march rhythms across their musical output demonstrates a level of integration between the varied musical disciplines with which they engage. While it is not unusual for film music to adopt a range of musical genres, it gains in significance here in light of the ability of the march to imbue a score with a 'quintessentially British' inflection through its art music heritage.

Commentators frequently acknowledge the influence of Elgar when they describe marches in film scores. Richards (1997, 36), for example, uses the term 'Elgarian' to describe John Greenwood's score for *The Drum*; Riley (2010, 254) uses it in relation to Bliss's *Things To Come* march, and the term positively proliferates in assessments of William Walton's output. Howes (1965, 133) and Palmer (1972, 249) use it in relation to his 'Spitfire Prelude'; Kennedy (1989, 113) to his march for *Next of Kin* (Thorold Dickinson, 1942); and Lloyd (2001, 227) to Walton's title music for *Richard III*. It is perhaps unsurprising that Elgar should be evoked so regularly in discussions of Walton's work, for not only was the younger composer to make the march 'peculiarly his own' (Lloyd 2001, 158), but he was to follow Elgar in achieving success with his ceremonial marches. Elgar had composed his *Imperial March* for Queen Victoria's Diamond Jubilee in 1897. Walton's coronation marches, *Crown Imperial* in 1937 for the coronation of George VI, and *Orb and Sceptre* for that of Elizabeth II in 1953, enjoy a continued popularity well beyond the ceremonial occasions that inspired them.

Moreover, when Howes hears in Walton's *Spitfire Prelude* an 'Elgarian march like *Crown Imperial*' (1965, 133), he acknowledges a musical influence that straddles the composer's work in different areas and closes the more arbitrary divisions between them. A wide use of the march across a composer's output may be most apparent with Walton, although his is not an isolated case. When Hans Keller writes about Arthur Benjamin's score for the documentary *The Conquest of Everest* (George Lowe, 1953), he notes the march as a 'characteristic preoccupation' of the composer, evident in both his film music and in his music for the concert hall (2006, 127). The march is a genre that can span the diverse areas of a film composer's musical activity and act as a point of intersection between them.

In the later nineteenth century, the military march was revitalised by the American composer John Philip Sousa (1854–1932), and by the younger British composer, Kenneth J. Alford (1881–1945), who in turn was influenced by Sousa. Kenneth J. Alford (a pseudonym for Major F. J. Ricketts) served in India as a cornet-player with the Royal Irish Regiment before studying at Kneller Hall and qualifying in 1908 to begin his career as a bandmaster. His first marches were published in 1912. After serving as Director of Music for the Royal Marines from 1927, Alford was brought out of retirement during the Second World War and continued to compose marches (Self 2001, 365). Alford's marches are 'notable for their clipped melodic phrases, economy of instrumentation, and unusually wide range of moods' (Lamb 2001, 815). One of his best-known, *Colonel Bogey* (1913) was used to good effect in David Lean's *The Bridge on the River Kwai* (1957), which exploited its popularity, and its common currency as a morale-boosting propaganda song with alternative lyrics. In this instance a pre-existing march is used within a film score, although a reciprocal cross-over also takes place, with military bands including march themes composed for films in their repertory. Lamb (ibid.) cites as examples both Eric Coates's march from *The Dam Busters* and Ron Goodwin's from *633 Squadron* (Walter Grauman, 1964). Thus the successive levels of influence come full circle, with the popular marches written as film themes taken up by the military bands which had first originated and popularised march music. Before moving on to explore some of the more popular march themes, I will begin with a brief consideration of the march when it is used as one component of a film's score, rather than its main thematic element.

Isolated Uses of the March

The simplicity of the strong beat and regular rhythm that typifies the march makes it an exceedingly memorable musical type. After first hearing Arthur Bliss's concert suite of the music for *Things To Come*, Christopher Frayling recalled that he 'was humming the *March* for days' (1995, 9). The first part of Bliss's march is heard in the opening section of *Things To*

Fig. 6.1 Marching soldiers in *Things To Come*

Come, where it scores a montage of shots that depict the mobilisation of forces and preparations for war, the attack and the ongoing conflict. The montage includes shots of the shadows of silhouetted soldiers marching across the screen in an expressionistic suggestion of the anonymous sacrifice of the men (Fig. 6.1). Donnelly notes that the march theme 'is not subordinate to the dynamics of any action, but occupies the foreground and articulates the visual proceedings'. In its recollection of 'the Victorian tradition of celebrative martial music', it is 'slightly reminiscent of Elgar' (Donnelly 2007, 16). The most familiar part of the march theme, the triumphal section, is reserved for the entrance of the swaggering Boss (Ralph Richardson), preceded on screen by groups of marching soldiers and drummers. The theme is subsequently restated as he returns to Everytown in triumph after the defeat of the hillmen. It plays again under his grandly declaimed speech and is reiterated briefly at the close of it. This rousing section of the march theme neither accompanies, nor is associated with, the spectacle of combat in the film. Instead, it underlines the arrogant triumphalism of the character of the Boss. The suggestion contained within the march rhythm of the onward progress of a group who move in unison and thus act as one body may be undermined by the association of its most memorable section with one individual. Alternatively, this can be read as acknowledging how the loyalty and patriotism engendered by the march is one of the means by which service personnel are encouraged to serve the interests of the ruling classes.

In an introduction to a BBC radio broadcast of his suite of the film music in 1950, Bliss felt that the march 'served as a motto theme for the whole film' (reprinted in Roscow 1991, 192), although this may overstate somewhat its thematic relevance to the film, as its association with the Boss precludes its return after his demise, a little after the halfway point in the film's running time. Nevertheless, Bliss's score remains highly effective, particularly in the film's striking montage sequences, where the music is permitted to determine the rhythm of the images. Although it does not act as the main theme of the film, the straightforward and stable rhythm of the march makes it the most memorable part of the score.

The martial origins of the march form are often reflected in orchestrations that favour instruments with military connotations, primarily those associated with the military band. The specific number and combination of instruments in the military band is not prescribed, but evolved to include wind, brass, and percussion (Herbert and Barlow 2013, 23). This derives from the historical use of these instruments in military life, as a means of communicating on the battlefield, regulating time-keeping, and identifying between friend and foe before the widespread introduction of national uniforms (Murray 2001, 686–7). These martial connotations can be exploited within a film score without the use of the march form.

For instance, in *The Four Feathers*, the young Harry Faversham (Clive Baxter) retires from the dinner given by his father, the General (Allan Jeayes), for his former military comrades. General Faversham has earlier confided to Dr Sutton (Frederick Culley) his concerns about his son—although the boy has been sent to a military school, he has been found reading poetry ('Shelley, of all people'), and needs to be licked into shape and 'made hard'. Miklos Rózsa's music enters with an eerie woodwind figure punctuated by pizzicato strings as Harry pauses outside the dining room to light a candle and then from Harry's point of view we see his shadow fall across a succession of military paintings, presumably of his ancestors, as he makes his way towards the stairs. When he reaches two paintings of men in bright red uniforms, the music adds a ghostly trumpet fanfare to highlight their military prowess and heighten by contrast Harry's sense of inadequacy. Dr Sutton interrupts the scene to offer his

Fig. 6.2 Military instruments conjure echoes of the past in *The Four Feathers*

friendship to Harry, and then as Harry continues the music returns, together with another trumpet fanfare as he pauses before a large painting of a cavalryman, the picture flanked by two suits of armour that further emphasise the military ambience that surrounds him (Fig. 6.2). The image cuts to a closer shot of Harry, and a steady drumbeat briefly joins the soundtrack as the scene fades to black. Herbert and Barlow note the particular status awarded to drummers and trumpeters in comparison to other military musicians. Prior to the development of the military bands, drummers and trumpeters fulfilled a military role by communicating messages to the troops, as well as being 'custodians of the cadence of the march'. In addition, until the mid-eighteenth century, they were 'usually multi-linguists' who were able to 'act as emissaries' and liaise with enemy camps (2013, 3). Rózsa takes advantage of these historical associations and uses the trumpet fanfares and drumming to point up the military expectations placed upon the reluctant Harry by his father and to emphasise the resigned melancholy of Harry's position. In this way, the military fanfare also encompasses a sense of patriotic duty. In the next shot, without music, a title indicates that ten years have elapsed and the adult Harry marches at the front of a red-coated regiment whose uniforms recall those of his forbears in the paintings.

Although this example from *The Four Feathers* proves an exception, an onscreen image that contains characters who march in a regular rhythm conventionally calls for music that marches in step with them. This provides an opportunity for the composer to demonstrate a clear coincidence between image and soundtrack and tie the two together in a moment of strong synchronisation. Points of closer synchronisation between music and image, Donnelly notes, 'constitute something of a repose, a default position of normality that furnishes moments of comfort in a potentially threatening environment' (2014, 73). March rhythms are able to provide such restful moments and thus reassure the audience of a level of connectedness between the screen image and the nondiegetic score. A brief example occurs in *Oliver Twist*, with the cue entitled 'Mr Bumble's March' and marked 'Pomposo – Vivace' (pompous and lively). On screen, we see Mr Bumble (Francis L. Sullivan) march Oliver (John Howard Davies) to Sowerberry's funeral parlour. Given that Bax struggled with the music, and Lean assisted him with extensive explanatory notes, it seems unlikely that the composer would have provided this cue prior to filming. Nevertheless, each beat of Bax's music coincides with Bumble's footsteps to match exactly the onscreen movement and a close bond is forged between image and music. The use of the march here accentuates the uneven balance of power between Mr Bumble and Oliver and heightens the former's sense of self-importance and the latter's innocence and vulnerability. Its inclusion in the score remains an isolated use, and it does not form part of the film's thematic material. The march rhythm, with its strong martial connotations bolstered by the use of instruments associated with the military, was to reach its fullest expression in the British war film, a genre that would gain in significance during the Second World War and the postwar era.

The March as Theme Tune

When the cinemas reopened after initially closing at the beginning of the war, the film industry, under the influence of the Ministry of Information Films Division, rose to the challenge of producing films that embodied the propaganda themes set out by the Ministry: 'I. What Britain is fighting for. II. How Britain fights. III. The need for sacrifices if the fight is to be won'

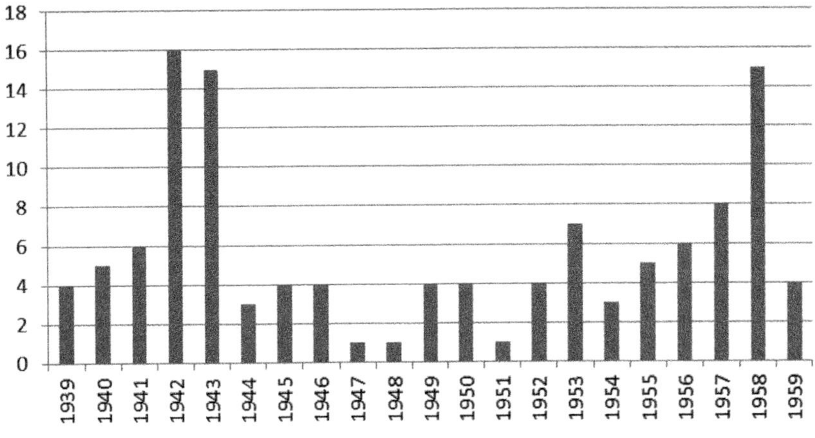

Fig. 6.3 Number of British war films by year

(memorandum reproduced in Christie 1978, 121–124). The industry responded with a 'surge of creativity' which saw attention focused for the first time 'squarely and continuously on the projection of Britain and the British people' (Aldgate and Richards 2002, 57). Along with 'comedies; historical films; and costume melodramas', the most dominant genre was the war film (Street 2009, 60), and the number of war films released rose sharply in the early 1940s (Fig. 6.3). During the first years of the war, *Convoy* (Pen Tennyson, 1940) and *The First of the Few* (1942) were the most popular British films of their years, while in 1941 and 1943, *49th Parallel* and *In Which We Serve* (1942) were the biggest box-office draws overall (figures in Gifford 1986).

Figure 6.3 illustrates the resurgence of the war film as a popular genre in the 1950s, when it reached a peak in terms of numbers comparable with that of the war years. War films again performed well at the box office, with *The Cruel Sea* (1953), *The Dam Busters* (1955), *Reach for the Sky* (1956) and *The Bridge on the River Kwai* (1957) proving top earners. During the Second World War, a 'solid tradition of popular British film marches' was established, a tradition consolidated by later British war films (Donnelly 2007, 27), and one in which the march became the default thematic option for the genre. The memorability of march tunes enhances their popularity, and makes them suitable for thematic use within a film score. Not only would a memorable march theme be a potential source of income from sales of sheet music and recordings, thereby raising the profile of the film more broadly, but in its cinematic context the audience would be sure to recognise the tune and to recollect its prior associations within the film.

This memorability is exploited by *Albert, R.N.* (Lewis Gilbert, 1953), whose title sequence introduces Malcolm Arnold's brisk march theme. The march is not heard again until nearly halfway through the film's running time, when it accompanies the scenes of prisoners-of-war being marched to bathing facilities outside of the camp's perimeter fence. The film's plot details the plan for a man to escape by hiding in the bathhouse when the other prisoners leave. Albert, a wooden dummy, takes the escaping prisoner's place when the men are counted in on their return to the camp, thereby delaying the discovery that he is missing. Arnold's march joins the scenes of the marching men, and follows the convention of matching their action and starting and stopping in alignment with their movements. Every aspect of the first journey to the bathhouse is covered in detail on screen: the men's journey from the camp, their arrival at the bathhouse, how the escaping man hides in a changing cubicle, how Albert is put together from the parts each man has hidden, and how two men flank Albert and carry him back to the camp in full sight of the guards. The journeys to and from the bathhouse are both scored by the march theme, which rings out stirringly as the men re-enter the camp. A second escape attempt is depicted on screen with far greater brevity, beginning with the men assembled ready to march back to the camp after bathing. The guard shouts: 'March!', and on cue Arnold's theme begins as the men start walking. The march theme recalls the triumphant success of the previous escape, it provides a unity with the earlier sequence and it enables a far tighter narrative economy in the illustration of the second escape. Arnold's march is heard in the opening and closing title sequences, and five times more within the body of the film, the first four of which accompany the first visit to the bathhouse.

In *Albert, R.N.*, the first restatement of the march theme is held back until the main narrative episode that the film has been leading up to. One interpretation of this would be as a form of what Guido Heldt has described as 'retrospective prolepsis' (2013, 228–242), in which the music in a title sequence acts as a foreshadowing, or prolepsis, of a key narrative event which only becomes apparent in retrospect. However, Heldt finds this most pronounced with music that is heard nondiegetically prior to entering the diegetic plane, while that which operates with 'nondiegetic music alone' constitutes a 'weaker version' of the formulation (ibid., 239). In the war films under consideration here, the opening music presents the main march theme, and it sets the tone of the film. Aligned with this mood-setting element is the sense in which music that prefigures narrative events implies a prior knowledge of them, and 'construes the narration as one in the past tense' (ibid., 235). This is certainly appropriate to the 1950s war films and their frequent dramatisation of real events that had occurred in what was then the recent past. Notwithstanding the implication of a 'past tense' narration, the holding back of the march theme in *Albert, R.N.* represents a level of deferral not found in Heldt's key examples,[1] and is a strong marker of the musical restraint shown by the film's score. It is a pattern paralleled by other films that employ a march as their main musical theme, two of which I would like to explore in more detail: *The First of the Few* (Leslie Howard, 1942) and *The Dam Busters* (Michael Anderson, 1955). Both William Walton's *Spitfire Prelude and Fugue* and Eric Coates's *Dam Busters' March* circulate outside of the films they first appeared in, and enjoy continued popularity in concert and on recordings.

After the opening titles of *The First of the Few*, Walton's Spitfire theme withdraws for an hour and a half before it returns to crown triumphantly a montage depicting the construction of the Spitfire. Walton's fugue, which in parts resembles 'the "revving" of the aeroplane engine' (Howes 1965, 134), was composed to accompany this sequence. Palmer feels the 'special function' of this march is 'to return at the main climax of the fugue, the fugal rhythm and figuration being maintained as counterpoint' (1972, 249). Ronald Howard (1981, 113) reports the disappointment felt by Adrian Brunel, an uncredited assistant director, that much of the material he had filmed for the montage sequence did not make it into the final cut of the film. This suggests the possibility that the montage may have been edited to fit Walton's music. In either case, there is no doubting the effectiveness of this sequence, culminating in 'one of Walton's finest marches' in a 'splendid performance' conducted by Muir Mathieson (Lloyd 2001, 184).

The restraint demonstrated by holding back the restatement of the march theme is echoed more than a decade later in *The Dam Busters.* John Ramsden (2003, 100) finds Walton's *Spitfire Prelude* 'appropriately close in feel' to Eric Coates's *Dam Busters' March.* The themes also find a parallel in that both are introduced in the title sequences of the film, and, in common with Arnold's march in *Albert, R.N.*, then retire, in the case of *The Dam Busters* for over an hour of screen time, before being heard again.

The Dam Busters exhibits further musical moderation; music joins the soundtrack, frequently unobtrusively, for less than a third of the film's running time, and the raid itself is for the large part accompanied only by the diegetic sound of engine noise. Ramsden (ibid., 102) attributes the restricted use of Coates's march to the film's director, Michael Anderson, and to composer Leighton Lucas, although he overlooks the contribution of musical director Louis Levy.

Leighton Lucas, I would propose, deserves a greater share of the credit for the success of the music in the film than history has accorded him. Ramsden (ibid.) praises Lucas's expert use of Coates's 'big tune' and notes that he 'also provided music of his own ... as backdrop to earlier scenes'. However, this understates the measure of Lucas's achievement, which was to write a film score, with its own discrete theme that was able to blend with and incorporate Coates's. Eric Coates himself had little interest in writing film music—for *The Dam Busters*, he revised a patriotic march he had written in 1943 'in honour of the Eighth Army's victory at the Battle of Alamein' (ibid., 99). Philip Lane (2012, 14) observes that Lucas's theme 'seems to play hide and seek with Coates's throughout the film, both vying for supremacy', and that the score 'predominantly comprises variations on the two themes, and little else'. At the end of the film's prelude and title sequence, Lucas's theme (a series of four rising notes) blends with Coates's theme, which then gives way to it. Lucas's theme dominates the scenes of Barnes Wallis's (Michael Redgrave) tests and dealings with government bureaucracy which occupy the first hour of the film. Overall, Lucas's theme, in varied form, is heard more frequently than Coates's (eleven times to Coates's eight), with the result that the familiar Coates tune does not seem over-used in the film, and the sense of musical restraint is maintained.

When Coates's march does return, it is first haltingly teased at and only stated fully when the day of the raid dawns and the men gather to be briefed. Thus Coates's *Dam Busters' March* is tied exclusively to 617 Squadron and to the raid itself, in the same way that Walton's Spitfire music is tied to the construction of the aeroplane in *The First of the Few* and Arnold's march is tied to the acts of escape in *Albert, R.N.* In *The Dam Busters*, Coates's march is heard in a minor key and at a slow tempo in the sequence where Gibson (Richard Todd) briefly mourns his dog. He finds the dog's lead and notices the scratches his pet has made on the doorpost, and here the music underlines a 'tug at the heart-strings harder than the film allows for any human bereavement' (Ramsden 2003, 80).

Fig. 6.4 Eric Coates's theme associated exclusively with the mission in *The Dam Busters*

The music synchronises gently with Gibson's onscreen action of dropping the dog's lead into the wastepaper basket, and thereby locks itself to the image. Coates's theme continues on the soundtrack to accompany the scenes of the men as they while away the time until the evening, heard on muted brass reminiscent of the *Last Post* as the evening falls. The theme then swells in orchestration and volume to a full-blooded statement of the tune as the men are transported to the Lancaster bombers for the raid, before it fades down when Gibson's truck slows and comes to a halt before the plane (Fig. 6.4). The scenes of the raid itself are accompanied only by the diegetic drone of the engines and the flak guns, and music does not return to break the tension until the success of the mission is revealed.

The tumultuous music (beginning with a jolting stinger) that scores the scenes of flooding and devastation incorporates both themes, and Coates's march is restated triumphantly for a quickly curtailed moment of celebration in the operations room. After the musical silence of the scenes that show the exhausted men coming back to the base, Coates's theme returns softly to accompany the radio broadcast that describes the raid and bridges the transition to the following morning. The film uses the actual BBC broadcast of 18 May 1943, by the wartime newsreader Frank Phillips, and Ramsden notes the strong claim it makes for the film's documentary authenticity (2003, 91–2). Both *The First of the Few* and *The Dam Busters* emphasise their factual credentials at the outset, in the opening sequence and the title sequence, respectively. *The First of the Few* begins with a montage of newsreel footage that graphically outlines the progress of the Nazi war machine and incorporates shots of Hitler, Goebbels, and Goering. Walton scores these with direct references to Wagner's Ring Cycle, drawn from the descent to Nibelheim in *Das Rheingold* and the Magic Fire music in *Die Walküre*, which in their evocation of steel and fire symbolise the industrial technology involved. This contrasts strongly with the musical silence as Churchill's speech fills the soundtrack ('We shall defend our island, and with the British Empire around us we shall fight on, unconquerable, until the curse of Hitler is lifted from the brows of men'). The potent propaganda of this montage reflects the morale-boosting function of much wartime British cinema, made at a time when the outcome of the conflict was uncertain. After the newsreel introduction, the film opens on 'Zero Day September 15th, 1940', at the height of the Battle of Britain, when Geoffrey Crisp (David Niven) introduces the main flashback narrative to explain to the young pilots the genesis of the Spitfire and its designer, R.J. Mitchell (Leslie Howard).

The original story from which the screenplay was produced had been approved by Mitchell's widow, who also attended and advised on the filming (Lloyd 2001, 183). *The Dam Busters* credits its source material, Paul Brickhill's book and Gibson's memoirs. In addition, it acknowledges the assistance of the RAF, the survivors of 617 Squadron and the next of kin of those who lost their lives, and thereby bolsters its claim to authenticity (Ramsden 1998, 50; 2003, 53). The film's director, Michael Anderson, has spoken of his efforts to cast the characters 'to their near physical likeness'. Where possible, Anderson 'spoke to survivors … [and] went to great trouble to try and get the people in each plane as near to those who took part in the raid themselves'. The director explains that he saw this striving for authenticity in his visual recreation as his responsibility 'to the people who were in the planes' (Anderson 1967). Both films deploy a similar iconography in their title sequences that emphasises their aeronautical themes by using shots filmed from above the clouds, although *The First of the Few* uses black titles on a paler background in an effects shot, in comparison to *The Dam Busters*, which uses white titles against an authentic darker sky. *The First of the Few* and *The Dam Busters* thus share many aspects in common: their use of a stirring march theme that has gained popularity beyond the film; their restraint in holding back the restatement of the march theme within the film; and their strong claim for the documentary authenticity of their narratives.

However, the two films also differ in certain areas of representation that reflect the times of their making. Put simply, war films made during the war tend to promote and celebrate the collaborative efforts of all sections of society in support of the 'People's War', whereas the focus of the war films made in the postwar period tends to foreground the achievements of the male officer class and obscure the contributions of civilians, the working class and women. Christine Geraghty notes the common theme of endurance in the war films of the forties and fifties, although those of the latter decade altered the focus on who was seen to be 'doing the enduring':

> In films of the 1940s, the war was fought by whole communities, including the working class, women and civilians, but the fifties war film tends to place an emphasis on a small male group, largely made up of officers and 'boffins' (2000, 181)

The active involvement of Mitchell's widow in *The First of the Few* makes it unthinkable that her role would have been side-lined in the film's representation of events in the way that women are marginalised in *The Dam Busters*. Ramsden notes that the last appearance of the only named female character in this film, Mrs Wallis (Ursula Jeans), occurs after only a quarter of the film's running time has passed, and the only women heard thereafter will be 'anonymous WRAFs offering bacon and eggs and cups of cocoa' (2003, 64). A similar marginalisation takes place in the film's treatment of the working class characters, evinced in the final credits, which list Gibson's batman (Harold Goodwin) at the end and deny him his name ('Crosby'), in contrast to the titles, decorations and subsequent ranks given in detail for each of the officers (ibid., 95). So apparent is this shift in focus between war films made during the war and those made in the following decade that Richards regards it as a 'new generic development', in which 'Britain's finest hour' is recreated 'conspicuously … as a celebration of the officer class' (1997, 144).

This altered emphasis is apparent in a popular sub-genre of the war film, the prisoner-of-war film. *The Captive Heart*, made during the war (although not released until April 1946) includes 'the experiences of working class characters … [and] the prisoners' emotional relationships with their wives and families at home' (Geraghty 2000, 183). With the exception of a later entry in the genre (*The Password is Courage* (Andrew Stone, 1962)), the 1950s prisoner-of-war narratives focus on officer-only camps, 'and hence avoid working-class characters' and concentrate on escape attempts rather than thoughts of home, and thereby tend to exclude female characters (Cull 2002, 288). Films that follow this pattern include *Albert, R.N.*, *The Wooden Horse* (Jack Lee, 1950), *The Colditz Story* (Guy Hamilton, 1955) and *Danger Within* (Don Chaffey, 1959). In this way, the broader and more inclusive representation of shared wartime experience shifts to become a distorted vision that ignores the contribution of the wider community. The marginalisation of the working class, civilians, and particularly of women, is also subtly contributed to by the predominance of the march rhythm in the musical scores of the 1950s war films. In contrast to the communal singing that brought together the group and upheld morale in the community films of the 1940s, typified by *Millions Like Us* (Launder and Gilliat, 1943), the march themes of the 1950s convey a revised perspective that implicitly discounts women and civilians. Although the form of the march may represent the group collectively in its expression of a body of individuals moving in unison, and thus may intersect with the role taken by group singing and music-making in the 1940s films, the powerful military (and pointedly masculine) associations of the march have the effect of excluding women and civilians from the span of its musical embrace. The revised and narrowed perspective of the 1950s war film may account for its more frequent use of a recurring march theme, in contrast with the films of the 1940s. March tunes were composed for films in the earlier decade (Walton, for example, provided them for *Next of Kin* and *Went the Day Well?*), although they were less likely to be the main recurring theme or to score the main narrative event of these films. Thus the march rhythm, when used as the primary recurring theme, operates as a means to efface the contribution of women and civilians in the war effort and to confer its uplifting sense of success upon the exclusively male officer class.

The musical simplicity of the march and the triumphant uplift it is able to convey belies the range of expressive possibilities it can encompass when it is varied and combined with onscreen events. The rhythmic stability and straightforwardness of the march and the image of marching it evokes can suggest a strong forward progression. This inherent sense of onward momentum makes the march rhythm a particularly appropriate musical theme for war films that feature a journey or military mission as their main narrative event. Typically, the restatement of the march theme will signal the continuation of the journey after some setback and will provide the audience with a level of reassurance. I would like to look more closely at two films from the 1950s that use recurring march themes in this way. Both *Sea of Sand* (Guy Green, 1958) and *Ice Cold in Alex* (J. Lee Thompson, 1958) build their narratives around the North African campaign of the Second World War; both introduce scenes of their protagonists negotiating minefields; and both include extensive location shooting in the deserts of Libya. In addition, both films incorporate march themes into their scores, although in notably different ways that produce different effects.

Sea of Sand was made by Tempean Films, a company set up by Bob Baker and Monty Berman, and was an exception to its usual output of 'B' features. Baker and Berman were both experienced cameramen who had met in the African desert when they were transferred into the Army Film Unit during the war, an experience they drew upon when making this film (McFarlane 2003, 177). The narrative follows a patrol of the Long Range Desert Group to destroy a German fuel dump behind enemy lines. In many respects, *Sea of Sand* is more closely aligned with the war subjects of the 1940s, which focus on the bringing together of a diverse group of people to fight for a common cause in the enactment of the concept of the 'people's war', than with the British 1950s war films which tend to celebrate the heroic achievements of the officer class. *Sea of Sand* charts the group spirit that develops between the ranks, regions, and levels of experience represented by the individuals who make up the team. It presents a more diverse group than other war films of the decade, although women remain marginalised, briefly glimpsed only in the photographs of the all-male cast. In *Sea of Sand*, the war-weary but pragmatic Captain Cotton (Michael Craig) is relaxed about the insubordinate manner of chirpy Cockney Brody (Richard Attenborough), who enjoys a bantering friendship with West Country family man 'Blanco' White (Percy Herbert). Cotton gets off on the wrong foot with his new second-in-command, by-the-book Williams (John Gregson), as the two men embody very different styles of leadership. Williams saves the group from discovery by speaking German, and offers moral support and encouragement to the innocent young Scot Mathieson (Barry Foster). Williams proves his worth and is integrated into the group as the film progresses, and then sacrifices himself in order to save his colleagues.

After the dark foreboding of *Sea of Sand*'s title sequence, Clifton Parker's score begins with a jaunty march theme. James Marshall (2005, 10) describes the march as one of the composer's catchiest film tunes, and it is heard only in the earlier, more optimistic sections of the film where it accompanies scenes of the convoy setting off cheerfully, and it stops and starts in alignment with the group's progress. Two further times the march theme accompanies the convoy as it restarts its journey after setbacks. The theme becomes progressively more lugubrious on each occasion, before it ushers in a more sinuous melody that slowly winds forward and banishes the cheerful mood of the march. As the film progresses, the tone of the music darkens as the drama intensifies and the narrative becomes more serious with each loss the group suffers. The main march theme drops out of the soundtrack after just over a quarter of an hour of screen time, and only returns to lend a brighter tone to the end titles.

In both *Sea of Sand* and *Ice Cold in Alex*, the main march theme, as well as being heard on the nondiegetic soundtrack, is also introduced diegetically. In *Sea of Sand*, the tune is whistled by Brody, one of the drivers, as the trucks depart; in *Ice Cold in Alex*, it is Tom (Harry Andrews) who whistles it as the ambulance approaches Alexandria (Fig. 6.5). The diegetic incorporation of the march theme in both films has four effects. First, it increases audience awareness of the theme and thereby marks it as significant. Second, it ties together the nondiegetic music and the world of the diegesis and confirms their interconnected nature. In both films, the march tune is whistled in synchrony with its nondiegetic presence on the soundtrack, as though the characters may be hearing the nondiegetic music and absent-mindedly accompanying it. The effect is to pull together the nondiegetic and diegetic soundtracks, melding them into a single entity and emphatically aligning the nondiegetic score with the experiences and emotions of the characters. Third, as it confirms that the march theme is part of the diegetic experience of the characters, and that they are sufficiently familiar with it to whistle its tune, these scenes introduce the further suggestion that the march theme may be one particularly associated with the regiment or unit that the men belong to. Soldiers felt a stronger sense of attachment and loyalty to their own regiments than to the British Army as a whole (Herbert and Barlow 2013, 219), and a march adopted by a regiment would therefore carry connotations of loyalty and patriotism, as well as the greater sense of commitment fostered by a shared group identity. Fourth, it conforms to Heldt's formulation of 'retrospective prolepsis', whereby the earlier nondiegetic statements of the march

Fig. 6.5 The march theme whistled in *Sea of Sand* (above) and *Ice Cold in Alex* (below)

theme foreshadow its entry to the diegetic plane and retrospectively imbue its previous hearings with greater significance (2013, 231).

In both films, the brief scene in which the march theme is whistled is post-synchronised. In *Sea of Sand*, Marshall (2005, 10) suggests that Richard Attenborough is most probably miming the whistle, and this is borne out by a closer viewing of the scene—Attenborough simply keeps his lips pursed throughout the shot. In *Ice Cold in Alex*, Harry Andrews takes a breath, and the whistling begins on the soundtrack as he purses his lips as though to produce the sound himself. In each film the scene is brief and no further synchronisation is attempted, although the effect would still have added an additional complication to the sound editing process. It is therefore a measure of the significance accorded to these moments that the filmmakers deemed them of sufficient importance to address the challenge required to include them.

Both *Sea of Sand* and *Ice Cold in Alex* initiate their narrative lines by establishing the nervous fragility of the officers in charge, and then assign them to journeys and situations that will push them to their limits. Andrew Spicer includes both in his discussion of a wider group of films that, in their portrayals of 'men-on-the-edge', reflect the time of their making. The Suez crisis of 1956 had rendered the notion of straightforward officer class heroism problematic, and a more sceptical tone prevailed, which was also expressed through location:

> The favoured terrain was no longer the crack unit on a daring raid or the stable microcosm of a ship or an air-force base, but the jungle or the desert where units were trapped, lost, or abandoned to their own devices (Spicer 2001, 45)

John Mills's portrayal of masculinity in crisis is central to *Ice Cold in Alex*. This element connects the film with the postwar pessimism expressed in British film noir, and by Mills himself in a key example, *The Long Memory* (Robert Hamer, 1953). *Ice Cold in Alex* charts Anson's (Mills) trials with alcoholism, fear, impotence, and vulnerability as he seeks to redeem himself after a moment of panic results in a fatal injury for one of the nurses he is transporting across the desert to Alexandria.

Leighton Lucas's march theme dominates the score of *Ice Cold in Alex*. The composer is adept at varying its pace and character according to the narrative situation and using it to hold together montage sequences. The march theme is introduced during the title sequence, and variations of it are then heard on seventeen further occasions throughout the film. It is incorporated into stingers and reverse stings, and brings unity to the episodic structure of the narrative. Its overriding connotation, in whatever guise it appears, is one of a steady forward momentum that mirrors the journey of the ambulance. The theme is appropriately slowed, curtailed or fragmented according to the challenge facing the ambulance at different times.

As the journey is led by Anson, it is possible to read the music as a mirror of his experience and state of mind, particularly as the march theme first occurs in the body of the film to underscore a wry comment he makes about 'dames and mines'. In addition, the scene in which Anson panics and tries to outrun the attacking forces is introduced with a loud orchestral stinger, then a fast-paced version of the march theme, and closes abruptly on a reverse sting when the ambulance's engine is switched off. The spiralling orchestral flourishes that accompany the theme create a sense of the chaotic situation as the other passengers shout at Anson to stop, but they may also be read as a more direct reflection of his panic and confusion. As Anson's quest animates the narrative and his success or failure is directly equated with, and measured by, the progress of the ambulance, a reading of the score as a melodramatic barometer of Anson's emotional state may not be as fanciful as it first seems. The score contains one instance of markedly different music, in the lyrical melody that underscores Anson's love scene with Diana (Sylvia Syms), and this too reflects Anson's emotional state. This romantic theme is held at a very low volume and the controlled approach allows the main theme to form the core of the soundtrack. However, variations on the march theme are also used to score sequences in which it cannot be read straightforwardly as a mirror of Anson's mental equilibrium, such as those involving the group working together to discover van der Poel's (Anthony Quayle) clandestine activities. Ultimately, the film's documentary aspirations and its restrained use of music argue against the more melodramatic reading of its score. *Ice Cold in Alex* resists the pull of the full-blooded male melodrama typified by Douglas Sirk's *Written on the Wind* (1956), in spite of it sharing a number of concerns with Sirk's film, not least in its depiction of alcoholism and impotence.

Ice Cold in Alex announces its claim to authenticity in a pre-title scene-setting prologue in which documentary footage shares the screen with a map of the area while an authoritative male voiceover narrates the progress of the campaign in North Africa: 'Two million men. Two million stories. This is one that happens to be true'. After the title sequence the scene is again set with documentary establishing shots of the conflict. Philip Lane (2012, 15) feels that the orchestral forces used for the film 'sound rather meagre', and this lack of richness in the sound itself confers a further documentary feel upon the proceedings. Viewing this film in the context of earlier productions from the Associated British Picture Corporation (ABPC), Vincent Porter notes its freedom from the influence of musical director Louis Levy, in whose hands the music was sometimes allowed to overwhelm the images and to 'undermine the narrative and visual strategies of ABPC films'. As Levy had died before he was able to work on the film, the producer and editor made the decision to use music 'only where it was absolutely necessary' (2000, 162–3), and this understatement contributes a further sense of documentary to the film. This view of Levy's approach, however, is somewhat at odds with his work on *The Dam Busters*, a film which demonstrates a comparable level of musical restraint.

Although *Ice Cold in Alex* provides opportunities for contemplation of the desert landscape, often filmed in long shots that dwarf the ambulance and magnify the scale of the journey, the most picturesque shots appear without musical accompaniment. This ensures a coherent use of music as a marker of Anson's state of mind and of the progression of the ambulance on its journey, and these silent landscapes emphasise instead the emptiness and hollowness of the indifferent landscape. The terrain is thus presented as a challenge to be met rather than a site for visual pleasure, and the resistance of the spectacular mode prevents the film from breaking the tension for the audience by taking the focus away from this narrative line. Fred Inglis reflects this virtue in the film by contrasting it favourably with *The Bridge on the River Kwai*, in which David Lean's 'indulgence of the picturesque fairly runs away with him into the lusciousness of Burmese travelogue' (2003, 48). *Ice Cold in Alex* resists this impulse and even foregrounds the centrality of its location in its narrative resolution. Gill Plain notes the 'unprecedented development' in a British war film of the Nazi spy van der Poel, who is not only saved from discovery by the British characters but vindicated in recognition of his contribution to a shared struggle against the '"greater enemy" of the desert' (2006, 159).

In addition to their prominent use of march themes, *Sea of Sand* and *Ice Cold in Alex* share further common elements. The most pronounced is the similarity of their narrative lines and the episodic structure of the challenges encountered on the journeys. Both films indicate at the outset the emotional tensions preying on their lead characters; for Anson, his alcoholism and the fact that he and a colleague are both in love with the same woman; for Cotton, his failure in love (indicated by the pieces of a torn-up photograph of an unnamed woman) and his jaded attitude to the war. However, whereas *Sea of Sand* harks back to the 'group' films of the 1940s with its regionally diverse mix of characters coming together against a common foe, the smaller group in *Ice Cold in Alex* is initially united by joint suspicions about van der Poel before working together to ensure the survival of all the characters regardless of the side they are fighting for. *Sea of Sand* has the more conventional narrative, and this conventionality is also evident in its scoring, although it is not without imaginative moments. The musical restraint of *Ice Cold in Alex* adds force to the music when it is heard and the consistent way the thematic material is incorporated unifies the sections of the film into a coherent whole. *Ice Cold in Alex* also stands out for the strong female character played by Sylvia Syms, an 'unusual role' in which the woman 'expects to take an equal part in the struggle' (Harper 2000, 86). The variations on the recurring march theme in *Ice Cold in Alex* include more sombre versions that colour the darker moments of the film. These bring forward a more lugubrious range of connotations that I would like to explore in greater detail by considering films that employ a slow march in their thematic material.

The Slow March and Funeral March

Just as the brighter march rhythm conveys the idea of uplifting progress, the march in a slower tempo can conjure the sense of an arduous journey that extracts a toll from those compelled to undertake it. The steady beat of the slow march has the resonance of the funeral march, and can infuse a film with a funereal atmosphere, as characters are pushed to the limits of their endurance. The funeral march itself is one of the most notable categories in which the march takes a non-military character—Schwandt cites the example of Purcell's funeral music for Queen Mary of 1694 (2001, 817). It was more usual for military bands taking part in state funerals to draw items from the art music repertoire. Herbert and Barlow record the use of the *Dead March* from Handel's *Saul* (1739) and sections from Mendelssohn's *St. Paul* (1836) at the funeral of the Duke of Wellington in 1852, as well as later uses of Beethoven's Funeral March and Chopin's *Marche Funèbre* at state funeral ceremonies (2013, 228, 230–1). The mournful atmosphere created by these funeral marches is similarly invoked by the slow marches employed in film scores to emphasise the challenging journeys of their protagonists.

For *The Captive Heart*, for example, Alan Rawsthorne provides a march theme that expresses the traipsing progress of the prisoners-of-war as they walk wearily and without optimism through France, Belgium, and Holland to the Rhine. Ernest Irving notes that musically it takes the form of a 'canon in two parts', that is 'the tune at the top and in the bass are the same tune, but the bass is half a bar behind the treble', and that it 'fits the dragging feet' of the men (1947, 51). This slow march theme is heard in the film's titles, it accompanies the first shots of the men and the opening narration, and returns as the men resume their journey on foot after travelling part of the way by train. Echoes of the theme recur through the film, and it is associated particularly with Geoffrey (Michael Redgrave) as it underscores his flashback recollection and returns to recall this moment again towards the end of the film when he meets Celia (Rachel Kempson) and retells his story.

In this way, the theme recurs not only to accompany each scene of relentless marching but also to connect the mood of exhausted tramping with the desperate actions taken by Geoffrey, and thereby both to explain his deception and to align him with the other prisoners-of-war. The introduction of such a sombre march rhythm in the title sequence of the film acts to temper any idea of optimism at the outset of the narrative. The unyielding progress of the march theme sets a tone of fortitude and stoic resignation in the film. This tone permeates the narrative and equates the men's experience of the extended march to the prison camp with the ongoing hardship of their day-to-day existence in captivity, and the sense of time suspended even as it moves forward. Geoffrey seeks to articulate this idea of being held in limbo in one of his narrated letters to Celia, where he writes 'it is not the duration, but the indefiniteness of duration, for if a man knew the length of his sentence, he could plan accordingly'. Like the prisoners' experience of time in the camp, the slow march moves steadily forward without conveying any sense of when it might end.

A comparable dark and plodding march creates a similar effect in *A Town Like Alice* (Jack Lee, 1956). The music again follows the convention of starting and stopping in alignment with a gruelling journey, here undertaken on foot by the group of women. Mátyás Seiber's slow march is one of the two main recurring themes in the score, the second being a theme associated with Alice Springs and used lyrically to represent the feelings that develop between Jean (Virginia McKenna) and Joe (Peter Finch), which Hans Keller suggests might be based on an Australian folk song (2006, 201). The lumbering march is introduced briefly when the women are first separated from the men, and it is heard more prominently as they begin their walk to Kuala Lumpur. It follows the pattern of marking a contrast between movement and stasis—it ends as they pause for a break and resumes as they set off again.

At the halfway point in the narrative, the two themes are directly contrasted. Jean steals a brief evening meeting with Joe, and as he speaks of the colours of the Australian landscape the 'Alice' theme begins softly on the soundtrack. The music continues as the camera floats across the image of sleeping children in the tent where Mrs Frith (Nora Nicholson) watches over them as Jean enters. Jean drops to her knees and tells Mrs Frith that Joe had talked about 'a town called Alice'. The music, which has been playing all the while, now surges in the strings to an emotional climax as Jean lets herself fall forward on to the rough bedding and lay her head down as though in a reverie. As the theme continues more calmly and at a lower volume, Jean understates her overwhelming feelings in the line—'he made it sound … alright'. Virginia McKenna (2000) praises the director Jack Lee for capturing in this scene the sensitivity and subtlety of the time, when meaning resided in 'what was perhaps not said and done … just a look says it all'. A look may say it all, but here it has the benefit of Seiber's music to raise the emotional temperature and operate melodramatically as a stand-in for Jean's unexpressed feelings. This emotionally uplifting moment contrasts with the slow plodding theme as the image moves to the following day, and the women resume their trek. The march theme holds together a montage sequence of their ongoing journey as the women seek a camp to take them in. The sombre theme marks the renewed progress of the women's seemingly endless journey and also conveys their steely resignation, in spite of their exhaustion, that they must continue on their way. Its direct contrast with Jean's rapturous meeting acts as a reminder that such moments of joy will be short-lived for the female prisoners, and soon overtaken by the return of their arduous trek. The juxtaposition of the two themes heightens the power of both, as each gains in intensity by its contrast with the other.

An equivalent sense of dogged determination in the face of obstacles is expressed in the slow march that scores the opening titles of *Scott of the Antarctic*. Vaughan Williams's theme is solemn and doleful, and suggests an effortful onward struggle. Ernest Irving sums this up as a 'stark primitive piece typifying strong and unflinching effort against nature and the elements' (1948, 146). The mournful tone is appropriate to the ill-fated expedition, and the statement of this theme at the start of the film sets the atmosphere for the tragedy to unfold. Christopher J. Parker dubs the piece the 'doom motif' and notes that much of the film's music is 'directly or indirectly derived' from it (2001, 13). Vaughan Williams uses the same theme to open his *Sinfonia Antartica*, the symphony he refashioned from the film music, and Ottaway feels that the way it recurs through the movements in this context encourages us to hear it 'as a "motto" basic to the whole work' (1972, 50). In his initial sketches, Vaughan Williams had labelled this theme 'Heroism' (Grimley 2010, 120). This should not, however, suggest an uncomplicated valorisation of Scott, as the composer's widow recalls that he had grown increasingly upset when he learned of the inefficiencies that contributed to the tragic failure of the expedition, and he 'despised heroism that risked lives unnecessarily ... such things as allowing five to travel on rations for four filled him with fury' (Vaughan Williams 1964, 279).

The opening theme recurs at least five times, although less than half of the music Vaughan Williams composed was used on the soundtrack of the film (Parker 2001, 13). This was because the composer preferred to start work before a rough cut or even approximate timings were able to be provided to him. Following a request for timing cues, the music director Ernest Irving wrote to Vaughan Williams in January 1948 to explain that 'no amount of bullying on my part will produce measurements of film that has not yet been shot'. Irving also suggested that when the editing had been undertaken, the composer 'may wish to synchronize some of the happenings a little closer than it is possible to do before shooting' (reprinted in Cobbe 2002, 422). In the event, the full score was delivered in April, and the rough cut of the film completed in June, before its premiere in December of 1948 (Parker 2001, 11). As the music had been written prior to the completion of filming, most of it 'had to be re-shaped after the location and studio shots had been cut together and the editorial department had done its work' (Irving 1948, 145). Parker (2001, 13) rather overstates his claim that Vaughan Williams's music has been 'butchered' into a 'patchwork of soundbites to fit the images and dialogue', given that the composer was at this stage sufficiently experienced in writing for films to be aware that the film would not be edited in order to accommodate the music. Furthermore, Vaughan Williams had himself approved the 'butchering'—Irving reports that 'all structural alterations were carried out under the censorship of the original architect' (1948, 145).

Opinion is divided over whether the slow march acts as a key theme for Captain Scott in the film. Kennedy describes the opening 'doom' motif as a 'great striving theme', and suggests that it may be a 'kind of *leitmotiv* for Scott himself' (2002, 6). This reading is supported by its powerful restatement in the film immediately after Scott has issued instructions to the men as to the route they will take to climb the glacier. While this sequence undoubtedly operates to tie the theme to Scott, I find its effect momentary rather than part of a cumulative pattern to achieve this connection. Parker also raises the possibility of equating the doom motif with Scott, as a means of highlighting 'the irresponsible behaviour of the individual to the detriment of the many', although the film's resistance to the use of music in a melodramatic mode argues against this. Parker's alternative conclusion, that the motif represents the 'fateful journey of the whole expedition party' (2001, 14) accords more closely to its effect within the wider score, where it tends to resist individual attachment, perhaps in part due to the collective associations of the march form. In common with the earlier examples, the slow march theme is associated with the group rather than with the individual, and it recurs through the film as a reminder of the ongoing struggles of the members of the group.

While the march form generally expresses the collective action and experience of a group of characters when used in a film score, the case of the funeral march proves an exception. Although the funeral march suggests a slow procession, a collective expression of memorial, when used in a film score it tends to attach itself to the individual character whose funeral it either accompanies, or, as we shall see, musically foreshadows. I would like to look more closely at two films that specifically associate a funeral march with their lead character. The extended funeral marches in both *Odd Man Out* (1947) and *Hamlet* (1948) are introduced at the outset and imbue their narratives with the sense of an inexorable journey to the grave that their protagonists are powerless to prevent. In both films the funeral marches play a significant role in structuring the narrative.

William Alwyn had been involved with *Odd Man Out* from the stage of its early planning. The director Carol Reed sent a copy of the novel to the composer asking for his thoughts—Alwyn recalls that they 'had often talked of the ideal picture we should like to make with music playing an essential part of the story' (quoted in Johnson 2005, 145). The significance accorded to the music is demonstrated by the reversal of the usual procedure of adding music to the edited film. *Odd Man Out* tells the story of IRA member Johnny (James Mason). Johnny is wounded in a robbery to raise funds for the organisation and falls from the getaway car. The film follows the last eight hours of his life as he trudges through the streets of Belfast meeting people who aid, avoid or seek to use him, before he is shot down by the police. Alwyn composed the main theme and leitmotif for Johnny, the funeral march, before filming began. Alwyn recalls that he and Carol Reed 'worked out the very pace of the music with a piano while I improvised' and that much of the film was 'shot to pre-recordings and transformed and orchestrated afterwards' (quoted in Johnson 2005, 148). James Mason remembers the 'relentless underscoring' that had been pre-recorded 'so that I would never escape from the beat as I played these scenes' (1981, 215). The process of filming to a pre-recorded track grants the music an unusual level of influence and prominence within the film, and contributes to the deeply integrated audiovisual match that the film achieves.

Johnny's theme dominates the score of *Odd Man Out*. It is introduced in the opening title sequence where it accompanies aerial shots of Belfast, and it is then held back from a restatement until more than a third of the film's running time has elapsed. From then on it is heard with growing frequency, and on each hearing it provides structural unity to Johnny's episodic journey 'by cueing each occasion when Johnny leaves a temporary refuge' (Johnson 2005, 149). As the film progresses, the funeral march increasingly overtakes the soundtrack. Dai Vaughan notes a corresponding progressive elimination of the diegetic sound when music is heard, which has the effect of causing Johnny's increasingly delirious state of mind 'to be mirrored in the fabric of the film' (1995, 44). Vaughan notes that the composition of the march prior to shooting allows it to exert a potent air of predestination over narrative events. The funeral march not only signals Johnny's journey to his death, but also grants us a level of access to his subjectivity that banishes the possibility of an alternative outcome. In the final sequence, as Kathleen (Kathleen Ryan) leads him along the railings to the safety of a ship in the dock, Johnny's theme plays steadily. The unwavering progress of the music through a cut to the advancing police-cars 'gives it a quality of the inevitable' (ibid., 63). It may be Kathleen who determines the moment of Johnny's death—she fires shots at the police in the knowledge that their response will be fatal for both her and Johnny—but from the beginning of the film Alwyn's funeral march has made clear that no other ending is possible.

If Alwyn's funeral march rings a slow death knell for Johnny from the start of *Odd Man Out*, a starker effect is achieved in *Hamlet* by the visual depiction of Hamlet's funeral in the opening scenes of the film. The images of the funeral in the title sequence are joined on the soundtrack not, in the usual manner, by a 'thematic exposition', but with an anticipation of the 'final E minor funeral march' (Keller 2006, 180). The dramatic opening of Walton's funeral march sounds as the film's white titles appear in front of a shot of crashing waves with cliffs beyond, and the march continues through the sequence. Several years later, when discussing with his publisher the possibility of compiling a suite from the film music, Walton expresses concern that the funeral march was scored for such an 'enormous' orchestra (quoted in Hayes 2002, 267). For the film soundtrack, Muir Mathieson conducts the Philharmonia Orchestra to striking effect. Palmer notes the 'warmth and intensity of emotion' in the music, as well as its 'grandeur and dignity' (1990, 6). The music continues as the screen fades to black after the title sequence, then a misty image emerges with a title that identifies the location as 'Elsinore' and the camera looks down upon a model of the castle. The mist returns and Olivier narrates the 'vicious mole of nature' speech as the text of it appears on screen. This image dissolves into a high-angle view looking down on the men carrying Hamlet aloft. The camera moves in to a closer view and Hamlet's lifeless body fills the frame as Olivier narrates the line 'this is the tragedy of a man who could not make up his mind'. This closer composition dissolves to a more distant view, and the pall-bearers and Hamlet fade from the scene to leave the empty battlements. A further dissolve shows us the castle and the fog enveloping it, and the next dissolve takes us to the staircase of the set. The string tremolos that draw the funeral march to a close are heard as Bernardo (Esmond Knight) climbs the stone steps and the music cue ends on the film's first line of dialogue.

By opening the film with a vision of its ending, Olivier emphasises the inevitability of the tragedy. Kenneth S. Rothwell (1999, 59) observes that Olivier 'liked to bracket his films'. This, he notes, follows the pattern set by *Henry V*, in which the action begins and ends in a theatrical performance at the Globe, while the body of the film transports us to an imagined, stylised France. In *Hamlet*, the framing device has a deeper impact on the narrative structure. As Hamlet is 'already dead' at the start, the whole tone of the film is rendered 'utterly fatalistic' (Howard 2003, 610). For Olivier, this cyclical structure offered a key as to how he might approach the film. He describes the way he 'suddenly visualized the final shot', and from this he saw 'how the whole conception of the film could be built up' (1948, 11). The symmetry of the return to the opening images and music at the end contributes a sense of predestination to the events that unfold, and casts the body of the film into the form of an extended flashback.

The sense of fatalism created by this narrative structure, through the introduction of the funeral scenes and the funeral march at the beginning, imbues *Hamlet* with the pessimistic air of film noir. This allows Olivier to reflect the contemporary uncertainties of the postwar years, and for his Prince to become 'almost a film noir hero … being swept along by Fate' (Sinyard 1986, 7). J. Lawrence Guntner highlights the visual influence on *Hamlet* of film noir and its source, German Expressionism—'deep-focus, the dazzling camera angles and the meandering camera' (2000, 120). For Olivier, the decision to shoot in black-and-white brought the advantage of deep-focus photography, which not only enabled 'unusually long scenes', but also lent itself to 'shots of extreme beauty' (1948, 12). The visual strategies adopted by Olivier form part of a wider framework and they are appropriate for the film to a large degree because the narrative is amenable to a noir sensibility. In this respect, it is significant that Olivier creates a flashback structure, and that he uses a first-person voiceover, for both are associated with film noir. Maureen Turim notes that flashback and voiceover narration are two of the devices that help to create the 'fatalism [that] pervades film noir' (1989, 170). Two types of flashback are typical of film noir: the 'confessional' and the 'investigative'. *Hamlet* employs the investigative structure, one which 'examines the past to solve a crime' (ibid., 172). Guntner highlights this investigative element, and proposes a reading of Olivier's Hamlet as an 'alienated sleuth' in the mould of Philip Marlowe or Sam Spade (2000, 119).

Within an investigative narrative, the usually authoritative perspective of the voiceover may be compromised. One consequence of the flashback narration is that the 'temporal separation of the moment of telling and the event told' creates a space in which the audience can assess the reliability of the voiceover narrator's version of events (Gledhill 1998, 29). The cinematic voiceover creates an awareness of a particular subjective position in the same way as the theatrical soliloquy—both inform the audience that one character's perspective is being shown. The 'reversed temporal order' makes the past a memory, a 'privileged subjective realm' (Turim 1989, 170). Olivier's technique of presenting Hamlet's soliloquies partially in voiceover matches the 'thinking aloud', musing quality of voiceover narration. These voiceover sections within the soliloquies reaffirm Hamlet's subjectivity and remind us of the prism through which we are viewing the events. Hamlet's opening voiceover narration aligns the audience with his subjective positioning, and also connects him with other film noir protagonists who narrate from beyond the grave and introduce flashback sequences that explain the events leading to their deaths, for example, Joe Gillis (William Holden) in *Sunset Boulevard* (Billy Wilder, 1950).

Fig. 6.6 Johnny's hallucination in *Odd Man Out*

In a further alignment with the world of film noir, both *Hamlet* and *Odd Man Out* share a central protagonist whose introspective confusion is expressionistically depicted visually and musically. Alwyn introduces harp glissandi to represent the wandering state of Johnny's mind when he hallucinates a prison warden in the air raid shelter. In the first shots of this sequence we not only see the prison warden as he appears to Johnny, but we see Johnny in the lower right hand section of the screen (Fig. 6.6). We don't simply witness the things that Johnny imagines, as we might with a straightforward point-of-view shot. Instead, we share Johnny's experience of what he imagines by visualising the scene with Johnny participating in it as he speaks to the warden. Johnny's confusion is indicated in Alwyn's music and the initial dissolve it accompanies that transforms the air raid shelter into the cell with its locked door.

A similar confusion is expressed when Hamlet envisions his father's murder during the Ghost's narration, and in common with Johnny in *Odd Man Out*, Hamlet shares the frame with his subjective imagining. The camera slowly moves towards the back of Hamlet's head, before the image dissolves into the vision, shot with an iris that contains the events within a

Fig. 6.7 Hamlet's vision in the visitation sequence

blurred-edged oval in the middle of the screen. Walton employs a Wagnerian sound world of 'lowering chords for six-part trombones, and … fogbound chromatic figures' that returns 'in almost identical form' when the crime is recreated in the 'Mousetrap' scene (Palmer 1990, 7). As the Ghost's narration draws to an end, we see the fading vision of it over Hamlet's shoulder, and thus we share his experience of seeing it, as he might say, in his mind's eye (Fig. 6.7). Hamlet's subjective imagining is prioritised, and through the association of the music with this subjectivity, it is recalled when the same music returns as the act is restaged in the play scene. In both films, the montages of music, sound, and image privilege the subjectivity of the lead character, and position the audience to share their experience, rather than simply to see what they see.

Both *Odd Man Out* and *Hamlet* are infused with a noir ambience, although it may be more accurate to locate them in the historical context of British film noir. In contrast to American film noir, the British version blends noir elements with social realism, and thus reveals the stronger influence of French poetic realism, 'with its emphasis on atmosphere, fatalism and existentialism' and a correspondingly reduced interest in the figure of the *femme fatale* (Spicer 2007, 9). Tom Ryall points out that employing a flashback structure as a means of 'inscribing fatalism into a narrative' pre-dated its extensive use in American noir. Ryall (2005, 102) cites the examples of Anthony Asquith's silent *A Cottage on Dartmoor* (1929) and the French film *Le Jour se lève* (Marcel Carné, 1939). Both use extended flashbacks to explain the desperate situations that their protagonists find themselves in in their opening scenes. The fatalism that the narrative structure and the use of music casts over *Odd Man Out* and *Hamlet* infuses them with the same pessimistic tone that characterises the postwar British film noir cycle.

The use of a flashback structure to create a sense of fatalism in cinema, and particularly the role of music in this, can be seen as a derivation of a similar musical formulation in opera. This is highlighted in modern opera productions by the tendency of productions to stage during the orchestral prelude a dumb-show that either encapsulates the narrative or explicitly details the tragic denouement presaged in the music. A recent example is a production of Pietro Mascagni's *Cavalleria Rusticana* in which the final tragedy of the death of Turiddu is staged during the orchestral prelude.[2] This has the effect of casting the main action of the opera as a flashback that will explain and ultimately return us to this tragic tableau. The framing of the narrative in this way is motivated and justified by the indication in the music of the inevitability of the final outcome, and unmistakeably in Turiddu's offstage song in praise of his illicit liaison with Lola, the cause of the duel in which he loses his life. He sings: 'The mark of blood is over your door, But I care not if I am killed, If through you I die and go to Paradise'.[3] The prescient nature of Turiddu's words suggests his acceptance of an unavoidable fate. This is perhaps not unconnected to a sense of divine will, as the action of the opera takes place on Easter day and is animated by Santuzza, the woman who loves Turiddu, whose association with him has caused her to be excommunicated, and who he has now wronged. The explicit religious association allows the sense of events beyond the control of the protagonists to reverberate through the work.

Correspondingly, religious, specifically Christian, imagery is a recurring visual element in films that employ a funeral march as a unifying or structural element. This is a measure of the affiliation between the ceremonial religious aspects of the funeral service and music that evokes the solemn processional of the funeral march. Johnson notes the equation of Johnny's progress in *Odd Man Out* with the Via Dolorosa, and that director Carol

Reed had drawn the mix of politics and religious allegory in F. L. Green's source novel 'towards an emphasis on the allegorical' (2005, 148, 151n). The film foregrounds its religious iconography. When we first see Kathleen, she is bounded by religious imagery. On the wall behind her to the left is a biblical illustration of Christ; on the right of her is the shadow of the cross as the bells chime the hour. Towards the end of the film, Johnny adopts the pose of the crucifixion, leaning against the railings in the snow with his arms outstretched.

The crucifixion is also evoked visually in *Hamlet*. At the end of the Ghost's narration, Hamlet, overcome, falls back on the stone turret with his arms wide. The next shot is an eerily-lit image of his face, filmed to appear upside-down in a composition mirrored in the closing scenes of the film as Hamlet's body is carried to the tower as the funeral march rings out. Hamlet's eerie close-up in the earlier scene represents a premonition of his death mask. In the corresponding image in the closing moments of the film, Hamlet's head hangs from the bier and comes briefly into a close-up framing as he is carried past the camera. The camera lingers on the open archway beyond and the chamber that contains the *prie-dieu* that Claudius had knelt at when Hamlet held back from killing him. The room is momentarily lit by a flash of lightning that synchronises with a climactic beat of the funeral march as it gains in intensity. An explicit crucifixion scene occurs in *A Town Like Alice*, when Joe has been caught stealing chickens from the Japanese forces. A raised platform is built and he is strung up to a tree, while Jean kneels at its base and Mrs Frith recites the Lord's Prayer. The scene is joined on the soundtrack by a slow drumbeat, a death march, and as the image shifts from Joe we hear the sound of hammer on metal and witness Jean's reaction to it. Christian iconography is evoked in an earlier sequence of this film, in which the boy Freddie (Cameron Moore) dies from a snake bite. Seiber's music enters softly on muted brass as the women weep for Freddie and the camera pulls back to reveal a composition that resembles a classical pietà (Fig. 6.8).

In all three films, crucifixion stands as a universal emblem of suffering. The Christian allegory is central to the structure of *Odd Man Out*, although Reed would later deny its influence (Johnson 2005, 156). Religion is referenced in *Hamlet* not as an index of morality but as a means to ensure that the murder would be fully avenged—Hamlet draws back from despatching Claudius while he prays only because Hamlet's father's life had been taken 'With all his crimes broad blown', not reconciled in repentant prayer. The religious allusions in *A Town Like Alice* convey the

Fig. 6.8 Pietà composition in *A Town Like Alice*

cruelty of the women's treatment by inscribing it with an epic dimension. The religious imagery employed in these films evokes both the suffering at the heart of the Christian story and the ceremonial and ritualistic aspects of the funeral service. It reflects visually the notion of divine will and contributes to the sense of fatalism and predestination in films that employ a funeral march as a structuring thematic element in their scores.

More generally, the march themes used in films carry with them connotations of loyalty and patriotism, together with a certain national character that they derive from their historical military connections and that run through the march in its wider musical incarnations. The range of musical compositions permeated by the march share these characteristics and are united by them. Martial connotations are brought to the fore in film scores that adopt a march as their main musical theme. These themes both draw upon and contribute to the continuation of a British tradition of military marches. The film marches have entered the repertory of the military bands and some have entered the national consciousness—Ramsden (2003, 101) reports, for instance, that the RAF has adopted Eric Coates's *Dam Busters' March* as a sort of unofficial anthem. This process erodes the boundary between the functional and ceremonial marches of the military bands and those composed for film scores. While it would be misleading to label the latter as 'fictional' given that the events they accompany on screen frequently have a factual basis, they are composed retrospectively and mimic the character of the earlier military marches in order to stimulate the associations and emotions that those arouse. The creative symbiosis between 'real world' marches and those composed for films is stronger than it may appear, and the distinction between the two is at best blurred. The simplicity of the march form—'essentially an ornamentation of a fixed, regular and repeated drum rhythm' (Schwandt 2001, 813)—militates against its becoming overly complex in musical terms, and ensures its accessibility. No musical division separates a march written for a military function or celebration, and one written for a film score. The numerous marches composed by William Walton, for example, demonstrate a stylistic consistency in both his film work and his overall musical output. The march is an area of intersection between art music and film music.[4] Both fields employ march rhythms in order to draw upon the tradition of military music and its connotations, and as the march is used by composers across the musical spectrum, it represents a point of connection between these areas of musical activity.

Notes

1. In neither *Far From Heaven* (Todd Haynes, 2002) nor *Breakfast at Tiffany's* (Blake Edwards, 1961) is a main theme introduced in the titles and then held back for more than a third of the film's running time, as it is in *Albert, R.N.*
2. Royal Opera House, Covent Garden, production directed by Damiano Michieletto, first performance 3 December 2015.
3. 'Ntra la porta tua lu sangu è sparsu, Ma nun me mporta si ce muoru accisu, E s'iddu muoru e vaju'n paradisu'. Libretto: Giovanni Targioni-Tozzetti/ Guido Menasci.
4. The cross-over between art music and film music in respect of the march is one that occurs within and across national film industries. I have noted John Philip Sousa's role in revitalising the march in American music, and his influence on Kenneth J. Alford. The march is also a recurring element in the film scores of John Williams, whose work has been instrumental in restoring the fortunes of the symphonic idiom of classical Hollywood scoring. In Williams's score for *Star Wars* (George Lucas, 1977), Mervyn Cooke notes the influence of Tchaikovsky, Prokofiev, and Shostakovich, as well as the 'more obvious classical model [of] the pounding triplet rhythms of "Mars" from Holst's *The Planets*' (2008, 463). Emilio Audissino similarly finds traces of Russian composers, together with Richard Strauss, Gustav Mahler,

and a number of British composers. In addition to Williams's admiration for Edward Elgar, Audissino mentions Ralph Vaughan Williams, William Walton, and Benjamin Britten, and notes that the '"Throne Room" music for the epilogue of *Star Wars* ... owes much to Walton's coronation march *Orb and Sceptre*' (2014, 124).

References

Aldgate, Anthony, and Jeffrey Richards. 2002. *Best of British: Cinema and Society from 1930 to the Present*. London/New York: I B Tauris.

Anderson, Michael. 1967. 'The Movies: Mr Anderson's War', Interview by Terence Heelas, Directed by Michael Philps, Produced by Barrie Gavin, First Broadcast BBC2, 8 May.

Audissino, Emilio. 2014. *John Williams's Film Music: Jaws, Star Wars, Raiders of the Lost Ark and the Return of the Classical Hollywood Music Style*. Madison: University of Wisconsin Press.

Christie, Ian, ed. 1978. *Powell, Pressburger and Others*. London: British Film Institute.

Cobbe, Hugh, ed. 2002. *Letters of Ralph Vaughan Williams, 1895–1958*. Oxford: Oxford University Press.

Cooke, Mervyn. 2008. *A History of Film Music*. Cambridge: Cambridge University Press.

Cull, Nicholas J. 2002. Great Escapes: Englishness and the Prisoner of War Genre. *Film History* 14 (3/4): 282–295.

Donnelly, K.J. 2007. *British Film Music and Film Musicals*. Basingstoke: Palgrave Macmillan.

———. 2014. *Occult Aesthetics: Synchronization in Sound Film*. Oxford: Oxford University Press.

Farmer, Henry George. 1950. *Military Music*. London: Max Parrish.

Frayling, Christopher. 1995. *Things to Come*. London: British Film Institute.

Geraghty, Christine. 2000. *British Cinema in the Fifties: Gender, Genre and the 'New Look'*. London: Routledge.

Gifford, Denis. 1986. *The British Film Catalogue, 1895–1985*. Newton Abbot/London: David & Charles.

Gledhill, Christine. 1998. *Klute* 1: A Contemporary Film Noir and Feminist Criticism. In *Women in Film Noir*, ed. E. Ann Kaplan, 20–34. London: British Film Institute.

Grimley, Daniel M. 2010. Landscape and Distance: Vaughan Williams, Modernism and the Symphonic Pastoral. In *British Music and Modernism, 1895–1960*, ed. Matthew Riley, 147–174. Farnham: Ashgate.

Guntner, J. Lawrence. 2000. *Hamlet*, *Macbeth* and *King Lear* on Film. In *The Cambridge Companion to Shakespeare on Film*, ed. Russell Jackson, 120–140. Cambridge: Cambridge University Press.

Harper, Sue. 2000. *Women in British Cinema: Mad, Bad and Dangerous to Know*. London: Continuum.

Hayes, Malcolm, ed. 2002. *The Selected Letters of William Walton*. London: Faber.

Heldt, Guido. 2013. *Music and Levels of Narration in Film: Steps Across the Border*. Bristol/Chicago: Intellect.

Herbert, Trevor, and Helen Barlow. 2013. *Music and the British Military in the Long Nineteenth Century*. Oxford: Oxford University Press.

Howard, Ronald. 1981. *In Search of My Father*. London: William Kimber.

Howard, Tony. 2003. Shakespeare on Film and Video. In *Shakespeare: An Oxford Guide*, ed. Stanley Wells and Lena Cowen Orlin, 607–619. Oxford: Oxford University Press.

Howes, Frank. 1965. *The Music of William Walton*. London: Oxford University Press.

Inglis, Fred. 2003. National Snapshots: Fixing the Past in English War Films. In *British Cinema of the 1950s: A Celebration*, ed. Ian Mackillop and Neil Sinyard, 35–50. Manchester/New York: Manchester University Press.

Irving, Ernest. 1947. Music and the Film Script. In *British Film Yearbook, 1947–48*, ed. Peter Noble, 47–52. London: Skelton Robinson.

———. 1948. The Music – An Interim Report. In *Scott of the Antarctic: The Film and Its Production*, ed. David James, 144–146. Neasden: Convoy Publications.

Johnson, Ian. 2005. *William Alwyn, The Art of Film Music*. Woodbridge: The Boydell Press.

Keller, Hans. 2006. In *Film Music and Beyond: Writings on Music and the Screen, 1946–59*, ed. Christopher Wintle. London: Plumbago Books.

Kennedy, Michael. 1989. *Portrait of Walton*. Oxford: Oxford University Press.

———. 2002. Booklet Notes to 'The Film Music of Ralph Vaughan Williams, Volume 1', Chandos CD CHAN 10529(3).

Lamb, Andrew. 2001. "2. 19th and 20th Century Military and Popular Marches" in "March". In *The New Grove Dictionary of Music and Musicians*, ed. Stanley Sadie, vol. 15, 814–815. London: Macmillan.

Lane, Philip. 2012. Booklet Notes to 'The Film Music of Arthur Benjamin and Leighton Lucas', Chandos CD CHAN 10713.

Lloyd, Stephen. 2001. *William Walton: Muse of Fire*. Woodbridge: Boydell Press.

Marshall, James. 2005. Booklet Notes to 'The Film Music of Clifton Parker', Chandos CD CHAN 10279.

Mason, James. 1981. *Before I Forget*. London: Sphere Books Ltd.

McFarlane, Brian. 2003. Value for Money: Baker and Berman, and Tempean Films. In *British Cinema of the 1950s: A Celebration*, ed. Ian Mackillop and Neil Sinyard, 176–189. Manchester/New York: Manchester University Press.

McKenna, Virginia. 2000. 'A Profile of *A Town Like Alice*', Written & Produced by David Lemon & Claire Thomas, Carlton Television Ltd., Special Feature on Network DVD 7952492.

Moore, Jerrold Northrop. 2004. *Elgar, Child of Dreams*. London: Faber & Faber.

Murray, D.J.S. 2001. Military Music. In *The New Grove Dictionary of Music and Musicians*, ed. Stanley Sadie, vol. 16, 686–687. London: Macmillan.

Olivier, Lawrence. 1948. An Essay in *Hamlet*. In *The Film Hamlet: A Record of Its Production*, ed. Brenda Cross, 11–15. London: Saturn Press.

Ottaway, Hugh. 1972. *Vaughan Williams Symphonies*. London: BBC Publications.

Palmer, Christopher. 1972. Walton's Film Music. *The Musical Times* 113 (1549): 249–252.

———. 1990. Booklet Notes to 'William Walton: Hamlet & As You Like It', Chandos CD CHAN 10436 X.

Parker, Christopher J. 2001. The Music for *Scott of the Antarctic*. *Journal of the RVW Society* 21: 11–14.

Plain, Gill. 2006. *John Mills and British Cinema: Masculinity, Identity and Nation*. Edinburgh: Edinburgh University Press.

Porter, Vincent. 2000. Outsiders in England: The Films of the Associated British Picture Corporation, 1949–1958. In *British Cinema: Past and Present*, ed. Justine Ashby and Andrew Higson, 152–165. London: Routledge.

Ramsden, John. 1998. Refocusing 'The People's War': British War Films of the 1950s. *Journal of Contemporary History* 33 (1): 35–36.

———. 2003. *The Dam Busters*. London: IB Tauris.

Richards, Jeffrey. 1997. *Films and British National Identity: From Dickens to Dad's Army*. Manchester: Manchester University Press.

Riley, Matthew. 2010. Music for the Machines of the Future: H.G. Wells, Arthur Bliss and *Things To Come* (1936). In *British Music and Modernism, 1895–1960*, ed. Matthew Riley, 249–268. Farnham: Ashgate.

Roscow, Gregory H., ed. 1991. *Bliss on Music: Selected Writings of Arthur Bliss, 1920–1975*. Oxford: Oxford University Press.

Rothwell, Kenneth S. 1999. *A History of Shakespeare on Screen*. Cambridge: Cambridge University Press.

Ryall, Tom. 2005. *Anthony Asquith*. Manchester: Manchester University Press.

Schwandt, Erich. 2001. "1. The Military March to the 1820s" and "3. The March in Art Music" in "March". In *The New Grove Dictionary of Music and Musicians*, ed. Stanley Sadie, vol. 15, 812–814, 815–817. London: Macmillan.

Self, Geoffrey. 2001. Alford, Kenneth J. [Ricketts, Frederic Joseph]. In *The New Grove Dictionary of Music and Musicians*, ed. Stanley Sadie, vol. 1, 365. London: Macmillan.

Sinyard, Neil. 1986. *Filming Literature*. Beckenham: Croon Helm.

Spicer, Andrew. 2001. *Typical Men: The Representation of Masculinity in Popular British Cinema*. London: I. B. Tauris.

———, ed. 2007. *European Film Noir*. Manchester: Manchester University Press.
Street, Sarah. 2009. *British National Cinema*. London/New York: Routledge.
Turim, Maureen. 1989. *Flashbacks and Film: Memory and History*. New York/London: Routledge.
Vaughan, Dai. 1995. *Odd Man Out*. London: British Film Institute.
Vaughan Williams, Ursula. 1964. *R.V.W. A Biography of Ralph Vaughan Williams*. London: Oxford University Press.

CHAPTER 7

Conclusion

This book has explored the influence of Britain's musical heritage on British film music, together with the impulse in British cinema towards documentary modes of representation and the notions of restraint that this implies. I propose that these three interrelated areas, of musical traditions, documentary influences, and restraint, mark the scores, and in turn the films, with a strong British inflection, and that film music of this era can be fully appreciated only when considered in the context of these historical underpinnings.

Each of the four categories of music considered in this study—pastoral, folk song, choral and the march—represents a national musical tradition linked either with the cultural concerns espoused by the musical establishment, or with the rituals of the church, or the military. The mission of the founders of the English Musical Renaissance to establish a national style of composition came to fruition with the composers in the second wave of the movement, spearheaded by Ralph Vaughan Williams. The integration of earlier British musical traditions into a pastoral idiom answered the challenge in three ways. The music was accessible and could maintain both its place in national life and the connection between composers and audiences; it was clearly differentiated from the modernist developments taking place in continental Europe; and above all, it could be claimed as national. The renewed interest in the nation's musical heritage brought folk song its moment of revival as part of the central myth of the Renaissance, a role it shared with the pastoral as the musical analogue of

P. Mazey, *British Film Music*, Palgrave Studies in Audio-Visual Culture, https://doi.org/10.1007/978-3-030-33550-2_7

the rural landscape, of harmonious communities, of lasting tranquillity. Folk song and choral sonorities often fall within a broad pastoral palette. These areas embrace a pastoral idiom and in doing so foreground the landscape and natural environment as key cultural symbols whose wider associations are evoked when combined on screen with landscape imagery. There are differences in the connotations most clearly foregrounded: gentle pastoral music most often accompanies the image of rolling hills and green fields typical of the south of England, whereas representations of other parts of the British Isles, such as Scotland's island communities or Wales, are distanced by the use of indigenous folk song in languages other than English, and their environments frequently presented as wild and untamed or as sites of potential danger. Notwithstanding these differences, the overarching connection between music that promotes a pastoral ambience, landscape, and rural communities is deeply forged and repeatedly reinforced. The composers associated with the English Musical Renaissance establish a style of national music that reflects cultural preoccupations with history, tradition, and landscape that, like the cinema itself, contributes to processes that construct notions of a shared heritage and national identity. The effectiveness of pastoral music in its cinematic guise is undiminished by our awareness of the constructed nature of the link between pastoral music and its connotations. Instead, the reverse is the case, for as with all audiovisual couplings, the pairing of pastoral music and rural imagery on screen naturalises and strengthens the bond between them. This holds true for all the musical styles explored, in that each enables a film to call on a plethora of cultural connections and to imbue its scenes with both musical and historical associations of Britishness.

When heard in a film score, each musical style recalls its broader cultural position, and allows the music itself to act as an authenticating element for the film. Across the range of musical types, music operates as an aural device within a film that validates the representations it is part of. This produces a documentary charge that is most pronounced when a film employs pre-existing music, as in each use of folk song and some choral and march cues, although it is equally present when the music takes on a recognisable style of British music and mirrors its 'real' equivalent. The approach to music scoring in the British industry accommodates music that unfolds to its own musical logic, and allows composers to write in their own musical voices, voices that are themselves influenced by prevailing musical attitudes. The composers' film music can be seen as a documentary element insofar as it resembles the music they produce outside of the studios, and we have seen a close alignment between their work for films and their wider activities, and reciprocal influences that flow between the different areas of musical activity.

Many British feature films aspire to a documentary aesthetic, a factor highlighted when both areas of filmmaking use music in similar ways. Across the musical styles we have noted the shared technique in documentary and feature production of employing music in a loosely-synchronised fashion that suggests it emanates from the wider community and the environment itself rather than solely from the characters we see on screen. The music speaks for the whole community, and repeatedly it emphasises not the experience of the individual but that of the group, the collective, the community. The pastoral idiom brings associations of communities living in a close relationship with the landscape, while it is in the nature of folk song, choral voices, and the march to connote communal rather than individual expression. The communal emphasis that the music fosters is bolstered by its place in social life as a group activity, and one that involves active participation. Whether in the form of choral singing, playing in a brass band or singing along to a factory radio, music is presented as a participatory activity, and one that is part of a communal experience in contemporary documentaries including *Spare Time* (Humphrey Jennings, 1939) and *Listen to Britain* (Humphrey Jennings, Stewart McAllister, 1942). This shifts music from a passive to an active pursuit and ties it to the lived experience of the audience, where the shared participation in music integrates individuals into a group culture. The willingness to engage in musical activity is clear in folk song and group singing, although it is equally reflected in the whistled march tunes that feature in *The Captive Heart* (Basil Dearden, 1946) and *The Bridge on the River Kwai* (David Lean, 1957). How the use of music in documentary has influenced its use in features in this era is a subject that deserves further research. This study reveals that by using culturally significant styles of music and adopting documentary audiovisual techniques, British feature films achieve a mode of representation that aligns them with documentary productions and enables them to accentuate the shared experience of the community.

Closely tied to the documentary aspiration in the British industry is the desire for the realistic portrayal of an emotional register in line with the audience's experience. In film music, this is expressed through an aesthetic of restraint, of understatement in terms both of the amount of music and in how it is used. British scores in this era tend to be shorter than their Hollywood counterparts, with a more sparing use of music that allows for a stronger contrast between scored and unscored moments. In a lecture given in 1958, William Alwyn regrets the alteration he finds in this situation:

> 10 years ago an average film score for a feature film was about 20 minutes – today it is normally 40 minutes to an hour. This cuts at the very root of film music as an *art* – without silence the composer loses his most effective weapon (quoted in Swynnoe 2002, 189)

As well as being sparing in the amount of music used, British films also demonstrate restraint in their orchestral arrangements, which frequently favour a more economic sound. Malcolm Arnold's music for *Hobson's Choice*, for instance, is scored for only twenty-two players, and Brian Easdale employs limited orchestral forces for *Gone to Earth*—in addition to the chorus, 'just four horns, two harps, percussion, and strings' (Lane 2011, 11). These films are not low-budget productions, and could have used larger musical forces had their composers wished. These creative decisions reveal the artistic intentions of the practitioners rather than economically motivated restrictions. We observe a similar restraint in the way music is employed on a film's soundtrack. I have noted how the tender love themes in *Ice Cold in Alex* and *Black Narcissus*, and the themes for the women in *Scott of the Antarctic*, for example, are all held at a low volume on the soundtracks of these films in comparison with other cues on their scores. This creative choice moderates their emotional impact, allows other soundtrack elements to occupy the foreground during these scenes, and illustrates a willingness to hold back and adopt a 'less-is-more' approach for artistic reasons. The documentary influence on feature production is bolstered by a system that facilitates a restrained approach to film music.

A further aspect related to creative decisions about how music is used in film, and one that this study has touched upon without being able to investigate in detail, is the place of music in theories of cinematic adaptation. I have noted Brian Easdale's musical response to the heightened prose of Mary Webb's *Gone To Earth*, and have also considered William Walton's musical setting of Olivier's Shakespearean soliloquys. This musical engagement with the literary and theatrical tradition reveals the English language as a central cultural concern, and cinema in the twentieth century as the medium in which it would find expression. In an era when many prestige projects drew upon classics of British literature and drama, a written heritage that dwarfs the nation's musical heritage in its ability to reassure audiences of Britain's enduring cultural contribution, the relationship between music and text in these adaptations is another subject that would reward further study. In the specific setting of words into a musical framework there is a parallel between film music and opera, and it is notable that a number of British film composers, including Ralph Vaughan Williams, William Walton, Brian Easdale, and William Alwyn, were also drawn to opera. Vaughan Williams highlights the shared musico-dramatic impulse of film music and opera when he references the Wagnerian concept of the *gesamtkunstwerk* (total work of art) and writes in 1945 that film 'contains potentialities for the combination of all the arts such as Wagner never dreamt of' (1963, 162). Alongside Benjamin Britten, the leading proponent of English opera, both Vaughan Williams and Walton composed operas based on classic texts, and in this respect we can see not only a stylistic parallel between film music and opera, but also a common desire to create a national musical voice in both disciplines.

I mentioned at the outset that a measure of 'drift' occurs between the styles of music considered here, which can blur the borders of their categories. Music cues can wander across the boundaries, as happens in the pastoral nature of folk song and in folk song arranged for choral voices, and this compounds their expressive potential. The musical styles can also create equivalent effects or they can share effects across their separate borders according to the way they are used on the soundtrack. The impact of the music is strengthened, for example, when it is used as a structuring element in the score, as a recurring theme or motif, or when the entire score is built upon one style of music, as I have noted with march themes and folk song, respectively. In addition, the various styles of music can individually or jointly foreground themes in a film in a nuanced way. Pastoral music, folk song, and choral music, areas in which Britain has a strong musical heritage, are all associated on screen with elements of the landscape and the natural environment, often in ways that amplify the sense of historical continuity, tradition, community values and spirituality that is attributed to landscape. This formulation, reproduced in celebrations of rural life that present the church at the centre of the community, is echoed repeatedly in films that emphasise their bucolic settings. The equation reinforces the connection between landscape as a national cultural preoccupation and music that evokes both the landscape and the qualities it is believed to encompass. These audiovisual combinations lend the films a distinct national aspect. The technique of using music as a means of laying claim to a sense of history, tradition, and national identity by accessing national musical heritage is reproduced in the use of march rhythms in war films. Each musical category is called upon to confirm a shared sense of national feeling.

This study began with the intention to explore the connections between the historical traditions of music in Britain, the English Musical Renaissance, and British film music, and I would like to consider here some of the threads that weave these areas together. There is a clear link through the music colleges between the generations of composers associated with the renaissance and those who subsequently worked in the film industry. We might also note that had the renaissance not revitalised and inspired confidence in British music, there would have been a smaller pool of noted British concert composers, and less recognition of the musical heritage they were able to bring to film culture. We may view it as a happy coincidence that the rise in fortunes of the British film industry followed and overlapped with an equivalent resurgence of critically acknowledged musical activity in Britain. The approach to music scoring in the British industry evolves in response to the more autonomous music provided by composers who were not film music specialists and accommodates a diverse range of musical voices. In turn this flexibility allows composers to work with a greater degree of musical logic and to create music that engages with images in a less tightly-synchronised, but sometimes more poetic way that extends the range of film language and establishes what we might class as a British approach to film scoring. This approach enables the film industry to exploit the evocative richness of the heritage of British music, and, in the sense that it resists a dominant model, it aligns the mission to raise the standard of British film music with the earlier project that initiated the English Musical Renaissance.

The national undertaking of the English Musical Renaissance that was reproduced by the practitioners of British film music was fortified by the onset of the Second World War. Regular musical activity in the country was curtailed, and the film studios offered concert composers not only an income stream but also a means of supporting the war effort. These factors, combined with the propaganda aim of films to celebrate British values and the British way of life, created the possibility for film music, by taking on the language of British art music and directly commissioning its most eminent purveyors, to adopt a particularly patriotic flavour and to promote a shared sense of national feeling.

The parallels between the mission of the English Musical Renaissance and the later movement to elevate the standard of British film music demonstrate, in the aims of both, a common impulse. The shared impetus behind these two movements enables us to see them as part of the same mission, and to view the desire to raise the quality of music in the British film industry as a late blossoming branch of the Musical Renaissance that had earlier revitalised British art music. British film music is part of the rich heritage of British music more broadly, an arena in which national cultural preoccupations are expressed for a mass audience, and one through which a deep imprint of Britishness is made upon a film.

A further force is at work here, one that is more challenging to write about within the framework of objective academic enquiry, but without which this consideration would be incomplete. It is the sheer affective power of much of the music discussed and the emotional pull it can exert in its cinematic context. It is not easy to define the sense of familiarity we may feel on hearing music in the styles explored, of a stirring recognition of something forgotten, or of a memory lying dormant. It is harder still to put into words the sense of this music meaning something to us in a way that evokes an emotional response that we can't quite explain. The feeling it arouses is of the proximity of the past, of a sense of continuity across time that is at once reassuring and yet paradoxically touched with nostalgia for the earlier time. A particular alchemy occurs when nationally significant musical styles are used in films, even when we understand the constructed nature of the elements associated with them. One of the most remarkable things about British film music of this era is how effectively it can convey ideas of national specificity, reflect back to the nation an image of itself and project a shared sense of community and national identity. The years between this era and our own have witnessed significant changes in British film culture and in the nature of British film music. In the 1950s television eroded cinema's dominant position as the primary medium of entertainment for adult audiences and the drop in cinema attendances led to a decline in film production and a change in the cinema-going demographic. Horror films proved popular with younger audiences, and the cycle of social realist films expressed the spirit of the times in their tales of working class alienation. These burgeoning genres brought a more contemporary sound to their film scores by embracing modernism, jazz, and popular music and called upon the services of composers versed in these areas. Elisabeth Lutyens, for example, found her brand of modernism well suited to accompany the horror films being produced by Hammer and

Amicus, while Benjamin Frankel employed the techniques of serialism in his score for Hammer's *The Curse of the Werewolf* (Terence Fisher, 1961). Largely though, with the notable exception of Richard Rodney Bennett, the close links between concert composers and British cinema were severed. The tradition of the full orchestral score was to return to prominence, although it was now in the hands of a new generation of British composers who specialised in film and television music. The musical traditions explored in this research have returned too, significantly in period films that associate them with the past and employ them to promote a sense of nostalgia for a bygone time. In spite of its being contained in a discrete historical period and set apart by the changing musical styles of the 1960s, British film music of this earlier era retains its evocative power, its poignant qualities intensified by its own passing into the heritage of British music.

References

Lane, Philip. 2011. Booklet Notes to 'The Film Music of Brian Easdale', Chandos CD CHAN 10636.

Swynnoe, Jan G. 2002. *The Best Years of British Film Music, 1936–1958*. Woodbridge: Boydell Press.

Vaughan Williams, Ralph. 1945. Composing for the Films. In *National Music and Other Essays* 1963, ed. Vaughan Williams, Ralph, 160–165. London: Oxford University Press.

Filmography

49th Parallel. Dir. Michael Powell. Mus. Ralph Vaughan Williams. Ortus Films. 1941.

633 Squadron. Dir. Walter Grauman. Mus. Ron Goodwin. Mirisch. 1964.

Above Us The Waves. Dir. Ralph Thomas. Mus. Arthur Benjamin. Rank. 1955.

Against the Wind. Dir. Charles Crichton. Mus. Leslie Bridgewater. Ealing. 1948.

Albert, R. N. Dir. Lewis Gilbert. Mus. Malcolm Arnold. Angel. 1953.

Alexander Nevsky. Dir. Sergei Eisenstein. Mus. Sergei Prokofiev. Mosfilm. 1938.

Appointment in London. Dir. Philip Leacock. Mus. John Wooldridge. Mayflower. 1953.

As You Like It. Dir. Paul Czinner. Mus. William Walton. Inter-Allied. 1936.

Black Narcissus. Dir. Michael Powell, Emeric Pressburger. Mus. Brian Easdale. Archers, Independent Producers. 1947.

Blackmail. Dir. Alfred Hitchcock. Mus. Hubert Bath. British International. 1929.

Blithe Spirit. Dir. David Lean. Mus. Richard Addinsell. Two Cities, Cineguild. 1945.

Breakfast at Tiffany's. Dir. Blake Edwards. Mus. Henry Mancini. Jurow-Shepherd. 1961.

Bridge on the River Kwai, The. Dir. David Lean. Mus. Malcolm Arnold. Horizon. 1957.

P. Mazey, *British Film Music*, Palgrave Studies in Audio-Visual Culture, https://doi.org/10.1007/978-3-030-33550-2

Brighton Rock. Dir. John Boulting. Mus. Hans May. ABPC. 1947.

Broken Horseshoe, The. Dir. Martyn C. Webster. Mus. Wilfred Burns. Nettlefold. 1953.

Brothers, The. Dir. David MacDonald. Mus. Cedric Thorpe Davie. Sydney Box. 1947.

Canterbury Tale, A. Dir. Michael Powell, Emeric Pressburger. Mus. Allan Gray. Archers, Independent Producers. 1944.

Captain Boycott. Dir. Frank Launder. Mus. William Alwyn. Individual. 1947.

Captive Heart, The. Dir. Basil Dearden. Mus. Alan Rawsthorne. Ealing. 1946.

Coal Face [documentary short]. Dir. Alberto Cavalcanti. Mus. Benjamin Britten. GPO Film Unit. 1935.

Cockleshell Heroes, The. Dir. José Ferrer. Mus. John Addison. Warwick. 1955.

Colditz Story, The. Dir. Guy Hamilton. Mus. Francis Chagrin. Ivan Foxwell. 1955.

Conquest of Everest, The [documentary]. Dir. George Lowe. Mus. Arthur Benjamin. Countryman, Group 3. 1953.

Contraband. Dir. Michael Powell. Mus. Richard Addinsell. British National. 1940.

Convoy. Dir. Pen Tennyson. Mus. Ernest Irving. Ealing. 1940.

Cottage on Dartmoor, A. Dir. Anthony Asquith. Silent. British Instructional, Svensk Filmindustri. 1929.

Cruel Sea, The. Dir. Charles Frend. Mus. Alan Rawsthorne. Ealing. 1953.

Curse of the Werewolf, The. Dir. Terence Fisher. Mus. Benjamin Frankel. Hammer. 1961.

Dam Busters, The. Dir. Michael Anderson. Mus. Leighton Lucas, Eric Coates. ABPC. 1955.

Danger Within. Dir. Don Chaffey. Mus. Francis Chagrin. Colin Lesslie, British Lion. 1959.

Dangerous Moonlight. Dir. Brian Desmond Hurst. Mus. Richard Addinsell. RKO. 1941.

Dead of Night. Dir. Alberto Cavalcanti, Charles Crichton, Basil Dearden, Robert Hamer. Mus. Georges Auric. Ealing. 1945.

Dim Little Island, The [documentary short]. Dir. Humphrey Jennings. Mus. Ralph Vaughan Williams. Wessex. 1948.

Drum, The. Dir. Zoltan Korda. Mus. Miklós Rózsa. London. 1938.

Edge of the World, The. Dir. Michael Powell. Mus. W. L. Williamson. Joe Rock. 1937.

Escape Me Never. Dir. Paul Czinner. Mus. William Walton. B & D. 1935.

Far From Heaven. Dir. Todd Haynes. Mus. Elmer Bernstein. Focus Features et al. 2002.

First of the Few, The. Dir. Leslie Howard. Mus. William Walton. British Aviation. 1942.

Flemish Farm, The. Dir. Jeffrey Dell. Mus. Ralph Vaughan Williams. Two Cities. 1943.

Four Feathers, The. Dir. Zoltan Korda. Mus. Miklós Rózsa. London. 1939.

Gone To Earth. Dir. Michael Powell, Emeric Pressburger. Mus. Brian Easdale. Archers, London, Vanguard. 1950.

Great Day. Dir. Lance Comfort. Mus. William Alwyn. Victor Hanbury, RKO British. 1945.

Great Expectations. Dir. David Lean. Mus. Walter Goehr. Independent Producers, Cineguild. 1946.

Great White Silence, The [documentary]. Dir. Herbert Ponting. Silent. Gaumont British. 1924.

Halfway House, The. Dir. Basil Dearden. Mus. Lord Berners. Ealing. 1944.

Hamlet. Dir. Laurence Olivier. Mus. William Walton. Two Cities. 1948.

Happiness of Three Women, The. Dir. Maurice Elvey. Mus. Edwin Astley. David Dent. 1954.

Henry V. Dir. Laurence Olivier. Mus. William Walton. Two Cities. 1944.

Hobson's Choice. Dir. David Lean. Mus. Malcolm Arnold. London, British Lion. 1954.

I Know Where I'm Going. Dir. Michael Powell, Emeric Pressburger. Mus. Allan Gray. Archers. 1945.

Ice Cold in Alex. Dir. J. Lee Thompson. Mus. Leighton Lucas. ABPC. 1958.

In Which We Serve. Dir. Noel Coward, David Lean. Mus. Noel Coward. Two Cities. 1942.

Jassy. Dir. Bernard Knowles. Mus. Henry Geehl. Gainsborough. 1947.

Jour se lève, Le. Dir. Marcel Carné. Mus. Maurice Jaubert. Sigma. 1939.

Kind Hearts and Coronets. Dir. Robert Hamer. Mus. Ernest Irving. Ealing. 1949.

Life and Death of Colonel Blimp, The. Dir. Michael Powell, Emeric Pressburger. Mus. Allan Gray. Archers, Independent Producers. 1943.

Lion Has Wings, The. Dir. Adrian Brunel, Brian Desmond Hurst, Michael Powell. Mus. Richard Addinsell. London. 1939.

Listen to Britain. Dir. Humphrey Jennings, Stewart McAllister. Crown Film Unit. 1942.

Long Memory, The. Dir. Robert Hamer. Mus. William Alwyn. Europa. 1953.

Love from a Stranger. Dir. Rowland V. Lee. Mus. Benjamin Britten. Trafalgar. 1937.

Love Story. Dir. Leslie Arliss. Mus. Hubert Bath. Gainsborough. 1944.

Loves of Joanna Godden, The. Dir. Charles Frend. Mus. Ralph Vaughan Williams. Ealing. 1947.

Madonna of the Seven Moons. Dir. Arthur Crabtree. Mus. Hans May. Gainsborough. 1944.

Malta, G. C. [documentary short]. Mus. Arnold Bax. Army Film Unit, Crown Film Unit, MOI, RAF Film Unit. 1942.

Man of Aran [documentary]. Dir. Robert Flaherty. Mus. John Greenwood. Gainsborough. 1934.

Mark of Cain, The. Dir, Brian Desmond Hurst. Mus. Bernard Stevens. Two Cities. 1947.

Matter of Life and Death, A. Dir. Michael Powell, Emeric Pressburger. Mus. Allan Gray. Archers. 1946.

Message from Canterbury [documentary short]. Dir. George Hoellering. Mus. Joseph Poole. Film Traders. 1944.

Millions Like Us. Dir. Frank Launder, Sidney Gilliat. Mus. Louis Levy. Gainsborough. 1943.

Mine Own Executioner. Dir. Anthony Kimmins. Mus. Benjamin Frankel. London. 1947.

Nanook of the North [documentary]. Dir. Robert Flaherty. Les Freres Revillon. 1922.

Next of Kin. Dir. Thorold Dickinson. Mus. William Walton. Ealing. 1942.

Night Mail [documentary short]. Dir. Harry Watt, Basil Wright. Mus. Benjamin Britten. GPO Film Unit. 1936.

Odd Man Out. Dir. Carol Reed. Mus. William Alwyn. Two Cities. 1947.

Oliver Twist. Dir. David Lean. Mus. Arnold Bax. Cineguild. 1948.

Overlanders, The. Dir. Harry Watt. Mus. John Ireland. Ealing. 1946.

Password is Courage, The. Dir. Andrew Stone. Andrew L. Stone. 1962.

Pimpernel Smith. Dir. Leslie Howard. Mus. John Greenwood. British National. 1941.

Pink String and Sealing Wax. Dir. Robert Hamer. Mus. Norman Demuth. Ealing. 1945.

Psycho. Dir. Alfred Hitchcock. Mus. Bernard Herrmann. Shamley. 1960.

Pygmalion. Dir. Leslie Howard, Anthony Asquith. Mus. Arthur Honegger. Pascal. 1938.

Queen of Spades, The. Dir. Thorold Dickinson. Mus. Georges Auric. De Grunwald, ABPC. 1949.

Reach for the Sky. Dir. Lewis Gilbert. Mus. John Addision. Rank, Angel. 1956.
Red Shoes, The. Dir. Michael Powell, Emeric Pressburger. Mus. Brian Easdale. Archer, Independent Producers. 1948.
Return to the Edge of the World [documentary short]. Dir. Michael Powell. Mus. Brian Easdale. BBC, Poseidon. 1978.
Richard III. Dir. Laurence Olivier. Mus. William Walton. London. 1955.
Rocking Horse Winner, The. Dir. Anthony Pélissier. Mus. William Alwyn. Rank, Two Cities, John Mills. 1949.
Scott of the Antarctic. Dir. Charles Frend. Mus. Ralph Vaughan Williams. Ealing. 1948.
Sea of Sand. Dir. Guy Green. Mus. Clifton Parker. Tempean. 1958.
Silent Village, The [documentary short]. Dir. Humphrey Jennings. Mus. Becket Williams. Crown Film Unit et al. 1943.
Silver Darlings, The. Dir. Clarence Elder. Mus. Clifton Parker. Holyrood. 1947.
So Long at the Fair. Dir. Terence Fisher, Anthony Darnborough. Mus. Benjamin Frankel. 1950.
Spare Time [documentary short]. Dir. Humphrey Jennings. GPO Film Unit. 1939.
Spy in Black, The. Dir. Michael Powell. Mus. Miklós Rózsa. Irving Asher. 1939.
Star Wars. Dir. George Lucas. Mus. John Williams. Lucasfilm. 1977.
Sunset Boulevard. Dir. Billy Wilder. Mus. Franz Waxman. Paramount. 1950.
Tales of Hoffmann, The. Dir. Michael Powell, Emeric Pressburger. Mus. Jacques Offenbach. Archers, Vega. 1951.
Tawny Pipit. Dir. Bernard Miles, Charles Saunders. Mus. Noel Mewton-Wood. Two Cities. 1944.
They Made Me A Fugitive. Dir. Alberto Cavalcanti. Mus. Marius François Gaillard. 1947.
Thief of Bagdad, The. Dir. Ludwig Berger, Michael Powell, Tim Whelan. Mus. Miklós Rózsa. London, Korda. 1940.
Things To Come. Dir. William Cameron Menzies. Mus. Arthur Bliss. London. 1936.
Third Man, The. Dir. Carol Reed. Mus. Anton Karas. London. 1949.
Town Like Alice, A. Dir. Jack Lee. Mus. Mátyás Seiber. Vic Films. 1956.
Train of Events. Dir. Basil Dearden, Charles Crichton, Sidney Cole. Mus. Leslie Bridgewater. Ealing. 1949.

Ulster [documentary short]. Dir. Ralph Keene. Mus. Richard Addinsell. Strand. 1941.

Waltzes From Vienna. Dir. Alfred Hitchcock. Mus. Hubert Bath et al. Gaumont British. 1934.

Went the Day Well? Dir. Alberto Cavalcanti. Mus. William Walton. Ealing. 1942.

While I Live. Dir. John Harlow. Mus. Charles Williams. Edward Dryhurst. 1947.

Whisky Galore! Dir. Alexander Mackendrick. Mus. Ernest Irving. Ealing. 1949.

Woman Hater. Dir. Terence Young. Mus. Lambert Williamson. Two Cities. 1948.

Woman in Question, The. Dir. Anthony Asquith. Mus. John Wooldridge. Javelin, Vic Films. 1950.

Wooden Horse, The. Dir. Jack Lee. Mus. Clifton Parker. London, Wessex. 1950.

Written on the Wind. Dir. Douglas Sirk. Mus. Frank Skinner. Universal International. 1956.

Years Between, The. Dir. Compton Bennett. Mus. Benjamin Frankel. Sydney Box. 1946.

Index[1]

[1] Note: Page numbers followed by 'n' refer to notes.

P. Mazey, *British Film Music*, Palgrave Studies in Audio-Visual Culture, https://doi.org/10.1007/978-3-030-33550-2

Printed by Printforce, the Netherlands